# THE STRUGGLE CONTINUES

Robbie McCauley in The Sedition Ensemble's *The History of the Universe According to Those Who've Had to Live It*, Dartmouth College, NH, 1981. Photo: © Nancy Wasserman.

# THE STRUGGLE CONTINUES

## SCRIPTS, ESSAYS, REFLECTIONS

## ROBBIE MCCAULEY

**EDITED BY**

*Alisa Solomon, Elin Diamond, and Cynthia Carr*

**CONTRIBUTORS:**

*Cynthia Carr, Marie Cieri, Elin Diamond, Daniel Alexander Jones, Omi Osun Joni L. Jones, Charlotte Meehan, Ed Montgomery, Erika Munk, Carl Hancock Rux, Maureen Shea, Pamela Sneed, Alisa Solomon*

**THEATRE COMMUNICATIONS GROUP**
**NEW YORK**
**2025**

*The Struggle Continues: Scripts, Essays, Reflections* is published by
Theatre Communications Group, Inc., 520 Eighth Avenue, 20th Floor, Suite 2000, New York, NY 10018-4156



TCG books are exclusively distributed to the book trade by Consortium Book Sales and Distribution.

Library of Congress Control Numbers:
2022040434 (print) / 2022040435 (ebook)
ISBN 978-1-55936-974-9 (paperback) / ISBN 978-1-55936-936-7 (ebook)

A catalog record for this book is available from the Library of Congress.

www.tcg.org
Follow us on Instagram @tcg_gram

Book design and composition by Lisa Govan
Front cover photograph by Peter Paradise Michaels,
pparadise@gmail.com
Back cover photograph by Vivian Selbo

First Edition, September 2025

Still enough time for ancient needs
like front porches and cement
corners.
The singer in the park hold'n a pan full'a coins full'a rhythm
play'n a blues harp harmony.
I feel blue too
cool and blue
and the blue tune still hangs
in the place between change
change and memory.

—ROBBIE MCCAULEY
JULY 17, 2019

# CONTENTS

## SOLO AND COLLABORATIVE SCRIPTS

## LEGACIES



## EPILOGUE

# EDITORS' PREFACE

In the summer of 2014, after Robbie had retired from her position as professor at Emerson College in Boston, she was, as she wrote in an email to one of us, "clearing my head for an effort I've been meaning to do for a while," namely, anthologizing some of her plays. She envisioned publishing three of them along with a "reflection" on each. She reached out separately to each of us—three white women who had written about and championed her work from the academic and/or journalistic platforms we were privileged to occupy—to ask us to write one. We all readily agreed. Obviously. The wider world needs to know Robbie's work.

We didn't hear anything further—Robbie apparently wasn't making any headway with publishers. Then, when all of us gathered in Boston in April 2017 to participate in celebrating Robbie's work at the idea- and love-filled symposium, "Robbie McCauley 'n Company: A Convening in Performance," organized by Charlotte Meehan, we felt with new urgency the need to get Robbie's work out there. We offered to take on the editing tasks, enabling Robbie to expand her vision for the volume, and to look back more fully on her more than five-decade career. We approached Theatre Communications Group, which immediately said yes.

We had the great good fortune of collaborating with Robbie on assembling this book. Each of us has contributed an essay, as Robbie initially had planned, and Robbie invited Maureen Shea and Charlotte Meehan to introduce the plays whose premieres they directed. We jointly conceived a "legacies" section and Robbie asked Daniel Alexander Jones, Omi Osun Joni L. Jones, Carl Hancock Rux, and Pamela Sneed to contribute. We added in a few earlier essays by and interviews with Robbie, and, to end the volume, we conducted a fresh interview and included what Robbie called her "iPhone Poems," short texts on acting, politics, and her body and health, many of which she composed while in the hospital.

On May 20, 2021, between the time we completed the manuscript and when it came to press, the world lost Robbie. Her death left a personal hole in the lives of those close to her, including everyone who participated in this book, and a chasm in the theater world more broadly.

About a year after Robbie's passing, we lost Maureen Shea, too. We deeply regret that they never held this volume in their hands, but we hope that it will help carry forth the productive provocations, and the commitments to honesty, justice, and meaningful encounter that Robbie's work forever exemplifies and inspires.

*—Alisa Solomon, Elin Diamond, and Cynthia Carr*
*New York City, 2023*

# THE STRUGGLE CONTINUES

# BEGINNINGS

*Alisa Solomon*

As an undergraduate at Howard University in the early 1960s, Robbie McCauley, like most college students, was trying to discover "who am I and what do I want to do?"[1] She stumbled onto the answer one day when, wandering through a campus building, she walked through a doorway and found herself on a stage. "Who are *you*?" asked the man in charge—who turned out to be the legendary Harlem Renaissance playwright and poet Owen Dodson, head of Howard's theater department at the time.

"I just walked in here," Robbie answered.

"Well, can you act?" asked Dodson.

"Yeah," Robbie bluffed.

"Good thing," Dodson told her. He was in the middle of preparing a production of *Medea* and had just lost his Chorus Leader. He cast McCauley on the spot.

Somehow, she was ready. "I felt when I walked on that stage that I was where I belonged," Robbie remembered. "It was natural for me."

Robbie soon added theater as a second major—on top of history—and after graduating, moved to New York in 1965 to begin a career that involved pushing open one door after another, and striding through with the same mixture of discovery, inevitability, and chutzpah that she brought to the stage at Howard a half century ago. In the decades since, as an actor, writer, director, and teacher, Robbie, in her own summation, sought "an organic relationship between charged content and experimental form in work that is personal, political, educational, and beautiful."[2]

Bringing together four of her solo/collaborative scripts, one example of her community projects, and two previously published essays—along with new commentary from colleagues, scholars, and critics—this volume chronicles Robbie's multifaceted and essential contribution to the American theater—and to America's ongoing experiment in democracy. This introduction sets the stage for Robbie's oeuvre, describing the first two decades of Robbie's work, when she blazed the path leading to the material presented here.

Born in 1942 in Norfolk, Virginia, and raised in Georgia and Washington, DC, Robbie entered Howard University at a flourishing time for its theater program. A vital force for developing African American theater since the early part of the twentieth century, Howard became even more prominent under Dodson's leadership, from 1947 to 1969. Dodson championed new Black writing—in 1955 he staged the first production of James Baldwin's *The Amen Corner*, for instance—and at the same time, he emphasized grounding in the classical canon, insisting not only that African Americans had as strong a claim to texts by Euripides and Shakespeare as anyone else, but also that these plays provided important models for Black drama. (His celebrated production of *Hamlet*, starring Earle Hyman, presented in 1951 in segregated Washington, DC, amply demonstrated the first point; his own play *Garden of Time*, an adaptation of *Medea* featuring a Black Medea and a white Jason and partially set in post–Civil War South Carolina, written when Dodson was a master's student at the Yale School of Drama in the late 1930s, proved the second.)

From Howard, Robbie carried into the vibrant New York scene of the late 1960s a solid grounding—in dramatic literature, in craft, and in sense of purpose. That purpose—to "shift views and break silences"[3] as she once put it—sharpened over the decades. Her first experiences of literacy, Robbie once said, involved knowing how to read WHITE and COLORED signs on water fountains, bathrooms, and so on, and "ripping down those signs became my life's work. Confronting, talking about, and attempting to change every vestige of ignorance about African Black people being made to feel inferior and European white people being made to feel superior as a result of slavery in the United States is the main material of my art."[4]

She arrived in New York at a time when there were doors to walk through leading to places where she could begin to define and pursue such a project. Two important theatrical streams had just breached conventional aesthetic and exclusionary barriers: the Black Arts Movement and experimental Off-Off-Broadway. In 1964, for instance, Amiri Baraka (also a graduate of Howard, who had studied with Dodson) established, in the wake of the assassination of Malcolm X, the Black Arts Repertory Theatre and School in Harlem, essentially a cultural wing of the Black Power movement. Militant, hyper-masculine, and activist, BARTS was short-lived, but it had tremendous influence, and Robbie was paying close critical

Robbie McCauley (center), Sarita Hunt (left), and Risë Collins (right) in a scene from Ntozake Shange's *for colored girls who have considered suicide / when the rainbow is enuf.* In the background: Laurie Carlos, Leona Johnson, Jonette O'Kelley, Roxanne Reese. 1977. Photo by Martha Swope © The New York Public Library for the Performing Arts.

attention. She involved herself more directly in the nascent Negro Ensemble Company, established officially in 1967 (after a couple of years in which its founding artists were making work together), defining itself as "a theater concentrating primarily on themes of Negro life, but also resilient enough to incorporate and interpret the best of world drama—whatever the source."[5] Robbie joined its apprentice company under the direction of Lloyd Richards. (It was there that she met her close friend and collaborator, Laurie Carlos; a decade later they performed together on Broadway in Ntozake Shange's *for colored girls who have considered suicide / when the rainbow is enuf* and they went on to form a collaborative company, along with Jessica Hagedorn.)

In proposing a Black theater as an alternative to the prevailing "pretentious theater elevating the narrow preoccupations of restricted class interests to inflated universal significance, tacitly assuming that its middle-class, affluent-oriented absorptions are central to the dominant human conditions,"[6] NEC's co-founder, Douglas Turner Ward, could have been writing a manifesto for Off-Off-Broadway. That parallel—or, thanks to artists like Robbie, *overlapping*—movement exploded into being, ignited by countercultural irreverence and a ravenous hunger for new forms and ideas. Between 1960 and 1965, some four hundred new plays by two hundred playwrights went up on the Off-Off circuit, the *New York Times* reported at the time.[7] The circuit included numerous spaces and companies, but primarily comprised four downtown venues within walking distance of each other—Caffe Cino, La MaMa, Judson Poets' Theater, and Theatre Genesis at St Mark's Church. Robbie performed in projects at three of those spaces. (And NEC soon set up shop in the same neighborhood.) While the work varied vastly between and within those venues—ranging from the glittery camp of the Playhouse of the Ridiculous to the radical spectacles of the Bread and Puppet Theater, from the anxious machismo of Sam Shepard to the jagged whimsy of Maria Irene Fornes—it shared a voracious spirit of exploration, low-budget scrappiness, and boho insouciance about making a buck. The work was highly collaborative, with actors frequently improvising or participating in other ways as playwrights reworked their scripts on-the-spot in rehearsals.

Never subscribing to separatism or polarization, Robbie worked in Black theaters and in the whiter avant-garde, bridging an abyss that, as far as she was concerned, existed only for those who wanted it to be there. Among white artists, she asserted and held fast to her commitments "to struggle for Black liberation and the best of human potential"[8] and her colleagues generally respected those principles and, often, stood in solidarity with them. In this formative period, acting in a single season in such disparate works as Archie Shepp's "jazz allegory," *Junebug Graduates Tonight,* and Lanford Wilson's skewed-naturalism of a family play, *The Sandcastle*, she soaked up—and poured her own talents into—the rigor, vivacity, camaraderie, and disputatiousness surging through the theatrical world.

All the while, she labored as a social worker. Apart from paying the rent, the job gave her a close-up view of the impact of social conditions on the most intimate aspects of people's lives. She regarded theater as an important place for speaking about that dynamic. The work also honed a skill that she'd later develop into a key component of site-specific collaborative community theater projects addressing local conflicts, what she came to call "participatory listening."[9]

By the end of the 1960s, Robbie was also beginning to teach at NYU—her replacement day job. Teaching turned out to be as profound a calling as theater-making and, over the years, a key part of her contribution to the American theater.

While Robbie acted in all kinds of plays, including dominant mainstream psychological realism, she was drawn most to experimental forms and, especially, processes. In a *Theatre Journal* forum in 2005 that asked "What is a Black Play," Robbie answered, in part: "good, hard work."[10] She wasn't being flippant. She was summing up the productive effort of making art that was not driven by an *a priori* program, despite its political engagement, but by the mutual exploration of all involved; she was talking about the labor of being in the room and confronting questions openly and honestly.

In the mid-1970s, Robbie was cast in a play that would prove highly influential, not least for combining a complex concern for Black liberation from a female perspective with dazzling theatrical innovation: Adrienne Kennedy's *A Movie Star Has to Star in Black and White*. Premiering at The Public Theater as a work-in-progress in 1976 under the direction of Joe Chaikin, the founder of the Open Theater and champion of an approach to performance highlighting the actor's presence, the play centers on Clara, a Black woman piecing together a fractured identity. Clara (like many of Kennedy's protagonists) is an aspiring writer confronting the social roles she is expected to play, the ideals that various cultural representations offer that grip her imagination, and the obstacles in the way of defining a self—racism, misogyny, and the intertwined specifics of one's own family background. Kennedy constructs the play in a nonlinear, kaleidoscopic way, showing audiences the images and thoughts that course through Clara's mind, some of them scenes from Hollywood movies that Clara projects herself into.

Chaikin's methods inspired Robbie in ways that had lasting impact. His actors worked from "an internal sense of the body," as she put it, and she began "going from the inside of my body out. I didn't realize that I was doing that until years later. Since then I've been experimenting with being present in the body while I'm working."[11] Robbie described the experience of playing Clara as "the highest light of my acting career."[12]

Apart from the play and the techniques for preparing performances, one reason was the rich artistic relationship Robbie forged with Chaikin. The next year, she joined his new communal theatrical workshop, the Winter Project. Meeting for improvisation, discussion, exercises, and eventually, rehearsals, participating actors, writers, and dramaturgs explored techniques like storytelling, focused listening, and devising work from found dialogue. Building on techniques Chaikin developed with the Open Theater, they worked on body, voice, and breath, on the eloquent power of movement and the need for physical expression to be absolutely precise, especially when the material was abstract.

Thematically, they grappled with mortality, the decisive yet fuzzy territory between life and death. Chaikin, who had suffered heart disease since childhood, had recently come back from a grave illness when he formed the Winter Project, and perhaps part of the deep affinity between Robbie and Chaikin involved to some degree their shared, if unspoken, experience of contending with a chronic, life-threatening condition. Of Chaikin, the playwright Jean-Claude van Itallie once said, "Death was always present for him, and making theater was life itself."[13] Chaikin's monologue, "The War in Heaven" (written with Sam Shepard), begins with the lines, "I died the day I was born [. . .] I am here by mistake."[14] I can't help hearing echoes in the opening line of *Sugar*, Robbie's play (her last performed piece, and included in this volume) about living with Type I diabetes (and about the sugarcane trade that was powered by slave labor): "You know," she says, introducing herself to the audience as she chomps on a candy bar, "I suppose to a been dead." She and Chaikin regarded the theater as an urgent business.

That urgency was always as political as it was personal. In Robbie's work in the 1980s with the saxophonist Ed Montgomery (her then-husband and the father of their child, Jessie) the politics were downright declamatory, as the very name of their group suggests: Sedition Ensemble. Montgomery played a funky style of jazz and in their performances together, which included other band members as well, McCauley sang and spoke lines that addressed pressing issues from a self-described "anti-imperialist" perspective. Drawing from newspapers, other found texts, and improvisations during rehearsals, McCauley and Montgomery scripted the material, but it

The Sedition Ensemble's *The History of the Universe According to Those Who've Had to Live It*, Dartmouth College, NH, 1981. Photo: © Nancy Wasserman.

felt spontaneous and immediate in performance. They made some half dozen pieces, which they toured around the country, playing on college campuses, in arts spaces, and elsewhere (affording McCauley the supreme pleasure, she once quipped, of entering a venue and saying, "I'm with the band."[15]) I remember encountering the Sedition Ensemble in the early 1980s at some kind of pro-Sandinista or anti-apartheid event. More vividly, I recall a lyric about the "arrogance of power" and an audience chant-along section: "USA, CIA: Out of Central America!"

In a survey on cultural activism in the mid-1980s in the left cultural magazine *Upfront*, Robbie wrote about the Sedition Ensemble's work: "Concern with U.S. involvement in Central America is essential in our search for images to expose the imperialist nature of the U.S. government. I'm concerned, however, that white artists may be using this issue to avoid their own and the society's systematic and now more subtle racism here against Blacks, Native Americans, and Puerto Ricans especially. I hardly ever see white artists confess their whiteness in all this, in their work. I see the denial of guilt and a trendy awareness of apartheid and oppression in Central America."[16] Robbie and Montgomery (who is white) created a duet performance called "Nicaragua in Perspective" to address this issue head-on.

At the same time, Robbie was beginning to feel the pull of storytelling about her own family background as a means of taking on, in the public forum of the theater, the persistent scourge of American racism, all the more tenacious for not being faced squarely by white people. By the early 1980s, the genre of performance art was an available framework for such inquiries. Generated in large part by feminist visual artists who were challenging both the commercial fetishization of the art object and their own silencing by a male-dominated, increasingly profit-driven art world, they began to claim space and voice within galleries, replacing collectible works on the wall with the ephemeral performances of their own bodies and words. From within the theater world, artists whose experiences were seldom honestly represented on mainstream stages crafted autobiographical pieces, flouting the restrictions of dramatic conventions and avoiding, too, traditional theater's big budgets for scenery, costumes, and a large cast. At their best, the personal revelations in such work didn't serve a narcissistic purpose of bringing the author/performer therapeutic closure but, rather, opened up an inquiry into larger, contextual questions for an audience, through the empathic connection with the story of the real, live person before them.

In this respect (among others) performance art extended the Off-Off-Broadway experimentation of the earlier generation. As in Chaikin's projects, in performance art, the actor does not seek to disappear into a fictional character, but to make the incontrovertible fact of her presence an acknowledged and rich source of the work. This was fertile ground for Robbie.

Another collaboration with Chaikin helped lead her to it: *Solo Voyages*, a collage of monologues from Adrienne Kennedy's plays, directed by Chaikin and presented at Women's Interart Theater Center in the fall of 1985. Culling material from *A Movie Star Has to Star in Black and White* along with *A Rat's Mass* and *The Owl Answers*, Chaikin (in his first directing project after suffering a stroke the previous year) distilled Kennedy's incantatory, poetic language into text

Robbie McCauley in a scene from the Interart Theatre's production of the performance piece *Solo Voyages* (New York). 1985. Photo by Martha Swope © The New York Public Library for the Performing Arts.

for a single actor. McCauley played Clara—Kennedy's recurring protagonist—and all the people she encounters, recalls, or imagines as she tries to discover her own legacy and chart a future. Robbie likened Chaikin to a conductor of the piece, helping to score the contours of her emotional connection to Kennedy's imagery rather than methodically (and Methodically) construct a psychological character.[17]

Robbie credited the example of Kennedy's work with inspiring her to write about her family, "not just biographically, but as a part of the bigger history we were born into. The personal parts of my story are a key to bigger ideas."[18]

And one more impetus: the Reaganite 1980s—years of backlash against the gains of the civil rights movement (among others) and a major shift in the American ethos away from the New Deal belief in the commonweal toward an everyone-for-themselves scramble for individual gain. Robbie was particularly stung by the depiction of Black people as menacing criminals. "How terrifying Black people were in the mind of the media—I was just mortified because as I remembered, growing up, the white people were the scary ones," she said. "My visceral impulse was to get the story straight. That was what was roaring inside of me, that the image of Black people is so wrong. So I started to tell stories about my family, who are so regular, but suffered dramas, in terms of racism, and then I started thinking—duh—not just my family."[19]

That distorting imagery—which combusted in a toxic mix of racism and mendacity with the infamous Willie Horton ads in George H. W. Bush's presidential campaign in 1988, and that festers openly in American politics today—became a direct topic of work Robbie made along with Laurie Carlos and Jessica Hagedorn in their company called Thought Music, which collectively created several major shows. *Teenytown*, for instance, first presented at Franklin Furnace in 1987, explicitly and disturbingly confronted the relentlessness of racist stereotypes by putting them in the audience's face. Projecting old stereotypical cartoons, singing minstrel songs, and telling offensive jokes in the context of a TV talk show, the trio of Thought Music summoned up the repressed to reveal its relentless grip on the American imagination.

Robbie's early pieces based on her family—she counted *My Father and the Wars*, completed in 1985, as the first (and later folded it into *Indian Blood*)—take a less confrontational tone, but are no less pointed in their critique of the battlefield that was everyday life for Black men in America like her grandfather and father (who also served in actual wars). In telling their stories, with moral complexity, political layering, sly humor, and frank theatricality, Robbie made something new and distinctly hers from the artistic wisdom she began accruing so many years earlier at Howard, when she stumbled into Owen Dodson's rehearsal of *Medea*. Climbing a rickety ladder in *Indian Blood* and with the Sedition Ensemble vamping behind her, Robbie says:

> I come to avenge
> avenge my father's death.
> To play Medea.
> Play Antigone.
> Play Electra.
> To play Medea, whose
> father was king.
> Medea, whose father was king, was considered a barbarian by the privileged Corinthians. I know Medea well.

And in her last performed piece, *Sugar*, in which she reflected on her own personal and professional history, Robbie asks, "How do I look back, go forward, and be here at the same time?"

Nobody knew better than she did that she answered her own question by standing on stage and posing it: Theater, after all, is an art form of the relentless present, but one that builds retrospection and anticipation as it moves inexorably forward.

This book, we hope, provides a partial answer, too: looking back as it reviews Robbie's substantial oeuvre and going forward as it provides texts for those who wish to study them and stage them in the future with new perspectives and extended purpose.

1. Robbie McCauley from a public interview I conducted with her on April 7, 2017, as part of "Robbie McCauley 'n Company: A Convening in Performance" at Emerson College, Boston.

2. Robbie McCauley described her work this way in the bio she provided for "What Happened?: A conversation between Robbie McCauley and Bill Rauch," *Theater* 31, no. 3 (November 2001): 109.

3. Robbie McCauley, "The Struggle Continues," in the Forum on Black Theatre, *Theatre Journal* 57, no. 4 (December 2005): 585.

4. Robbie McCauley, "Mississippi Freedom: South and North," *Theater* 24, no. 2 (Summer 1993): 88.

5. Douglas Turner Ward, "American Theater: For Whites Only?" *New York Times*, August 14, 1966.

6. Ward, "American Theater: For Whites Only?"

7. Elenore Lester, "The Pass-the-Hat Theater Circuit," *New York Times*, December 5, 1965.

8. McCauley, "The Struggle Continues," 584.

9. Robbie McCauley and Vicki Patraka, "Obsessing in Public," *TDR* 37, no. 2 (Summer 1993): 36.

10. McCauley, "The Struggle Continues," 585.

11. Interview, "Robbie McCauley 'n Company: A Convening in Performance."

12. Robbie McCauley, "Swirling and Connecting Since the '60s," an essay included in the Soho Rep. publication of Daniel Alexander Jones's *Duat* (On Stage Press, 2016): 127.

13. Jean-Claude van Itallie, contribution to "Joseph Chaikin (1935–2003)," *Village Voice*, July 8, 2003.

14. Joseph Chaikin, Rick Harris, and Sam Shepard, "The War in Heaven (Angel's Monologue)," *Performing Arts Journal* 9, no. 2/3 (1985): 249.

15. Interview, "Robbie McCauley 'n Company: A Convening in Performance."

16. Robbie McCauley with Ed Montgomery and the Sedition Ensemble, response to "Cultural Activism: Movement or Murmur?" *UPFRONT: A Publication of PADD (Political Art Documentation/Distribution)*, no. 12/13 (Winter 1986–87). *UPFRONT*, which began in 1981 under the name *First Issue*, ceased publication in 1986.

17. David Willinger, "Developing a Concert for the Spoken Voice: *Solo Voyages*, and an interview with Robbie McCauley," *Intersecting Boundaries: The Theatre of Adrienne Kennedy*, ed. Paul K. Bryant-Jackson and Lois More Overbeck (Minneapolis: University of Minnesota Press, 1992).

18. McCauley, "Swirling and Connecting Since the '60s," 128.

19. McCauley, "What Happened?: A conversation between Robbie McCauley and Bill Rauch," 109.

# THOUGHTS ON MY CAREER, *THE OTHER WEAPON,* AND OTHER PROJECTS*

*Robbie McCauley*

> Sometimes I feel I'm walking on three feet,
> one in survival, one in rebellion,
> and a third one for balance.
>
> —FROM *SAN JUAN HILL* / THE FATHER PARTS

One day in New York I saw some men working, making a delivery of walls to a storefront space. Men from inside came out. They were all intending to carry the walls into the store. First they greeted each other. One had a cup of coffee. They all seemed uncomfortable. When one started to pull a wall from a flatbed truck, another approached him and asked, "Why are you doing it like that?" The first man turned the wall on its long edge, stooped under, and began to walk his hands along it. The other guy got in front of the first and let the wall land on his shoulder. When they

* "Thoughts on My Career, *The Other Weapon*, and Other Projects" was originally published in *Performance and Cultural Politics*, ed. Elin Diamond (London and New York: Routledge, 1996), 265–82. Reprinted by permission of Routledge/Taylor & Francis.

In this piece, Robbie states she chooses not to capitalize "black." We honor that preference in this twenty-five-year-old essay. In the rest of the book, we follow the contemporary convention of capitalizing "Black" as a proper noun or adjective.

—eds

stood up the sight was spectacular. It reminded me of actors working together.

The performance theater work I have been doing for the last many years has involved a conscious process wherein I sought to address certain assumptions about art, history, community, the personal, and the political. Those assumptions had seemed to me to be an official attitude in this society, mouthed by numerous people educated in the United States—the idea that art about social issues and community either must be done a certain way and must say certain things in order to be relevant, or that such art is doomed to "preach to the converted" and is not good work. I wanted to do a kind of theater I felt I remembered from before I was born.

## I THINK PERHAPS

It came through my mother's memory of the wagon shows. Or maybe it was that there was always live music at the house parties Mother and 'em went to. The house would come alive with perfume, shiny jewels, cigarette smoke, and whiskey smells as she and her sisters slipped themselves into magnificent dresses and splendid shoes. There was good food, a pecan tree, chickens, a fig tree, and the dirt. There was no talk of struggle or freedom. I thought we were already free. Memories that faded too soon.

## I'VE BEEN

Always concerned about power and control, being on the bottom of the heap, fighting, rising, no time to be tired, concerned about the big invisible thing, right people, tiny streams of light, and hidden terror. Scarier still are monsters that smile in the bright day and steal from us.

I'm shy and struggle with a problem of low self-esteem. The problem has puzzled me because I was brought up to advance myself, think for myself, be proud. Well, what your family teaches you is so full of contradictions. I knew very young that I am not only the people I come from, but the world I was born into. As a black girl in the United States in the mid-1940s and 1950s, I felt the contradictions of life in this country were brutal and confusing. What I internalized out of the situation was that I was not all right, but if I got all right, I could be accepted. That is why I think the fault for my problem lies not entirely in myself or in my family but in the government. Government as idea, reality, metaphor. The people my mother called THEY.

## LIKE DIABETES

Low self-esteem may be a condition that has no cure. Like diabetes it may be something you have to control in order to function. Like diabetes, I'm sure there are many biographical reasons for the condition. Like diabetes, I believe the condition also has political reasons. The triangular slave trade in the Americas was largely based on sugar.

A politically conscious woman shared this anecdote with me: I was once at a party with members of an old rich family. Their money had been made from sugar. The waiter put sugar on the table for coffee. One of them pushed it away and laughed. "Poison," another of them said, and they all laughed even harder. Hearsay probably, but I like gossip. Stories that reflect feelings of the insiders and outsiders. Personal stories are usually political. "My father was in the war when I was born . . ." Causes and effects are stated passionately. "My mother wanted to be a lady, but had to work." Despite the general belief in individual choices, people are affected probably more by the wars they are born into than anything. Talking about wars one gets a sense of her own power or lack of it.

People often ask, "Do you eat a lot of sugar?" when they discover I have diabetes. I sometimes answer, "Well . . . partly." Diabetes is not a result of eating too much sugar. The causes for it are a combination of genetic, psychological, and dietary things, and each case is individual. Its cure may lie in the recognition of it as a condition of imbalance, of each person learning how her whole body ought to be nurtured. Yet, I've become dependent on western medicine to maintain my life, and though I am in good shape, I do have annoying problems. Even the excellent internist with whom I'm finally working is puzzled by the extremes of my case. I'd have questions about balance if I did not have diabetes. The tightrope image for me catalyzes clear thinking and change.

I want to continue in the tradition of performance art, which encourages people to learn from the past and to challenge the stories. I want to follow a tradition that heightens the connection of art to life. I have particular obsessive urges to analyze the world I was born into. I've had certain key, gut artistic influences. I call myself an artist to demystify the term. I always imagine my mother in the audience. Art is work. I'm also a mother, which is extraordinary. I want to build on a form of performance as discourse. The first Last Poets, whom I saw in 1969 in a loft on downtown Second Avenue, New York, who consisted of Gylan Kain, Felipe Luciano, and David Nelson, initially inspired me to create my own work.

As luck would have it, with my interest in charged form and content, I arrived in New York City in 1965 at a time when experimental theater and black theater were present up and down the city. By 1979, I had gained some reputation as a "good actress," had received an Audelco Award in 1974. I worked at the Judson Church on Washington Square; Circle in the Square on Bleecker Street; the Caffe Cino, a crowded bar, and sometimes theater, on Cornelia Street all in the West Village; La MaMa E.T.C., when it was the experimental theater club in a second-floor loft on Second Avenue, catty-cornered southeast of Gem Spa [a newsstand] and later in a basement on East 9th Street; the Negro Ensemble Company then on the northwest corner across from Gem Spa; and The Public Theater at Lafayette and Astor, all in the East Village. I lived first at 3rd and MacDougal and later on East 9th Street. The fire of change and rebellion in the world at that time was reflected in the theater. Downtown. Uptown. I had a chance to observe work by the Open Theater under the direction of Joseph Chaikin and the New Lafayette in Harlem under the direction of Robert Macbeth.

I would have been dead or crazy years ago had I not become an actor. A bewildered young black woman with a do-gooder attitude, I crossed into a world where I saw that one's talent helped to define one's identity, a world where I felt encouraged to follow my impulses to find beautiful ways to express hard feelings. I came to New York in my early twenties to seek new experiences, but had been brought up well enough not to fall all the way off the edge. I literally tuned in to my insides, as was the mode of the day, and seized upon the stirrings inside me as raw material.

Performance theater work fulfills my desire to make a contribution to the world of culture. In 1979, with composer Ed Montgomery and his musical group, Sedition Ensemble, I began to create musical performance-theater pieces. Since then, I've concentrated on engaging the audience and performers to face charged issues. I do have concern for the essentials of time, money, and status in work, but I've often felt immobilized by the majority of well-meant advice offered over the years on how to be successful in the theater.

## IN MY FAMILY

. . . A passion for history, a sense of connection with the past. No great scholars in the family, but stories survived from the time of slavery told in snatches around the breakfast table, as answers to mine and Sister's constant questions, and even as declarations in my father's drinking rages: "We fought for this country for you to be free, so don't be giving me no lip." Things like that.

Ed Montgomery and I felt almost the same way about the drama inherent in political text. He had already started a collection of startling passages from pamphlets, rallies, and news reports from which we selected tell-able stories. Avowed anti-imperialists, we followed the events of political prisoners in current U.S. history including Geronimo Pratt, Leonard Peltier, Assata Shakur, and Lolita Lebrón as protagonists, with Uncle Sam, the FBI/CIA, and several right-wingers as antagonists. We worked with several musicians and performers in the New York area. Even with a range of political and spiritual beliefs among us, and very little money, nobody was turned off from the views of history Ed and I espoused. Bern Nicks, Martin Aubert, Bob DeMeo, Valois Mickens, Verna Hampton, April Green, Crystal Joy, the late Jay Oliver, Jaribu Hill and Ngoma Hill, Sharita Hunt, a host of dedicated artists . . . affirmed my belief that what is performed *about* is essential.

## BACK THEN IN GEORGIA

Dr. B. was the best-educated, nicest man. He made house calls. A black man to look up to. He got killed, downtown, stepping in between the police and another black man they say the police were getting ready to shoot on Broad Street, or something like that. They say white folks came to his funeral. Not much was said about what happened downtown, and no justice was done. After that, not much foolishness was tolerated. My Aunt Jessie started using the phrase, "Do like the white folks do."

Sedition Ensemble terminated from natural causes. Groups get to the end of their time. I now miss the uncompromising politics as the source of the work, but then I missed the personal stirrings. I continued to seek a way to balance both. Ed and I worked with the late performer Bob Carroll from 1982 to 1984. In a piece of his called *Dirt*, I began to create *San Juan Hill.* This became the basis of a series about my family's survival since the nineteenth century, "Confessions of a Working-Class Black Woman," and included *My Father and the Wars*, *Indian Blood*, and *Sally's Rape.* I was revved up by the stories my family had told me. My imagination kicked in. I began to see possibilities of teaching history in a non-academic way.

## BUFFALO

I did this series out of the obsession for examining my feelings about survival. The work was structured like jazz music with black and white players. In 1988 we played at Hallwalls, an art center in Buffalo, with *Indian Blood.* By then I was already impressed with how audiences of many races identified with this work. Riding around in the town, I observed the racial separations of neighborhoods, as usual in U.S. cities.

I was influenced to open up the connection with the audience by a conversation with Ron Ehmke, who curated the work at Hallwalls. I asked him if there were any stories in Buffalo concerning race that the community shared. Ehmke told me about the "riots" there in 1967, and told me about a sociological study of it based on interviews with people in the town. The concept of working with actors was my own. Having taught for several years, I was anxious to share some of the work I'd been doing with students, how one's personal biography is part of history and how that affects the actor's voice. Ehmke applied for and received a grant from the New York State Council on the Arts for such a project. *The Buffalo Project* was the first work I did with text from local witnesses.

*The Buffalo Project*, Hallwalls Contemporary Arts Center, Buffalo, NY, 1990. Left to right: Laverne Clay, Tom Dooney, Catherine Horton, Barry T. Burts, Lorna C. Hill. Photo: © Hallwalls, Inc. Photographer: Paul DeFrain.

There is always a personal and political investment in work. Having grown up in the southern United States and having moved to the North later, I was affected by the out-and-out all-day-long racism in both areas. I wondered how events I was told about, known as "the riot" in Buffalo in 1967, reflected racial attitudes in a northern industrial city. Ed Montgomery, whom I had by then married and who is the father of my daughter, is a second-generation member of an Italian working-class family of Buffalo. This intensified my curiosity about the place.

The assignment for each actor was to interview one or more people in Buffalo about the riots. This would include a variety of people, whether or not they experienced it. For instance, the actors themselves, who either grew up in the community or had come later and heard stories, were witnesses. The script would be a basis for talking about racial relations in Buffalo today. I knew that the performance would include choral passages. I like the idea of modern events having the choral voice. In Buffalo the cast consisted of ten people from age seventy to age twenty-two, with several stated identities—men and women, black, Jewish, Protestant, Catholic, mothers, fathers, Italian. Thus began a way of working that became basic for subsequent projects. The actors and I declared a safe space in which to express thoughts and feelings about the subject matter, and to listen to each other.

Some have asked me about the relationship of my "histories" work to that of Anna Deavere Smith (author and performer of *Fires in the Mirror* and *Twilight: Los Angeles, 1992*). The recognition of the way people talk about the charged issues in the United States is something I think we're both exploring. We also share a certain intelligence about acting and, of course, blackness. Aside from feeling naturally jealous of her fame, I like the similarities. Her particular talent and work is so fine-tuned that mine does not compare. The truth is I have neither the skill nor the interest in being so precise. Working with actors in the places I am investigating, the personal response of the actors to the content of the witnesses interviews, the mirror reflecting the community back on itself and dialogue about it, are my priorities. I am eternally grateful to the actors who engaged with me in exploring their towns, so many actors on various levels willing to learn, give up other work, take risks to succeed or not. Unlike Smith, I seldom identify witnesses in the piece. They are given the option as to whether they want to be identified even in the program. I enjoy the question that has emerged about Smith's work. Is it writing? I think that her ability to hear, script, and sculpt what people say is indeed legitimate, possibly great, new writing. My work, though, developed quite separately from hers.

I select an event that stirs me, like the riot in Buffalo, and work with the producer or curator to seek out people in local community and artistic organizations and request meetings with them to talk about collaborating on a project. When we first get together I usually describe my intentions with the image of the Trojan War. It was an event of real and mythical weight that affected not only the participants but also people way beyond that time. These meetings are best when they result in the exchange of images, stories, and philosophical comments. The potential co-sponsors actually get a taste of how the performance allows different points of view to be talked about while retaining passion. Here is where I get the first suggestions for actors and witnesses.

## PRIMARY SOURCES

A series of work, "Primary Sources," produced by Marie Cieri (The Arts Company) from 1991 to 1994 followed *The Buffalo Project. Mississippi Freedom*, about the freedom rides and the voting rights struggle in Mississippi in 1964; *Turf*, about court-enforced busing in Boston in 1974; and *The Other Weapon*, about law enforcement and the Black Panther Party in Los Angeles in 1969 resulted. The event itself, not necessarily as factual history, but as witnessed by people in the place is the clay for the work.

With producer Cieri, there were hours in cars talking about our own likenesses and differences. Once in a Mississippi motel room I badgered her to tell me what it is that white people want. One of the choicest bits of information she told me was that white people have the power and don't intend to give it up. What a relief that was! That made working with her much easier. I have not made up my mind about the role of the producer in performance theater. I know part of her work involves the creative aspect. That was the uneasiest part for me, because I've always been nervous about holding on to what belongs to everyone. What guided me in these projects was to stick to what I wanted to accomplish in the work. The work is valuable in so many ways. Ownership in this work is uncomfortable. I put my name on it to take responsibility for and identify myself as the gatherer and shaper.

Making the transition from the dialogues to the performances is always shocking. The task of the actor is to identify and try to work through resistances and see how material plays from the inside out. The key is the material itself. I try to be fair. I try to be honest. The work is to get actors to be present with information and their own vulnerability in the face of it. As much work as possible must be done to play the material with one's intellect, voice, body, and sense of connection to others. Here is a process by which the actors can learn and teach history.

In a Mississippi meeting, two community leaders actually flinched when I described the way I work. Why work with actors rather than "real people"? I felt that question was an insult to the work of an actor, but I understood the prejudice because of how actors are often perceived. Implied in that question is the discomfort about bringing up painful subject matter and ownership of experience. I explained that I identify myself as the outsider and try to share my passion for the subject matter of each work to help cut through people's resistance to the outsider. I explained that I felt the work of artists was to connect to the community and try to interpret and reveal history. I explained that I wanted to find among them, perhaps, people who may want to act, and to support the proposition that storytelling is real work. Later both of these leaders welcomed the final project. Theirs were two of the most responsive audiences. The assumption seems to be that actors are some strange creatures that do not walk among regular folks. I assume that actors are everywhere, like musicians.

## ONE MIGHT SAY

My family is conservative. This takes many forms among black people. It often has to do with words. African American is a conservative name. Negro capitalized. I like language. I like black uncapitalized. I lean to the left politically. Brought up in a reasonably well-functioning, reasonably intact black family in the U.S., I saw later in life what a prized condition that was. Still, angry and rebellious impulses began to inhabit my persona.

## I STILL GET BITTER

Exhaustion from too much humiliation. Rage is healthy, more active. As an actor, I'm interested in the range of emotions that emanate from anger. Jean Paul Sartre, the French philosopher, once wrote that love and fear were the only emotions. Maybe. I work with emotion as if it is energetic material at the source of my being. Moving through it is a journey that is sometimes beautiful, can keep one from sinking into it.

Acting is basic to work I create. Intelligence is a valuable element of the craft. It is an element that ought to be identified and nurtured. I believe it is an element that is, especially in the anti-intellectual culture of the United States, systematically undervalued. The best teaching of acting too often impedes the thinking process. "Don't think," is a common admonition to the actor. This makes sense in many cases where tension and judgment are inhibiting her. The question, "What are you thinking?" whether answered or not, may be more useful. However, in eliciting the actor's presence, I find it valuable to explore what is being thought. Uncharted dialogue, daring talk, not humiliation, but fiery personal analysis of ideas, is raw material for work.

Becoming intellectually engaged with new details can be empowering for actors. In the Los Angeles project, there was a lot of resistance from the performers, especially the men. I usually welcome resistance, especially from men. I have a talent to recognize, name, open up, and explore the information inside of the resistance. Resistance is information. Perhaps bitterness, too, is information to be picked apart and used.

I use what people already know, what they may not know, surprising details, strong images, a sense of the absurd, and that we are all a part of different stories. I aim to neither bash, nor to forgive the privileged, neither to praise nor blame the underprivileged, but simply to include more stories. I do have a prejudice in favor of those who've been systematically denied. How history is taught continues to be challenged. The powers that be in the academy, who naturally fear change, still stifle stories, and isolate contributions of those not in the official versions. In the new theater, performers are teaching history. This work need not diminish academic versions, but it may include more people, more life and more sense of continuity from one time to another.

Actors can rather safely explore the painful, the sad, the fearful, the so-called negative conditions and be able to perform them with energy, joy, beauty, power. Recognition of blocks and belief in the ability to penetrate them are craft elements. For instance, you may visualize a stone block and imagine you have a hammer and chisel. The block is full of things you are resisting—learning lines, feeling the emotions that the words bring up, listening to the director, whatever. Your will to move toward what you are resisting is the hammer and chisel. Moving or pounding at the block can transform one's resistance to a meeting with what's inside the block. From inside there, something new may be made. This work, basic to acting, is useful for audiences as well—to see examples of people grappling to think clearly.

I've been fortunate to work with master directors. Lloyd Richards persuaded me to say to myself: "I am an actor." To admit that felt scary and strangely powerful.

Gilbert Moses, who'd trained directly with Viola Spolin (author of *Improvisation for the Theater*), spoke the language of animal imagery in a down-to-earth tone that my body responded to. "You're like a goat," he told me one day, rehearsing Ed Bullins's *The Taking of Miss Janie*. Right away I began to move more freely.

Bill Duke, for *DREAM* at the Negro Ensemble Company, gave the actors situations that put such a demand on our imaginations that we learned to perform a piece that was never written down. I still remember the lines from it.

Carl Weber, who directed the original Ed Bullins's *Jo Anne!*, one day called me over and described how he was making the story move. Whether he sensed that I needed to feel part of the creation of the play, I don't know, but I could feel my resistance move away, and thought he was very clever.

Joseph Chaikin some years after, said to me, "You have many voices inside you," and gave me a tape of Marian Anderson singing spirituals to listen to, not to sing he said, just to hear.

Conversational music, choruses, dialogue, poetry, monologues are new and old forms at my disposal. This work is endemic to the poetry, politics, and music of the 1960s black cultural movement.

It requires a willingness and some technique in involving oneself personally with the content of text. I am still experimenting with how to articulate it. The mystery of it has to do with the commitment to explore the subject matter. These projects work more or less on that basis. Giving voice to the range and subtlety of feelings about charged issues is the task here. Mainly educated in western culture I use all I can, including a visceral imagination out of my blackness. Certain images emerge consistently. The human heartbeat and color are basic. Jazz is the major inspiration. Each actor is an instrument whose keys when played resonate her experience and imagination. Being willing to tune her instrument to the material (or score), to enter a time and space to play herself with others is basic to acting. I experience jazz and theater as a source of infinite manifestations with an African American center.

## A CHANGE IN MOTION

I miss dancing for the hell of it. Except for my Aunt T, who drank too much and was great fun, my family tightened up so much in Georgia that it became hard to let go. My confessions come from that. I had to admit the murderous jobs people take in order to survive. My grandfather and my father were soldiers for the government. I hate that I was the one born with the bad pancreas and so many sad feelings. I inherited my father's wars. Men are little gods propped up to play the role of savior. I have never been able to just jump up and down. It would make me cry so uncontrollably to be happy that I'd miss it anyhow. I've been diagnosed as irritable. Still, the sources of my rage are political. I will not rest until confessions of privilege come from all sides.

White supremacy is a better term for the kind of racism I'm dealing with. The idea that white people are something special and that to identify with the white condition is a good thing has been so much a part of European colonial thinking that so-called white people and colonized people all over the world have internalized the thought for centuries. People easily bristle at these statements. People who consider themselves white may be tired of being put in the role of oppressor, and may feel there's nothing they can do about it anyway.

We know that black slavery and Indian land were the reasons for the success of U.S. and European capitalism. If we all have ancestors who somehow gained or lost from that story, we may be able to continue with less irrational prejudice. I am amazed at how much in denial people in the U.S. are. It makes the general population, black and white, seem hopelessly ignorant. We relate to one another in a reactive mode. We seem terrified of facing the truth about class. Whites seem as if they may disappear if they had to admit they're nothing special in relation to other peoples. Native American people seem to have withdrawn (which may save us all), and other populations, especially blacks, seem exhausted and desperate.

I encourage white actors to take the material of how their families participated in, or received privileges from, the horrors of racism and take time to think about it. I announce at the start of all these projects that I will not try to be objective. Black people by necessity are smart about social conditions. I encourage black actors to look for and admit what they don't know. Certain recognitions about craft come up in this work. There needs to be a healthy arrogance about one's ability to dialogue about the subject matter. Coupled with that arrogance is the recognition that vulnerability is the source of strength for the actor. The ability to grapple with vulnerability and arrogance comes as a result of extensive dialogue between us.

## *THE OTHER WEAPON*

February 1994. It is the day I hand out the first few pages of *The Other Weapon*. It is the day the actors see their names as characters. It is the day the group resistance seems impenetrable. However, I trust that such resistance is full of energy. It is shocking, I know, to see one's name in print, especially connected to words stated out of context. It shocked the actors in Buffalo, Boston, and Mississippi too. That I had explained before that this was the way I would write means nothing at this moment. Almost to a person, the actors feel somehow ripped off, betrayed, or unrewarded for their contributions. I do not take time to defend or explain the script pages. I literally have to pry people from the walls in order to lead a warm-up. A sullenness permeates, but the warm-up is effective. Then I assign the actors to tell personal stories with elements related to the charged subject matter of race. We were working in a dusty, dark alternative theater space on Venice Boulevard called Beyond Baroque. "Barely," I say, looking around, reaching for a cheap laugh. No takers. I take a deep breath. The personal story, I think, is the best way to go today. We'll get back to the script later. The actors are thrown back on their ability to listen to each other, to remember, to tell the truth, and/or lie compellingly.

I immediately choose some of those stories for the performance. I consider bebop, the jazz form, popular in the 1940s and 1950s, characterized by improvisation, as a direct source for putting a performance together. The melody may be just a fragment. Push through, I tell myself. Familiar forms can be a way to chip at the block of resistance. Trusting the actor's ability is a craft element for the director, I think grandly. In other words I am desperate to keep on playing. What a day!

In *The Other Weapon* we were concerned with three dramatic events about law enforcement and the Black Panther Party in Los Angeles, 1969–71. The story from that time is that the police attacked a BPP headquarters at 41st and Central Avenue and the Panthers held the police off without anyone getting killed, unlike what happened in Chicago a few days earlier with the infamous police murder of Fred Hampton and Mark Clark. The story res-

*The Other Weapon*, Hollywood Moguls, Los Angeles, CA, 1994. Left to right: Gregory Binion, Lyvingston Holmes, Jane Zingale, Robbie McCauley. Photo by Martin Cox, © and courtesy of The Arts Company.

onates the idea that Los Angeles had a strong black community and that these events signified a victorious moment. A strong point of the story for me was that when the Panthers finally surrendered and emerged from the headquarters, numbers of people from the community were there bearing witness. At the end of this performance, the actors improvise an interview with one of the original women in the headquarters, Sister Somayah "Peaches" Moore-Kambui, who happens to be a performer and agreed to work in the project. The interview segues to the dialogue with the audience. A delightful woman, Sister Somayah helped me to deal with the absurdities and realities of trying to do the work in this way now.

I have had such good experiences working in theater that I tend to expect them. As a director, my struggle for personal strength has been put to the test. I've discovered for myself that the director is not a position of power. It is more Zen than that. The director is a guide and an actor. She has a sense of the world in which she is working. She lets the material and the actors guide her. Sometimes, in order to get things done, she acts like the powerful one. This is the most risky part. The energy of actors comes from so many sources. I continue to aim for processes wherein trust, nurturance, and imagination are basic and effective. Clearly stating what you need to happen inspires actors to be creative.

Kristin Linklater, author of *Freeing the Natural Voice*, received a Ford Foundation grant in 1968 to train people in the United States to teach. As a member of the apprentice company in the early years of Negro Ensemble Company, I had already fallen in love with her work. She had stated that she wanted particularly to work with black people. She had identified something I understood. It was that American actors—especially black American actors—exhibited a good ability to connect with passionate impulses, but not so good an ability to transmit the full power and range of such connections through their voices. She felt that the British actors were more articulate but not so passionately connected. Of course, this was general, and possibly reflected a cultural metaphor. At any rate, it made sense to me. Without question, I responded to her handwritten note on the wall for anyone interested in teacher training with her to write their name and number. The grant allowed me to quit my day job and change my life. The teacher training taught me how to teach how to learn.

## L.A. LESSONS

There are more screaming matches than I would have wanted in this project. In the script I use testimony of one of the actors referring to Rodney King and the killing of a young black woman by a Korean shopkeeper. When the Asian woman protests against the passage, on the grounds that many Asians had responded constructively to that incident, the young black man states his point of view that Asians don't work hard enough against the model minority status they enjoy. I was, as usual, cutting off the white man in the group whenever I felt he was trying to have the last word. In a previous exercise wherein we admitted prejudices I had not admitted that particular one—white men getting the last word—and don't know if I was aware of it then. The older black woman sighs to the young black man that he's being too hard on the Asian woman. The two Latina women complain that again their issues are being ignored. The white man keeps trying to give *the* solution. The older black man agrees with the older black woman that the younger black man is being too hard. The two of them and the two Latina women begin to do a physical manifestation of what is going on, one climbing on top of the other, trying to be the winner. I yell over and over, "L.A. is fucked up!" My losing it lightens things up just a bit.

## UNTIL THIS DAY

Black people get caught into behaving—acting—in order to get along. I met an intelligent, mature black woman painter in Mississippi who had a few white friends. Their affection and support for each other seemed genuine. However, I noticed that the black woman's behavior was full of bad acting, using bad white grammar, as opposed to good black English, all in all an unconvincing portrayal of southern earthiness. After she saw the show and discussion there, she walked up to me with her face discontorted, breathing easily, and simply said, "Thank you." I hoped we had given her permission to relax. I hoped she would begin to be more honestly present with her friends.

Rather than avoid stereotypes, I study them. Stereotypes are based on how people perceive others. People are also consciously or unconsciously driven to act them out. Stereotypes of white people include the idea that they are all extremely self-involved, uneducated about people other than themselves, are unable to understand complicated ways in which people who are not white survive, and are in deep denial about racism. Some of that is sometimes true. Black people are seen as angry, hostile, finding racists behind every bush. There's some truth in some of that. Down south until quite recently it was often a matter of life and death for black people to behave in a prescribed manner. Blacks could not express arrogance, anger, or hostility without risking a violent death.

## IN THE EARLY DAYS

The signs that told you where you could not go. WHITES ONLY. Black people down south who say they did not adhere to that are lying, or they came along when official apartheid was over. We had to. It left a deep mark on my psyche. If there is a collective memory of slavery, harassment, and humiliation among black people, I certainly got my share. My folks worked against the signs by striving to be better. Not so strictly Christian, but strictly patriarchal. Internal ambiguities . . . good Negroes . . . military values . . . southern food . . . bad nigger in there somewhere . . . better not come out. The class and race strivings, that I believed were required, and my rebellion against them, the contradictions remain.

Actors can be effective collectors and transmitters of the meaning of history. The aim is not "to tell real stories from real people," but to create something that emerged from the process of the actor's examination of, and ability to give voice to, the essence of events. *Organized improvisation* is how I describe the connection between that theater art and bebop. The actor herself is the instrument. Her act of thinking becomes physical. She plays herself. She is committed to and has a heightened consciousness of the theme. This work, like bebop, depends upon the mind as an important element of the playing. Each instrument is alone, but is present with all that is being played. Bebop reflects the art of black survival.

> The oppressor is smarter than we thought.
> He's made it passé to be oppressed
> Out of style to be emotional about injustice
> Absolutely boring to wish for his death,
> So we pull ourselves by fashionable boots,
> And try to get over with a hustle or two
> In a world turning backwards, in a world
> turning backwards, in a world turning . . .
>
> FROM *MY FATHER AND THE WARS*

In Mississippi the history of the freedom riders who came from outside the state to help stir up change was the material of the piece. It was an obvious metaphor for my relation to the community. This work, of course, is in no way the same as the political action of the freedom riders. I do not call the telling of stories and making a place for dialogue a political act. Some would say it is. The aim of the work is providing continuity from one generation to the next. The aim of the work is not to gain power for a particular people. The fact that I create work from my black experience is what makes it universal. Many people of all races have internalized the idea that blackness is a limitation. People are able to get beyond that idea.

## L.A. AGAIN

If this city were a character, it might reveal quite clearly the political reality of how the police are used to perpetuate racism and class prejudice in American cities. Black people are definitely targeted as criminals. I, a rather mild-mannered artiste (well, somewhat mild), found myself in a screaming match in a Santa Monica drugstore with a white store manager who physically handled me and accused me of stealing. Most black people I talked to there, no matter what their lifestyle, had had a variety of such occurrences with or without the police. Many felt the attitude of businesspeople reflected that of the police. A Los Angeles Police Department former officer, a white man, gave testimony that young black men are targeted as gang members, are murdered indiscriminately, and that the average police officer has "more respect for a dog" than he has for a young black man.

According to other testimony, many Latino people also had hard times with the police. Asians generally had not. A Japanese man I interviewed told me that he grew up in an L.A. with many Latino hangout buddies. They were periodically picked up by the police, as often happened with young men, especially blacks and Latinos. He said if he were picked up with his Latino friends, he would be dropped off and told to go home, whereas the Latino guys would be taken to headquarters and harassed. One of the most volatile exchanges in the work was an ongoing dialogue between an Asian and a black performer about Asians being seen as, and getting privileges from, being the model minority. The young Asian woman did not like being stuck in this role. The young black man saw her as being in denial of that role. I know it was frustrating to both of them that neither of them won the fight. I hoped that eventually the two got the point, that a lesson from the Panthers is that the class struggle continues, and that more people are becoming consciously affected by it.

The new right wing shows little movement away from the basic position of white supremacy in the United States, or the denial and distortion about it that Malcolm X made plain.

At The Vision Complex, after the first performance of *The Other Weapon* in L.A.'s Leimert Park area, a black community, a fourteen-year-old girl with a pen and pad in her hand stood up and told us how grateful she was about what she was learning. How could she learn more? A woman in that same audience said it brought back parts of her life she never talked about, when she worked in the Black Panther Party programs. A sophisticated black male artist was disappointed because for him the form was nostalgic.

The organized improvisational form took another route in a later performance at the Southland Cultural Center in Inglewood. Included in the piece was a personal story by the Asian woman. She told how her white employer had made a racist remark about Rodney King. She first ended the story by saying how hard it was to say something back to the person who hands out the paycheck. For some reason, she began ending the story by saying that she quit the job. I had told her I thought the first telling was strongest because black and other people could identify with having to keep a job. Well, on one night when she did the revised version, the young black man went at her verbally about revising the story, about not admitting to the model minority status. She went back at him about not hearing the whole story. It played like a good fight scene. In the moment I remembered that he'd warned me he might do this. Maybe my forgetting was convenient. I liked thinking that both actors were in on a possible improvisation. The moment was live and fresh. The performance went on. Another actor jokingly accused me of beaming when it happened.

The L.A. project was by then not what I wanted. My exhaustion made me impatient. Patience is part of the process, and I tried to hold on to it. One actor told me privately that their careers, their images, were always on the line. At Hollywood Moguls during the audience talkback, a white male audience member complained about the portrayal of whites in the piece, whom he perceived as negative characters. I pointed out that there was plenty of okay stuff about white people, but the piece was more about the brutality of the LAPD against black people. Well, I probably was not that clear. The white male actor stated that he'd never left the company no matter how hard it got for him. Clearer.

The best parts of this project for me happened during audience discussions. Many people have asked how this is done. I started this work before I knew what interactive theater was. Having been around a long time, I often have the feeling that I invented something that others caught on to. The truth is that things are in the air. Serious conversations happen often now in public. Talk shows on television, however maddening, are a part of this. I try not to get hung up on who came first, but it is a sensitive thing for me, being black and getting credit. We are all reshaping material, catching things from out of the air. It has been difficult for me to own and then to release ownership. Perhaps generosity is a craft element. The more one shares the work, the more one learns, I keep telling myself.

In L.A. the talkbacks often went on as long as the show, which was about an hour and twenty minutes. At the University of California Los Angeles, several students expressed dismay that they knew few, if any, facts about the 1969 shooting there that was dramatized in the piece. In Hollywood, previous members of the Black Panther Party came and talked back with enthusiasm about how useful the work was in being specific about the Los Angeles Black Panthers. Still others criticized the fact that we did not tell the whole story, or parts they would have liked to tell. I feel there is a balancing act in the work between the artist/outsider and the local artists, the witnesses and the audiences. The tightrope sways also between the parameters of the personal, the aesthetic, the political, the scholarly, and the hearsay. All these elements spill over into each other and surprising things happen. Sometimes the artist has to compromise her aesthetic concerns for the sensitivity of community members.

Learning from mistakes was almost a cliché with the L.A. project. How personal is one able to get without messing up? Personalizing frees the actor's voice. That is the purpose of it. It is not the same as substituting one's own personal experience for one in the performance. It is the work of exercising one's imagination and giving voice to what comes up in response to the issues of the work. This process can weed out what is irrelevant. Artists need to make unique connections with the issues.

A Mexican American woman in the cast had a story about confronting the insults of so-called society women in Beverly Hills. Her story was strong because it was honest and repeatable and because it allowed her imagination to respond to the humor in it. In the performance it was placed as a moment of contemplation, the passing of refreshments to the audience, and a transition to one of the more tragic stories in the piece. The balance of all those elements was my favorite moment.

One night in the after-show talk a black man started to speak and broke into tears. "Take your time," we echoed from the stage like folks do in church. He thanked us for showing what he said he no longer heard people speak of. The end of the work is often the beginning. The L.A. project was not what I wanted it to be. Maybe that is better.

# COMMUNITY PROJECTS: MISSISSIPPI FREEDOM

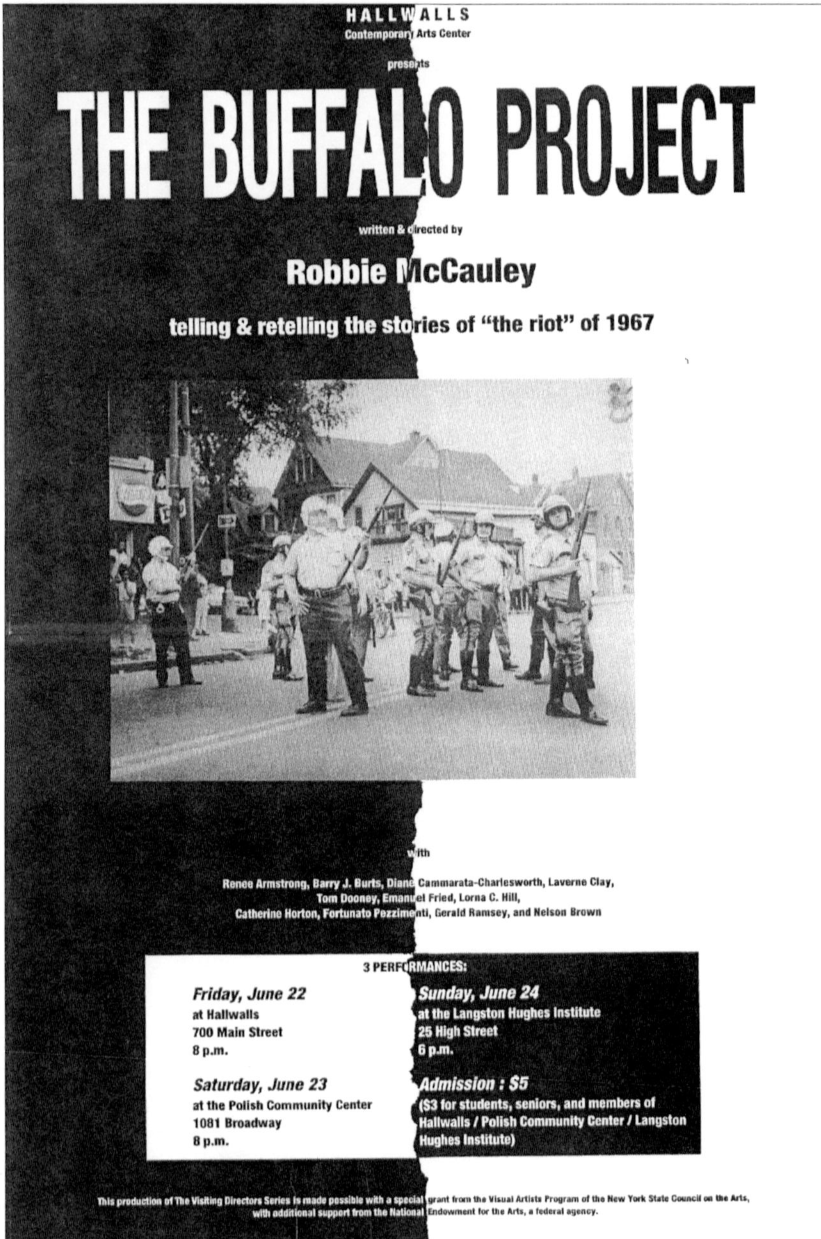


Image courtesy of the Poetry Collection of the University Libraries, University of Buffalo, The State University of New York.

# EDITORS' NOTE

This section offers an example of the community projects Robbie McCauley refers to in the essay "Thoughts on My Career, *The Other Weapon*, and Other Projects." Beginning in 1991, she worked with local actors and community members on researching a past racial conflict that continues to have repercussions in the area (although they often remain unspoken), and devising a performance piece based on that research and on rehearsal workshops. The first of these pieces, *The Buffalo Project* (1989–1990, Hallwalls Contemporary Arts Center, Buffalo, NY), investigates the issues and events of the so-called "Buffalo Riots" of 1967.

From 1991 to 1994, Robbie worked with The Arts Company to create "Primary Sources," a trilogy of new mixed-media performance theater works looking further at race relations in the 1960s and 1970s in different parts of the United States. All three works were made in close collaboration with local artists and grew out of stories collected from the local communities.

The first in this three-part series, *Mississippi Freedom*, focused on the voting rights struggle and toured to seven locations in Mississippi in 1992 (and to the 1993 Whitney Biennial in New York and to Houston in March 1996). The second, *Turf*, addressed the issues of education, race, and class, using stories of the Boston school-busing controversy of the 1970s as its starting point. It was presented at four neighborhood locations in Boston in 1993 and, produced in June 1996 in association with WGBH Radio, Boston, was distributed to public radio stations nationally, often airing along with live local call-in sessions with Robbie and some of her Boston collaborators. The third piece, *The Other Weapon*, centered on stories of the Black Panther Party and was seen at four locations in Los Angeles in 1994.

In 1995, the Fund for New Performance/Video supported Robbie's work in the Czech Republic; she led workshops in Prague with Czech, Romany, and other residents. The result, *Pribehy/So Has, So Hin (Stories/What Has Been, What Is)*, was performed in Prague in 1995.

The example here, is *Mississippi Freedom*: the script, published for the first time, along with Robbie's reflections on the piece in an essay and an interview and some principles about making participatory work developed by Robbie and Marie Cieri (producer of The Arts Company).

# NOTES ON PARTICIPATORY THEATER*

*Marie Cieri and Robbie McCauley*

## TYPICAL PARTICIPATORY THEATER (PT) PROCESSES

### ORIGINS

- PT is grounded in sustained artistic practice.
- PT artist-researchers are dedicated to making theater informed by material compelling to participants and their community or communities.

### PREPARATION

- Identify research location and topic.
- Talk to local theater people and potential community partners.

* The "Notes" are excerpted from: Marie Cieri and Robbie McCauley, "Participatory Theatre: 'Creating a source for staging an example' in the USA," *Participatory Action Research Approaches and Methods: Connecting People, Participation and Place*, eds. Sara Kindon, Rachel Pain, and Mike Kesby (London and New York: Routledge, 2007). Reprinted by permission of Routledge/Taylor & Francis.

- Seek funding and in-kind support (actor-collaborators will be paid for their work, affirming the value of their contribution and the community stories they tell).
- Basic tool: audio recorder.

### Script Development

- Recruit actor-collaborators through people you know or locate at local arts, educational, and community organizations.
- Start PT with repeatable processes:

  "Talk-abouts" focus on the event and why it was chosen.

  Actor-collaborators and artist-researcher(s) record interviews with local citizens who have stories about the event and its aftermath.

  Hold story circles where collaborators dialogue about the stories collected and add their own material (minimum twelve hours per week for three weeks), all recorded.

  Scripts are developed from transcriptions and shaped by artist-researcher(s) in collaboration with actors in a narrative collage informed by jazz rhythms.

### Rehearsal, Performance, and Purpose

- Rehearsals proceed from talk-abouts (minimum twelve hours per week for two weeks). Music, movement, set design added as budget allows.
- Actor-collaborators variously play themselves as well as other characters.
- Modes for addressing the audience with subtlety and/or directness are proposed. Goal is to engage audiences theatrically as well as inspire more stories and dialogue about the targeted event and its legacy.

- Performance spaces are secured in places where stories resonate.
- With the help of actor-collaborators and others in the community, word is spread on the ground and in the media about the performances.

## PRINCIPLES THAT GUIDE US

These are not hard and fast rules, but ones that can inform Participatory Action Research as practiced through theater. Such repeatable guidelines are needed for the process to do what it will and to release us from focusing on the end product so much.

### Commitment and Respect

The artist-researchers and the community commit to the process and agree to consider differences and transformation as core values.

### Humility and Connection

Stories are celebrated as being both personal and bigger than any one individual (i.e., it's not just your story).

### Subjectivity and Objectivity

Subjective understandings and perspectives are as valuable as apparent objectivity.

### Listening and Hearing

These strenuous and essential practices heighten the physical, mental, and sensory aspects of being present with, and paying attention to, what others are saying. Attention to content and presence with one another make for dynamic dialogue that can crack walls between people. Willful acts of listening and hearing are transmissible to audiences and can provide an example that can transform behavior.

### Collaboration and Exchange

Personal exchanges about charged issues during the making of the work are welcome and must be grounded in respect for differences. Such exchanges provide examples for actor-collaborators, researchers, and audiences to continue the conversation beyond the performance space, thereby enhancing possibilities for creative social change.

# MISSISSIPPI FREEDOM: SOUTH AND NORTH*

*Robbie McCauley*

**NOVEMBER 1991.** I am drawn to Mississippi because I fear it. More an actor than anything, I long to confront that fear and talk out of it. Riding the roads here, I can't help thinking about Emmett Till, Fannie Lou Hamer, and Goodman, Chaney, and Schwerner.** At night I think of the darkness. They were taken into the woods, the trees, basements of jails. I am overwhelmed by sadness and pain, but I can't cry. Riding the desolate trek from Philipp to Money, Mississippi, along the Tallahatchie River, where they dumped Emmett Till's body. Marie is driving. Younger and white, she's affected, too. I wonder if I were a Martian, would I feel it. I swear it's in the air,

* "Mississippi Freedom: South and North" by Robbie McCauley was originally published in *Theater* 24, no. 2 (Summer 1993): 88–98. Copyright © 1993 by Robbie McCauley. *Theater* is published by Duke University Press.

** Fannie Lou Hamer (1917–1977) was a community organizer and a leader in the civil rights movement. She cofounded the Mississippi Freedom Democratic Party served as its delegate at the 1964 Democratic National Convention. Hamer was one of the organizers of the Freedom Summer of 1964, a massive, interracial effort to register Black voters across Mississippi and advance Black freedom more generally. Three of its activists—the local Black organizer James Chaney, then 21; the white Jewish civil rights workers from New York City, Andrew Goodman, 20, and Michael Schwerner, 25—were tortured and murdered by members of the KKK and local sheriff's office.

the terror. And there are still no lights on this road. The river is thick and brown. It is almost night in Money. We stop outside the store with the faded Coca-Cola sign where fourteen-year-old Emmett Till allegedly looked at or said something to a white woman, for which he was subsequently tortured and killed by some local white men. By the time we get to Money, I am full of rage. I breathe into it, and know this, too, is why I had to come here.

**FEBRUARY 1992.** *Mississippi Freedom* by Robbie McCauley, produced by The Arts Company, executive director Marie Cieri. We are at Delta State University to do some preproduction work for the tour. I perform some excerpts from *My Father and the Wars.* They are warmly received, the audience largely faculty members. Sentimental and intelligent, sympathetic, good short discussion follows. Large men and gracious women. One cries when I say the actors in Jackson kept talking about healing. Healing, I say, healing. She keeps asking me to repeat it. One of those faces from a southern novel, one of those hard/soft images they use for women down here, steel magnolia, or peaches, which everybody knows have a hard pit at the center. She comes up and touches my Navajo beads and cowrie-shell necklaces. "You are protected," she says, crying. "We may never be able to heal," she says. "You look so young." I let her touch my hand and notice the exquisite way her checked blouse matches a ribbon she wears carelessly about her upswept hair. Her hands have never picked cotton. Later, encircled by sympathetic dowagers, I am shocked to hear one of them say, "I don't know if we *can* heal what our men did to your men in our name."

How I got into this goes back to where I come from. Born in Norfolk, Virginia, with Daddy just gone to war and my grandmother taking Mother, Sister, and me on "the first thing smoking" back to Georgia, my first moments of literacy had to do with knowing how to read WHITE and COLORED signs on water fountains and bathrooms, in train stations, wherever. Ripping down those signs became my life's work. Confronting, talking about, and attempting to change every vestige of ignorance about African Black people being made to feel inferior and European white people being made to feel superior as a result of slavery in the United States is the main material of my art. I am fascinated by denial, confession, and people's attempts to release social and political chains. I am still

Some of the Mississippi-based participants in *Mississippi Freedom*, near Jackson, MS, 1991. James Green, Veronica Cooper, Leroy Divinity, Kay King Valentine, Deborah Imboden, Sameerah Muhammad, Kent Lambert, Clarie Collins Harvey, Sadat Muhammad, Sheila Richardson. Photo: © Marie Cieri, courtesy of The Arts Company.

attempting to codify a process so that it is repeatable for myself and others. Also, for the sake of performance art history, I am naming the process: content as aesthetic.

**THE EARLY 1980S.** Two decades of other people's plays behind me, hearing images inside me connect to the pain of people all around about identity, I start to write, perform in, and direct my own stuff, with composer Ed Montgomery: *The History of the Universe According to Those Who've Had to Live It*, and *Loisaida War Party*. I begin to hear music, jazz or African American classical music, in everything. History defines the present if it is unknown, as some philosopher said. In the work I'm doing, it is essential to study images from history and to listen to what resonates from them. The work is not new by any means: It's in plays by Adrienne Kennedy, by Aishah Rahman. It's work that the men who've played the horns did long ago; that Amiri Baraka is the professor of; that the real original Last Poets played in a loft on Second Avenue in 1969. It is, of course, an African American aesthetic, and therefore universal. Its source is the banned drum and the obsession to communicate. The slave ship, the middle of the ocean, rage, hope, and creative solutions to oppression are the aesthetic's central images. Willingness and ability to use a particular experience of living, to tune into the memory of ancestors, to identify and confront history are the material. The content informs the form. It is personal and political. It is ritualistic and unfixed.

So begins a series of performances about my Black working-class family struggling to survive in the United States, fighting their wars, living with the contradictions of freedom (*San Juan Hill*, *My Father and the Wars*, and *Indian Blood*). On tour with *Indian Blood* to Hallwalls (Contemporary Arts Center) in Buffalo I talk to performance curator Ron Ehmke about my interest in doing something about racism in Buffalo, a city I'd heard rumors about, but did not know firsthand. Hallwalls curates *The Buffalo Project* in 1990. The subject is the 1967 riots in the Black community bordering on the Polish community, and I begin the method I continue to develop in Mississippi.

In both Buffalo and Mississippi, I connect with African-American theater companies who use both Black and white actors: Ujima Theatre in Buffalo and Potpourri in Jackson. The process centers on meetings between their community-based actors and me while we are interviewing witnesses to the historical event. The stories that emerge from the interviews become the basis for our conversations. I create the texts directly out of these dialogues.

Intimacy is more important than truth in theater. Who is telling the story is more important than truth. None of this means that truth is not important. It means that intimacy and presence are more important. One's willingness to speak makes the truth resonate. In the meetings with actors, we learn to listen to each other in every way possible. Eventually these processes permit the audience members to hear things from people they are not used to listening to, about issues that have been barriers between them.

There were eleven actors, four white and seven Black, five men and six women, from various parts of the state, all except one with some professional or community theater experience. None of what was exchanged between us in rehearsals was any more sensational than what happens in other Black or white lives in this country, but it was all informed by the extremity of Mississippi's apartheid and historical isolation. The willingness of the actors to give up resistance to confronting that history, to engage in relentless dialogue about it, and to admit cultural secrets, made the work rich.

I initiated this work with the American Festival Project in Mississippi in 1990, whose organizer, Barbara Nayo Watkins, helped me contact people there. Cieri's Arts Company subsequently came on as producer and raised money through the NEA, the Rockefeller Foundation, and the Ruth Mott Foundation to finance us. I knew that I wanted to work with people who were directly affected by the history, and to make sure that they got paid for it.

Marie drives through Mississippi with me and we've had artist/producer and, yes, Black woman/white woman tension throughout, but not to worry, just par for the course.

**MARCH 1992.** With the actors in Jackson. Improvisational dialogue among the actors and me is essential. I am impressed by how easily they all accept the edgy form I am proposing, requiring them to play themselves as characters. That they are part of the community is the point. The civil rights movement of thirty years ago is treated like the Trojan War. Everybody knows something about it, whether they want to say so or not. We begin to develop questions to guide interviews with witnesses. One of the Black women suggests that we concentrate on body functions: How did people eat, go to the bathroom, get their clothes washed? She relates how her mother didn't want her and her sister to have anything to do with the freedom riders, but they did anyway. They'd put some of the stranger's dirty T-shirts in their laundry. She thinks her mother knew and that saying nothing was her action.

The first chorus in the piece is from the testimony of a Black, middle-class businesswoman and Christian activist in her seventies who tells how the freedom riders were headed to New Orleans, but had to stop at Jackson because they had to go to the bathroom:

> . . . They were never able to relieve themselves. So when they got here to Jackson . . . and all this was in the trial . . . the sign on the black toilet said OUT OF ORDER . . . and in their urgency, they went to the white restroom because there was no sign on the door. And in the process of relieving themselves . . . the freedom riders were arrested.

The first dialogue comes out of a dynamic confrontation during the workshop between the same Black woman actor and a young man actor who happens to be her twenty-ish son.

SON: Wait a minute . . . I'm glad that we're doing this project. It seems there hasn't been enough told about this era . . . I don't know . . . People are trying to forget about it for some reason. I don't know about that fear . . . But it's hard for me to imagine how bad it was . . . being so scared of some men in sheets.

MOTHER: You're just weak. We failed to pass it on. We were tired of fighting. We didn't give it back. You're just weak because it's not as hard.

Another strong moment comes the same night from a thirty-ish white woman who's recently returned to college. It turns into the first improvisational confrontation between the actors.

DEBORAH: Whose point of view is all this? I have some contradictions. I don't feel comfortable. How are we supposed to make people feel? Whose truth is this? What is the truth anyway? Why don't I know the same history you know?

The student never says the line quite like that again in the performance, but her questions raise the level of confrontation between Blacks and whites in the group.

Sitting on two queen-sized beds in my hotel room, eating punch and popcorn, the atmosphere is intimate and comfortable. A white Christian activist actor woman relates how keeping her father's job was important enough to prevent her from having a Black girlfriend in her wedding. Most of us hear how hard it is for her to admit that. I keep repeating that I am more interested in learning how to listen than in being "objective." I say that the project will be from the African American point of view, that there will not necessarily be equal time for the white view. I've already admitted my guilt about not having been a freedom rider. I am surprised by the lack of knee-jerk objections to my lack of objectivity.

**MAY 1992.** A rehearsal at Smith Robertson Museum in Jackson. We are close to opening, yet the process continues. There is enough in place to go from beginning to end, but I resist the "professional" practice of having the show "locked in" by now. Jazz improvisation as a mode of theater is what I am pursuing at the moment. Playing the interlocutor role, I go too far with the general contractor/actor who jokingly calls himself the resident redneck. He does an "admittance," a personal image that reveals a cultural secret. The admittance may or may not be part of the performance. It is mainly for the sake of filling the actor's well, so he can draw upon it in discussions with the audience. In an earlier rehearsal, I had asked the two white male actors to be like scared rabbits running through the woods with dogs chasing them—I didn't put that image in the performance, but used it as an emotional reference. Today, the contractor tells a story about being taught as a youngster by older teenagers to watch out before hitting a Black man to make sure he's not "a blue-gum nigger 'cause a blue-gum nigger had bacteria that could poison your blood."

I'm supposed to give notes. For the first time, after many visits and dialogues between us, my rage comes up. Bringing up the scared rabbit image, I batter him verbally, right into his face: "How did it feel to be the lyncher? . . ." Shaming him. He is hurt and tells me so without breaking the rhythm. I stop the rehearsal and apologize too fast, too furious, bad acting. Both the Black and white Mississippians in the cast assure me many of them had heard the "blue-gum" image before. Without further discussion, the actors shape the moment by responding to the image. Some of the Black actors tease him by pulling their lips open to show off their gums. This moment remains a strong one in performance, where he can be counted on to pick up after the teasing, and say, "I don't know if it's funny or sad, but looking back, I can recall that I did not recoil in horror," like a rhythmic coda.

**PREMIERE. SMITH ROBERTSON.** We planned the show as interactive with the audience, to demystify the form. Because of last minute this and that, light cues are not ready. I trust that the content is the compelling element, so I start by talking to the tech crew out loud, calling out cues.

This establishes a repeatable improvisational style, and the top of the show from then on is different each time. We didn't realize how hot and dry the room would be, or how hard it would be to hear the actors. The audience sits throughout and leans forward, or calls out for the actors to talk louder. This helps when the moment comes for actors to talk to the audience about school integration. I say we want to know not only about what happened in the late 1960s when schools in Mississippi were federally legislated to desegregate, but also about the schools in Mississippi now, the successes and failures of desegregation, whether mixing with whites was valuable for Black people.

One Black college professor says he doubts the value of integration for Blacks except as a means of getting better facilities. A white woman, a health worker, I think, talks about how school integration means nothing if Black and white people do not go to church or socialize together.

A white male actor, a philosophy professor at a traditionally Black college, says he feels integration has not yet begun, but he sees value in it. In an earlier admittance, this actor had responded to the whole issue of the rape of slave women. He told how he'd discovered, as he'd suspected that many white men had, that the stereotype of Black women being mysterious, exotic sexual objects was not true, but many were brilliant and powerful. He admitted that if white men in power were to systematically admit such a thing, they'd have to give up the whole illusion of supremacy. I'd argued that the material privileges were even harder to give up, but was impressed by his admittance. I felt it helped his statement in performance on the value of integration to resonate, to have more grit.

Witnesses' names and characters are not revealed in the script, but are listed in the program. Tonight, many of them are in the audience. An actor asks them to stand and calls out their names. Ms. Annie Devine, who accompanied Fannie Lou Hamer to Atlantic City in 1967 when the Mississippi Freedom Democratic Party challenged the Democratic Party, is there. She had come two hours before the show and sat silently in the second row waiting as the preparations were made. She is in her eighties. After the witnesses we name sit down, she stands up with the aid of two younger men on either side of her. Then she tells them to sit down. Her back is straight. She speaks, congratulates us, says she feels good to see this because we are telling the truth. I feel we have been blessed.

**SEPTEMBER 1992.** The tour. I realize that the two white guys, one a rock-and-roll sound man and the other a good ol' boy with a thick drawl, are who'll travel with us on the tour. I feel this is my fault since I'd insisted to Marie that we use local people. They are trying to figure out how to hook up the lights. Guy two is going to work the slides in the show, which he tells me he's never done, but by tomorrow, he'll be an expert. I sense his humor and ease about my being his boss. This ease seems to make him feel okay about making ignorant, defensive comments about Black people. I learn to answer him, in the style of the show, by trying to make him think. On the ride to Alcorn State University when Marie is out of town, I'm in a van seated on a lawn chair between them. He makes a statement about criminals (read: Black men). "In the old days you knew what to do—beat 'em, run 'em out of town, or get a rope." Sitting between the two on an empty road, I ask about the crop growing all around. It's not cotton. "Soybeans," they chorus. When we get to Alcorn, I tell him that white people have to recognize that Black crime is a white problem. He grunts, "You would say that." He is aiming the slide projector toward the ceiling. Let's show them on the ceiling, I say, it's a risky choice.

**THE UNIVERSITY OF SOUTHERN MISSISSIPPI AT HATTIESBURG.** The first show is poorly attended and technically a disaster. The young Black woman actor from Jackson State has transferred to Northwestern and is commuting to the tour sites from Chicago. She shows up five minutes before showtime. I'm trying to remember her lines. The lights are a mess. The space in the science building is absurd. The one sound cue comes up very late. Even so, the audience participates, and many stay afterward. The second night is better. Afterward, a Black woman tells me the story of Clyde Kennard, a Black man who registered at USM in 1969, and was not accepted. That part, she tells me, is officially acknowledged. What is not told, she says, is legend in the Black community: He was subsequently framed by the city government and given a long prison sentence for allegedly stealing a chicken. He got cancer while in prison and became too weak to walk, so he was carried to the fields to work, but he was never allowed to see a doctor. He worked with fellow inmates to help them understand their rights. He died in prison. She also says that white officials who were in on the frame-up are alive and well in college and government jobs in Hattiesburg, and the campus has many Black students now who don't know this story. "They have a lotta guilt," she says. Another Black woman tells how her parents housed freedom riders, and her mother lost her job as a result. These are college-educated women who laugh at the absurdities of the terrors as they talk. "My mother and father kept finding places on the floor for folks to sleep. Mama said, 'God took care of us before I lost my job. He'll take care of us now.'"

During the audience dialogue about school integration, a young white woman from the local high school says, "I used to have many Black friends from the time I was very young, but then as we got older, about sixth grade, we went apart." She says this with her hands raised parallel to describe *together* and then spreads them up and separates her arms away from each other.

**HOLMES COUNTY.** Lexington, Mississippi. Rural Organizing and Cultural Center (ROCC). The audience is full of children, older people, and young parents, three generations of Black people in the room. There are only a handful of white people, all of whom work with us or with the center. In rural Mississippi, no social integration of Black and white people exists. Since legal desegregation, the white children go to private academies. No Blacks attend the academies. There is one integrated county school.

An older man says he feels that we'd gone backwards since the 1960s. An older woman says she feels the children need discipline. There is talk of the fact that people from up north send their children down to relatives here, resulting in drugs and gangs in this rural Mississippi town. A young woman talks about how hard it is for working women to help their children in schools, to see that the schools are doing the right thing. One woman talks about how hard people have struggled in Holmes County to elect Black officials. She describes how when Black people go to a certain office headed by a Black official, they have to wait until the white people get waited on.

She says she is not going to name names, but the audience chuckles with recognition.

A white woman in the cast comes to me saying she wants to quit the show because she doesn't feel necessary. I assure her that she is, that the work is about Black and white people talking about race relations in Mississippi. I point out that she is probably feeling excluded and that many things are being said by people in the audience she may not be hearing because of that feeling. I tell her how I worked the previous year at ROCC with teenagers, helping them dramatize interviews they'd done with older people about the civil rights movement in Holmes County. A book of those interviews, *Minds Stayed on Freedom: The Civil Rights Struggle in the Rural South, An Oral History,* by the Youth of the ROCC, was published by Westview Press in 1991, and is a great source of pride for the people at ROCC. Now, I tell her, we are near Tchula, the home of the late Eddie Carthan, activist mayor, known nationally as the subject of a frame-up by county officials. His wife and child are in the audience tonight. Also, some of the first Black people to register to vote in rural Mississippi in the early 1960s, people who took the circuit judge to trial at the risk of their lives. This evening is special because we are in the presence of living libraries and the future. I tell the cast member to examine her feelings in light of all that. "I hear you," she says. I am particularly fond of this evening.

**ALCORN STATE UNIVERSITY.** A young white man, accompanied by his mother, speaks up asking the obligatory, "Would I be accepted here at Alcorn?" Immediate murmurs of, "Yes, why not?" in the midst of which a Black woman student played like a trumpet blast, "Would you be accepted? . . . You got a car, sure you'll be!" Alcorn is a long way from the nearest pizza, convenience, or supermarket. The hilarity of this response eases the subsequent talk. His mother asks about a T-shirt she'd seen that said, "The Blacker the college, the sweeter the education." Is this fair? What if it had said, "The whiter"? I say the struggle is not about equal experiences or equal solutions, and that I suspect she knows that. She admits that she does, but says she wanted to bring it up anyway. The mother and son are among a smattering of white people in a small, filled theater.

The older Black woman actor, who is a spiritual healer, asks why the students there had chosen to attend a Black college. Their responses include self-esteem, comfort, more sensitivity to their needs, and support of their African American identity. One woman student says she'd been accepted by a highly accredited white college, and chose Alcorn because she felt she'd get a better sense of who she was before going out in the larger world, that by going to a Black college she'd be better able to compete. Another woman says she felt after two years at Alcorn, she'd like to go to a white school to further prepare herself. A male student complains first that he didn't think a white teacher could teach humanities to Black students, then raises his hand later and says he was just "frontin'," saying that he knew it depended on the teacher because he'd had a white teacher in high school who'd taught him Black history better than anyone else.

By now the performers are just listening, calling on people, throwing in comments. After days on the road, setups, missing cues at Hattiesburg, waiting on the commuting actor who once again came in at the last minute, after all that, I see that the audience dialogue is working as part of the aesthetic—open, risky, rhythmic, essential, passionate, beautiful, jazzy.

**CULTURAL CROSSROADS** is an active community center in southwest Mississippi with an extensive program based in art and community. Gorgeous quilts, made there, surround the space. A white woman is the director, and she has over many years established a program that includes both Blacks and whites. She and her husband, one of the white faculty at Alcorn, seem to have made a life's commitment to the center. I have visited several times, and in spite of the cultural contradictions, it seems to be a haven for humanistic, creative possibilities too rare in this country.

The audience is well mixed with Black and white, and people readily speak up. An older Black man calling on the scripture says, "We are like the Israelites coming out of bondage on the way to the promised land, but getting lost in the wilderness . . . and it is up to us to find a way out." A forty-ish white man asks if he should let himself feel pride about his participation in the movement. The Black woman actor mother answers, telling the story of a white guy who is now a bus driver in Seattle because he could never go back to his father's business after participating in the movement. John Brown, she says, was considered crazy. "So, yes, be proud of your contribution, and don't be worried about what people say about it." She describes herself as African-centered. A young white woman stands in the back. "I was the only white at a Black school for a long time. I was naively integrating because my parents believed in it. I want to publicly thank them, because I learned so much." Her parents, the center director, and her husband, sit snugly together down front. I feel myself among down-to-earth, regular-extraordinary people. Two years ago the center's theater group gained notoriety for presenting *Romeo and Juliet* with a racially mixed cast.

**OCTOBER 1992.** Back in the Delta. A neon sign on Highway 8 right outside Delta State University flashes "*Mississippi Freedom* 7:30 P.M." A TV interviewer from Greenville asks me why I am doing this play now since so much has changed. I answer that people don't talk to each other enough about the painful past and that this drama can help them do that so changes can continue. I am particularly careful to be clear and smart. Marie, who is white, is called over by him to sit next to me and point her finger out. He says that we need not say anything. I automatically look where she points. What appears on the six o'clock news is nothing of the interview, only the shot of Marie pointing, me looking, and a white male voice saying, "*Mississippi Freedom* directed by Robbie McCauley." After the interview, the reporter tells me he thinks white people should ask for atonement. I think, but do not say, "They ought to give up some power." As if answering my thought, he says, "But the problem here is that Black people have gotten all this political power, and a few white people have the land and money, and neither is giving up anything."

Driving through the Delta in the midst of the cotton harvest, we take backroads from Money, where Emmett Till was observed, to Glendora, where he was killed, and back over to Phillip, where he was put in the river. The river is brown. Especially brown and full of currents. Marie tells me somebody said, "The Tallahatchie is full of niggers." The river is narrow. The river looks like grease on thick gravy. We'd passed three barbecue places—the "Pig Pit" was one. Neither of us can eat pork after that river.

Glendora is divided into Black and white sections with the railroad track in between, the Black side so poor I beg Marie not to take pictures. We are intruders not having to, or even willing to, stay. I feel the sense of my own privilege more than ever before. On the deep road out, I imagine what it was like during slavery, how there was no way out of there, too far from the North Star.

At Delta State a young white man had asked, "In the West they teach you about the future, in the North and Midwest, they teach you the present, and in the South they only teach you about the past, why is that?" In the midst of the awe and dismal weight of the question, which I sensed to be a distraction, I answered like a trumpet: "Don't trust any curriculum that separates the past from the present and future."

# ARTISTS HAVE TO DO THIS*

*Robbie McCauley Interviewed by Erika Munk*

On May 12, 1993, *Mississippi Freedom* was performed at the Whitney Museum of American Art at Philip Morris as part of *Say What: The 1993 Biennial Performance/Theater Project.* Afterward, Erika Munk spoke to Robbie McCauley:

**MUNK:** This performance seemed very different from what you describe in Mississippi, partly because the Whitney is such a large, chic, corporate space, and every word and gesture was mediated by the big mics the actors carried.

**MCCAULEY:** Our main priority is to work with the audience. The Whitney's a problem—its acoustics are impossible. The mics became a serious joke. We didn't want to use them and tried every other possibility, but yelling would also have been distancing and body mics would have picked up so many sounds in the atmosphere, we'd have gotten police calls. I'm always talking about content as aesthetic,

* This interview originally appeared as an addition to "Mississippi Freedom: South and North" by Robbie McCauley, which was originally published in *Theater* 24, no. 2 (Summer 1993): 88–98. *Theater* is published by Duke University Press.

making form and function equally compelling, and going with content when there's a problem. We went with the mics.

**MUNK:** What else did you change for New York?

**MCCAULEY:** We thought from the beginning that the piece was transferable, that it could work outside Mississippi or the south. Take the line about the end of the Cold War, "Didn't we crack that wall?" People everywhere keep forgetting the importance of the civil rights movement. But with five of the cast members absent because we had no money to bring them, we were performing other people's performances of still other people's testimony about events in the past. The piece became about the actors as well as the witnesses—always was, but more so. We decided for some parts that we'd talk about so-and-so's story in rehearsal, start telling it as this other person's story, and then do it as oneself.

**MUNK:** Did you modify the script?

**MCCAULEY:** We rewrote it. The testimony came out of Jackson, and when we did the piece there it was full of references to people, stories, and incidents the community knew, in which we tried to find what was universal. For New York we brought in the Delta and broadened the references.

The actors were sensitive to how people in the North perceive the struggle in the South differently from the way southerners see it, that gestures which seem conciliatory here are perceived as momentous in the South, where the NAACP had been essentially radical. The Black middle class was in the vanguard years ago, by necessity, because they could wear the mask effectively. For example, the piece on Claire, our main witness in Jackson, has a section about her husband, who was ostracized by young people in the 1960s because, as he was teaching at a Black college and his wife was a businesswoman, she did the civil rights work for the both of them so he wouldn't lose his job. One line says, "That's how the Black middle class could negotiate"—but underneath is a recognition that his struggle went back further than hers.

Also, the Holocaust came up more in rehearsal and turned into part of the dialogue when we were preparing to come to New York,

*Mississippi Freedom*, The Whitney Museum of American Art, NYC, 1993. Photo: © Paula Court.

but finally we said, it's cheap, and didn't use it. Gave us a lot to talk about, though. The Christian activists Claire visited in Germany in the 1930s brought Jews out, distracting officials by acting niggerish. We didn't want to use this, either. Of course, the Holocaust museum** came up in the audience's questions anyway—"Why isn't there a slavery museum?"

**MUNK:** How much did having so many white middle-class arty-lefty spectators affect the post-play discussion?

**MCCAULEY:** The audience was really very mixed. I found out at the door that people from a Brooklyn shelter were there, organized by some guy who knew my work, as well as Black students and artists. Part of what happens at the Whitney is the fulfillment of the whole idea of a diverse audience. My work is always to make sure that a participant feels safe enough and brave enough to talk, in this case in front of this diverse audience. If a white woman talks, then another white woman talks. For example, when that woman at the Whitney made her speech about the universality of oppression, how she as a woman felt burdened in the same way as Blacks, people just

** The United States Holocaust Memorial Museum in Washington, DC, opened in 1993 and was much in the news at the time of this performance of *Mississippi Freedom*. In 2016, the National Museum of African American History opened nearby.

groaned inside. I had to start articulating the problem so that they'd ask their questions.

Audiences arrive with seventy percent of their opinion preformed—if they go away with a less stereotypical view of people in the South after hearing the dialogue of class and race on stage, we've succeeded. I felt a gratifying and pretty phenomenal attention—they were straining to hear, rapt. My last note to the actors was, be clear in what you say. That's what worked, and not only to overcome the acoustics.

**MUNK:** Why didn't you do the piece in Harlem or Brooklyn?

**MCCAULEY:** I'd have liked to, if we'd had the money to stay. When John O'Neal and the Roadside Theater performed to young Black New Yorkers, their first reaction was, what are these white people doing here with this Black performer, but after five minutes they settled down, they were into it. We have false ideas of what the audience can take. It's up to artists and presenters to trust them.

**MUNK:** The projections didn't follow the chronology of the period and sometimes were only flashes—like that quick image of Chaney, Schwerner, and Goodman. What do young people make of these references?

**MCCAULEY:** Moving the historical chronology back and forth, away from a timeline, was purposeful, to force people to look up the answers. When I read *Hamlet* as a kid, what did I know? Also, I wanted to keep the actors as the focus. Their improvisation between sections is the glue holding the piece together. The real story is what happens among them in between telling the civil rights stories.

**MUNK:** What is this story?

**MCCAULEY:** Its center is that we're messengers—the actors change before and during the collection of testimony, during the rehearsal period, during the performances. Sadat, though his mother was an activist, started from, "Why were you people so scared?" He'd heard this stuff all his life and thought he was bored by it. Then he was

*Mississippi Freedom* on tour, The Rural Organizing and Cultural Center, Lexington, MS, September 1992. Left to right: Sameerah Muhammad, Robbie McCauley, Dick Johnson, Kay King Valentine (background), Willie Horton. Photo: © Marie Cieri, courtesy of The Arts Company.

transformed by gathering the testimony. Deborah wasn't a screaming racist by any means, but she came from a mixed acting company and was uninterested in Black points of view. Now she undresses psychically. She's so obsessed with not being negative and not being perceived as the problem. When she cried after the Emmett Till speech, I didn't want it to become about her tears so I moved on, and she was strong enough to take it.

**MUNK:** What kind of long-range effect do you want to have?

**MCCAULEY:** We're setting the audience an example of ways to research and perform their own community's history. I'd like to keep this kind of work going in places where we've performed. Not just where they live, though that's fine, but crisscrossing the country with their stories. I hope the whole business of community theater work—which is being done by many others, including Charles Dennis, Celeste Miller, Liz Lerman, John O'Neal, and Jawole Willa Jo

Zollar—doesn't become an art-world fad with a built-in end point. Actors can do this, go to Hollywood, and come back.

The idea that we're preaching to the converted is just an excuse for not doing the work. In Mississippi—all over the country!—people are exhausted, people don't remember or talk about history or make connections between then and now. In Mississippi people asked, why bring it up again? But our kind of theater makes everyone part of that specific history and cuts against the antihistorical nature of American society. Artists have to do this. It looks like no one else will.

# MISSISSIPPI FREEDOM

## A Performance Theater Work

*Robbie McCauley*

## PRODUCTION HISTORY

Produced by The Arts Company, *Mississippi Freedom* was first presented in 1990 at the Smith Robertson Museum, Jackson, MS, and toured to seven locations in western Mississippi in 1992, to the 1993 Whitney Biennial in New York, and to Houston's Diverse Works in March 1996.

*Mississippi Freedom* was devised through improvisation by the acting company in response to prompts, and then edits, from Robbie. The script changed from performance to performance: some sections retained elements of improvisation; in addition, the original full acting company was not present for every performance.

## PROLOGUE

*Any time after 1990. A troupe of actors. The text is testimony collected by the actors.*

*Some of the script is improvised tellings. The actors who do these will be playing themselves: Sameerah, Sadat, Veronica, Robbie, Willie, Ona, Dick, Kay, Deborah, Kent, James, Sheila, Leroy, and Jane.*

*Actors will also play: SNCC* Brother, Businesswoman, Professor, Tougaloo Official, Delta Lady Doctor, Conscious Caucasian Woman, Bright Woman Child, Mr. Sam, Hecklers, Integrators, Father, Mother, Chorus, and others.*

*Director organizes who plays what, when, and where.*

*Actors enter the space. Conversational music. Sadat and Sheila lean chairs and then themselves against a wall. Ona takes her time finding a place to be.*

*Deborah takes one of the chairs, sets it for Ona, then places herself between the audience and the playing area like an interlocutor.*

* Student Nonviolent Coordinating Committee.

*James, Kay, Kent, Dick, and Leroy are present throughout the space.*

*Veronica enters as latecomer, sits with audience.*

*Conversational music is improvised talk among the actors, like musicians, warming up their instruments, play dialogue, listen to each other. Robbie and Sameerah enter.*

*Actors set chairs around Ona like seats on a bus. Kent is driver.*

VERONICA *(Still in audience)*: They told me at the New Stage audition that with my accent I should go to a Black theater. If I'd been auditioning with a Russian accent, would they'd a sent me to Moscow?

CHORUS *(Singing)*:

If you're looking for me in the back o' the bus,
I ain't going nowhere.
Look for me in the front o' the bus.
I'll be riding up there, O Lordy,
I'll be riding up there
I'll be riding up there.
Look for me in the front o' the bus
I'll be riding up there.

*(By now all are seated in the bus.)*

The freedom riders did not intend to test Jackson. / They were headed to New Orleans. / But there had been no toilet facilities since North Carolina / and whenever one of the men went up to say, / You know we would like to stop at the service station, / they were laughed at and told to / "Go on and use the back of the bus . . ." / "Well, we got ladies on here . . ." / And they laughed at that . . . / so the riders were never able to relieve themselves . . . unless they did it in their clothes or whatever. They were never able to relieve themselves. So when they got here to Jackson . . . / all this was in the trial / . . . the sign on the black toilet said OUT-OF-ORDER / . . . and in their urgency, they went to the white restroom because there was no sign on the door. / And in the process of relieving themselves . . . the freedom riders were arrested.

# PART ONE

ROBBIE: Light change!

SADAT: Wait a minute! Just as a point . . . I'm glad that we're doing this project. It seems there hasn't been enough told about this era . . . I don't know . . . People are trying to forget about it for some reason, and I think some things need to be known. I don't know about that fear. I deal with pressure. The tension is still there. But it's hard for me to imagine how bad it was . . . being so scared of some men in sheets.

SAMEERAH: Your mother said, You're weak. You're not weak. We just failed to pass it on. We were tired of fighting. We didn't give it back. You're just weak because it's not as hard.

DEBORAH: Change the lights!

*(Ona remains. Others disperse. SNCC Brother watches.)*

SAMEERAH *(Walks with Sadat all around)*: Herbert Lee, a Black man, a landowner, in Amite County near McComb, was killed for organizing people to register to vote. Killed outside in a public place, by a white man, E. H. Hurst, a Representative of the Sovereign State of Mississippi, who called Lee to a public place and told him to stop . . . They had been childhood friends—fished and threw rocks in the woods the way young Black and white boys did back then in the rural South . . . But now they were grown and . . . in that confrontation between the two men, Lee had said, my responsibility is to proceed to do what I feel is appropriate and right, and Hurst couldn't deal with that, so he shot him . . . at a public place . . . as a very public statement of what happens to a Black man who does not behave. That was September 25, 1961, and it was one of the horrible things that began the ending of the horrors. *(Leaves Sadat standing before SNCC Brother)*

SNCC BROTHER: So that Mississippians who had lived all their lives under that fear were not terribly motivated to want to die like that . . . It was us dumb naive folk . . . *(Laughter)* who came in with all of this spiritual motivation and feeling of being right because of our cause and history and the natural fairness of life that enable many folk in Mississippi to say . . . perhaps we can try this.

ONA: Most Mississippians were horrified . . . even the possibility of getting involved . . .

SADAT: Hold that. I really want to get that . . . Mississippians were horrified . . . So it took those people who were coming in from other places?

CONSCIOUS CAUCASIAN WOMAN: It was a closed society . . . how segregated my life was . . . I only saw Black people working in my neighborhood or my home as domestics or gardeners or something . . . I asked my bishop, "Did you know there were Negro Episcopalians?"

*(Piano/bird sounds.)*

DELTA LADY DOCTOR: I'm PhD now. I'm from the Delta, and I think there is one script for most people who lived in the Delta. We were born either on plantations or the little towns that the plantations built. Cotton fields and mules . . . before tractors came along . . . and hot days and mosquito-filled nights, of popping water until it turned cool, and thinking that was the best thing that God had provided for people.

I never remember having a dream about life being different till I was almost twelve. Then I'd seen in a book someplace this woman who was in an office with a telephone, and she was a secretary, and I thought that would be a wonderful life to have. She had on her church clothes, and you could wear them, I understood, every day. And you didn't have to get hot and sweaty in the fields with salt running down your brow and in your eyes, and you didn't have to have corns on your hand from holding that hoe handle. You didn't have to have a backache from picking cotton.

We did go to school . . . walking . . . while white kids came by riding. I wanted to be grown. They were taking advantage of all of our hard labor because we weren't keeping records. We had never cleared any money. I told my father that we needed to keep records. He humored me. Got me a blue horse . . . You remember those little record books?

JAMES: When it came to the day of settlement?

DELTA LADY DOCTOR: Well I would listen to a radio broadcast every day that told what cotton was selling for, what soybeans and corn were selling for. You could know whether it was short staple cotton or long staple or medium . . . and I knew all of that. I knew a standard bale was five hundred pounds. I knew that if you came in with a six-hundred-pound or six-hundred-seventy-pound bale, which I remember one time we had, that the man only gave you credit for five hundred and he took the other one-hundred-seventy pounds which represented a lot of money, for himself.

When the cotton started to be harvested, you listened at what they were making, and this was a good year for cotton. At one point that year, cotton went for forty cent a pound. And you knew that half of every bale or all the bales you picked went to the man. So you did that.

And I put in a generous amount for plantation expenses which was this unnamed category of expenses that the sharecropper never knew what went into it, but it was whatever the man wanted to charge you, so we did that. I was sure that even with him taking half of the cotton, and taking more than he deserved for all the rest of the expense and everything, that we had to come out of there with five or six thousand dollars.

So the day of settlement, I went to school . . . and you have to understand my father couldn't read and write . . . but I went over these figures with him in detail. Here's what we owe, and up and down, the night before and the morning of the settlement, and I went off to school.

I don't know what Daddy thought about it because he didn't say anything. He took my blue notebook, and when I came back from school . . . I couldn't wait all day, 'cause I was just sure we were gon' have lots of money, and I was gon' be able for the first time to have nice clothes and everything . . . I'd begun to speak in church, and I had discovered boys, so it was important to look nice . . . There were kids coming down from Chicago with nice clothes . . . I wanted those things. When I got back that afternoon, I rushed in and I say, How did the settlement go?

My mother knew how much I'd been putting into this stuff. She said, Well, we came out, and cleared some money. It was the first time in my life that we cleared money, and oh I was so excited because I was sure she was gon' say thousands of dollars. I say, How much? We cleared two hundred and forty dollars . . . I was devastated.

I never asked Daddy, but I'm sure now he never brought my figures up because it would have been out of his place. That's one of the most painful memories I have of that time. And I realize afterward that the pain really wasn't for not getting money. It was for the unfairness of the system. It was for an image that I had about what we needed to do to exact fairness, being destroyed. Since I've been an adult, my pain over that incident has grown because as a parent, I realize how much I must have hurt my parents, asking them to challenge a system that they knew was totally unfair, and that my childish challenge meant nothing to. And they never put me down, never said, This won't work, get this mess and get out of here. They never vented their frustration. In a way they gave tacit and quiet encouragement to me for questioning this system. I never forgave those white folks for taking our money.

*(Laughter.)*

JAMES: I know you didn't.

DELTA LADY DOCTOR: It was the first real protest, I think, I'd ever been in, and I think it set the tone for my life. Sometimes you know you can't change things, but there's something in you that makes you know that you have to speak to the oppressors and let them know you know that what they're doing is wrong.

BUSINESSWOMAN: My aunt, my father's sister, went to Rust College, a Black college, in the 1800s, in Holly Springs, Mississippi. She was so moved by her experiences there, which were positive, that she came back at the end of the year and was so changed in everything, and she said to her parents, whose pictures are up on my wall, I want to not go back to Rust . . .

CHORUS: Why? . . . Don't you like it?

BUSINESSWOMAN: Yes . . . ah . . . no. I want my baby brother to go . . . Baby Brother became my father. And they said, Well we can't send both of you. So she says, I'll stay at home and work so that he can go. So in the 1800s, everything he owned was packed into that trunk there and he went to Rust College. He graduated in 1909 in the field of mathematics. His father was born a slave and he could figure. He'd go down to the commissary and he would not get the money he thought he should get back, and he'd say, Mr. Sam?—he'd back away like you had to do—and he'd say, Mr. Sam, Ise don't git watchu git.

MR. SAM: Where's your paper?

FATHER: Ise don't got no paper. I figures.

BUSINESSWOMAN: And every time he would be right. I say this to talk about my father and mathematics. My father could do mental arithmetic, you know, long columns and all that . . . because he had this native thing . . . and also that made it possible for him to go into business. My mother's family . . . already businesspeople. Two generations. Before her was plantation owners and . . . merchants. Then she went to Hampton and then she went to Tuskegee . . . That was her trunk . . . See how much bigger her trunk is?

DEBORAH: Robbie . . . I don't feel comfortable. How are we supposed to make people feel? Whose truth is this? What is the truth anyway?

ROBBIE: You wanna talk about it?

DEBORAH: No . . . um . . . not now.

*(Robbie cues Actor playing Bright Woman Child.)*

BRIGHT WOMAN CHILD: Pain that has been buried inside of me . . . Not like the average person that goes through one or two experiences. I'm talking about bad massive, massive doses of hate dumped on me as a child for two years in a row. If you can come through that and still be sane, and still be loving, and still be respectable, and you can still make something out of your life, you know it's by the grace of God.

DEBORAH: Provine Senior High School hallway lights!

*(Deborah, Kay, Dick, and Kent become hallway. Veronica and Sadat walk through. Robbie selects and directs audience members to play Hecklers and Integrators.)*

BRIGHT WOMAN CHILD: I was fifteen.

It was such a traumatic experience. I haven't been back in that school. Provine. It's like I closed a chapter in my life and I've never looked back. I shall never forget the first day 'cause they had lined up on both sides of the hallway . . . They had given us our lockers when we registered the week before . . . and I never will forget walking down that hallway, the first major hallway to the left when you walk in the Provine building, and they had lined up on both sides of the hall, and it was all the football players, all the guys in the school, and their little girlfriends, and the girls were like behind them . . . and they were all heckling . . .

CHORUS OF INTEGRATORS *(Led by Robbie, Sadat, and James)*: They called us everything under the sun . . . and it was just like being paraded down in front of an aisle of folks, and they were throwing things, and they were spitting, and they were heckling, and they were just . . .

CHORUS OF HECKLERS *(Led by Deborah, Kay, Dick, and Kent)*: You niggers ought to go home. Who do you think you are? You bitch this, and You son o' so and so that, and da da da. You'll never stay here. We gon' kill yo' assess. We gon' lynch y'all right out here in this schoolyard. Blah blah blah . . .

VERONICA: . . . And you going through hearing all of this heckling and noise and you wondering, Where are the teachers? . . . The administrators? . . . Nobody is saying anything 'cause they are agreeing with what the children are doing.

*(Deborah and Kent walk through.)*

VERONICA, SHEILA, AND JAMES: Would we coulda . . . Could we woulda . . . would we coulda been like that?

*(Sadat and Robbie thank audience participants. They return to their seats.)*

SADAT AND ROBBIE: Lights!

*(A slide show of Black men who've been executed in Mississippi, including lynching photos; national fighters like Martin Luther King, Jr., John Brown, and Chaney, Goodman, and Schwerner; and the international perspective like Lumumba and Biko.)*

ROBBIE: Let me paint the emotional picture for Black men in Mississippi. You have to understand that Mississippi had simply lynched Black people for whatever reasons. Emmett Till . . . the manner in which Black men were killed was not in any kind of ordered manner by the State . . . accusation, trial, and quickly over? . . . No. The pictures of Emmett Till taken out of the river were gruesome. You had a slow torture . . . eyes and head so swollen that it was difficult to recognize who he was . . . beaten severely about the head. His testicles were extremely swollen where he was repeatedly kicked. Many parts of his body was burned . . . and bruises. He died a very painful, slow execution. Mississippi responded to any effort of Black folk to assert their right to exist free of fear and intimidation and domination with a slow execution, and that was periodically done to remind Black men to stay in their place so that if one contemplated challenging any white man, didn't matter whether it was someone of some sort of public notoriety or not. They did it with the clear knowledge and expectation that they would be taken and slowly and painfully executed . . . And I'm probably understating it.

DEBORAH: Robbie . . . I do want to talk about it now.

After everybody knew it was illegal to segregate bathrooms, I had to "go" bad one day in Wendy's and a Black woman went in just ahead of me. The white women started running out like there was a fire. I felt shocked . . . and ashamed.

*(Robbie leads talk of white people's admittances.)*

ROBBIE: Kay talked about how she considered their housekeeper a member of the family. And Sameerah challenged her, asking if she ever asked her housekeeper if she felt the same. Kay thanked Sameerah.

DICK: As a white educated man, I always knew segregation was wrong, but it became personal for me when I fell in love with a beautiful, smart Black woman. Uh, no, she wasn't interested in me, but I had to wonder who was I if she was all of that. It was no privilege to be a white male if Black women were equal to and often better than us.

*(Robbie cues Actor playing Delta Lady Doctor.*

*Lights change. All make story circle. Actor playing Delta Lady Doctor is at the center.)*

DELTA LADY DOCTOR: And there was a very strict ordering of behavior. I think I remember as early as I remember the cotton fields and the hot sun and the mosquitoes, this whole concept, which I am not even sure was ever spoken directly to us, about our place and their place, *their* being white folks' place . . . One of the earliest things that I remember as a child was fear. When somebody had been lynched or something had happened on the plantation.

CHORUS: At night in their houses with their doors fastened and the shades drawn, Black folks talked about it in whispers.

KENT: . . . as if the white man's ears were like giant microphones that could pick up whatever was being said . . .

DEBORAH: . . . and you sensed the fear, you sensed the fear, you sensed the fear . . .

VERONICA: When you'd watch Black folks talking to other Black folks, they would stop, put their hand on their hip, laugh, and talk, be relaxed . . . There would be this tension whenever they would meet these white folks. They would look down, they would be a little different in the way they held themselves. I didn't understand it when I was seeing it, but I knew it was fear.

CHORUS *(Singing)*:

O, Freedom, O Freedom, O Freedom over me
And before I'll be a slave I'll be buried
in my grave, and go home to my Lord and be free . . .

JAMES: In the sixties, the white folks who came and the Black folks who came were relaxed with us.

VERONICA: There was no tension when you talked to them. There was no sense of something impending happening. There was no consciousness of the power difference.

ROBBIE: To have folks come and ask you about your feelings, how you thought the world ought to be bordered, what you felt about this unfair system everybody was forced to deal with . . . nobody ever done that before.

ONA: To see people moving in mass . . . I mean . . . I'd never had that full religious thing . . . that people have when they get happy . . . when you see people get together at a mass meeting . . . all of that fervor . . . would move people . . . I mean I still get chills . . . It was like church moved closer to Heaven.

*(Song fades out . . .)*

DICK, DEBORAH, KAY AND KENT: Summer, 1961. Bob Moses came to Pike County, Mississippi.

Invited by the NAACP there to establish a voter registration drive in McComb.

SNCC BROTHER: How everything came to a head that summer was that a wing of SNCC was established in McComb with Marion Barry, Dion Diamond, Diane Nash, Charles Sherrod, James Bevel, and there was at that time an intense dialogue in SNCC about whether we should concentrate on freedom rides, voter registration or sit-ins . . .

VERONICA: I don't want to be stupid, but what is Snick?

DEBORAH: I'm glad you asked that.

ROBBIE: Listen.

SNCC BROTHER: Anyhow, at a meeting in North Caroline, Ella Baker, Fundi . . . had the wisdom to keep us together. In McComb, Mississippi, students who'd been inspired by sit-ins and freedom rides elsewhere staged a sit-in in a Woolworth store and were arrested.

WILLIE, SHEILA AND SAMEERAH: Brenda Travis, Hollis Watkins, Curtis Hayes had the nerve to stage a sit-in in rural Mississippi in 1961. And the Student Nonviolent Coordinating Committee . . . SNCC . . . came to a consensus to come to McComb and support those students.

VERONICA AND DEBORAH: Bob Moses, Dion Diamond, Charles McDew, Charles Sherrod, Diane Bevel came in. James Bevel, Bernard Lee, Marion Barry had been there, and there are one or two others . . . and Bob Zellner, the white student from Memphis was there. It became apparent after we had talked among ourselves that we had to support the kids.

SNCC BROTHER: And we arrived in McComb. Herbert Lee had been killed about a month earlier. The students were in jail. The principal of the school had been instructed by the white superintendent, of course, not to let the students back in school . . . because they had petitioned for freedom . . . and the people were not quite sure what to do. It was in that context that we drove into McComb . . .

DEBORAH: Kay says, ". . . which is not to say there were not very strong committed and motivated Black males who were standing tall . . . during and prior to that period. What you will find in the history of Mississippi is that . . . there were many men who did stand up . . . not a lot . . . but they were almost all lynched or executed in various forms."

KENT: As a teenager we learned to hate Black people. We'd ride in old cars and call out—it's hard to say now—to any Black boys we saw. We'd laugh and call 'em either blue-gum niggers or red-gum niggers. The ones with blue gums were the worst.

*(Silence.)*

SADAT: I just want to listen, you know.

SNCC BROTHER: The group that I mentioned—McDew, Sherrod, Dion, myself—we had decided to come to Mississippi because of those factors that I mentioned . . . Bob Moses . . . the students . . . voter registration . . .

SNCC BROTHER: We all took a couple of weeks and did whatever we felt we needed to do in anticipation of coming to Mississippi. *(Sharing some male stuff)* I went down to Acapulco and hung out for a couple of weeks. All the members of that group went different places . . . and did whatever they felt was the last thing they'd want to do . . . *(Ironic laughter)* and with whomever they felt they wanted to do it . . . *(Sharing a naughty laugh)* before coming to your fair city.

So we met up in New York and drove south. We came through Alabama. Just outside of Anniston, Alabama, a white lady's dog ran out into the road. I was driving and I swerved to miss the dog, almost ran into another car, and I think we hit the dog anyway.

ROBBIE: She called the police. They came. She said, They purposely tried to run my dog down.

DICK: This is 1961. Now you will recall that the first wave of freedom riders who had come through Alabama, the first bus was stopped right out of Anniston by members of the Klan who took everybody off and beat them severely and burned the bus.

SADAT: We were about five miles from where that incident had taken place. This had been the year before, so suffice it to say we were worried.

DEBORAH: Fortunately, a neighbor of this woman had seen the whole thing and stepped forward, and informed the police that "they did everything possible to avoid hitting the dog . . ." They decided, based on what the neighbor said, not to charge them with anything.

SADAT: We got back in the car after that, wiping our sweaty brows, and proceeded to Mississippi. And as we approached the state line, the sign said THE GRAND DRAGON OF THE KU KLUX KLAN AND THE GOVERNOR WELCOME YOU TO MISSISSIPPI.

CHORUS: . . . With a Klan robe on the huge sign . . .

SADAT: We went past that state line and everything became totally silent as each of us contemplated where we were and what we were doing and why . . . and Emmett Till . . . Herbert Lee . . .

and all the men who had been lynched. We drove in silence for about five or ten minutes . . . and all of a sudden Chuck McDew started singing . . .

> Ain't gonna le-et no-o-body turn me around
> oh no-o, turn me around, oh yeah, turn me around . . .

We all joined in.

*(Chorus joins in softly.)*

And for the next three hours *(Laughing)* . . . we sang unceasingly all the way to Jackson . . . dealing with that fear . . . and it was in that fear that we moved throughout Mississippi when we first came . . . 'cause there was no organized movement of any sort, there was no contact with the press, there was no way to yell for help.

We were it.

We had made contact with the Kennedys, who were president and attorney general at the time . . . and Harry Belafonte, who had arranged for us to get together and analyze the best ways to do things, but those people were quite far away, so we came into Jackson, went out to the airport, which was the only place we knew was federal property, to eat, and deal with that fear until we were ready to go on down to McComb . . . which we did.

*(Chorus out.)*

# PART TWO

*Robbie starts a "Welcome Table." Chorus joins in.*
*Actors pass out cookies and fruit.*

BUSINESSWOMAN: Okay. Get me back to center.

CHORUS: The trip!

BUSINESSWOMAN: Where I met my husband?

SAMEERAH: Well, yes, but in terms of the experiences that you had that would lead you . . . I want the experiences such as that . . . being the only one to travel from Mississippi to that particular . . . because there's a lot . . . the history is there as to why you felt so secure in doing what you did.

BUSINESSWOMAN: I finished college at Spelman in '37. So . . . I got on a tangent . . . the trip . . . The Y group was looking for persons who had some experience . . . the First World Conference of Christian Youth . . . in Amsterdam, Holland, in 1939. My father had been in a car accident. Mother was saying she can't go, my husband's ill, I need her here and so forth . . . and he raised up in bed and he said . . . she's going, you find the money . . . and he died while I was over there.

*(Dick puts on captain's hat. Deborah and Kent play Jane and her father.)*

BUSINESSWOMAN: Going over . . . I was assigned to a cabin on a ship . . . see, there was no flying in those days . . . with Jane . . . both our last names started with "C." Something I didn't know . . . Her father was German from Pennsylvania . . . he brought her aboard the ship. And when he found there was a Black among the group, he tried to get her not to stay . . . She telephoned me just last week. We talked about how she had got to the place where she could defy him and stay. I didn't know that. Here it's fifty years later, I'm finding it out.

JANE *(Sits next to Businesswoman)*: We landed in Britain first. We visited the prime minister . . . 1939 . . . Chamberlain . . . We saw him as a group . . . first time I saw television was in London . . . Anyway, we go on to Copenhagen . . . *(To Businesswoman)* They said when we get to Berlin, we're going to join up with the Methodists and Martin Harvey is in that group.

BUSINESSWOMAN: I didn't pay attention until they asked me, "Do you know Martin Harvey?" Then I knew he was a Negro. They thought all Black people who could read and write knew all other Black people who read and write . . .

DEBORAH: Aw, come on . . . I'm not like that.

BUSINESSWOMAN: She likes me to tell . . . because I'd come aboard a ship and they didn't have all these permanents for Black hair, that mine was looking like that . . . all frizzy . . .

DEBORAH: You mean it wasn't straight . . . Okay? When you say permanent, you mean straight, when we say permanent we mean curly.

VERONICA: How 'bout that . . .

*(All talking, mumbling at once: I didn't know that . . . Umm hummmm . . . Yeah . . .)*

KENT: That's something us men talk about . . . white women more curl their hair and Black women more straighten their hair, they never satisfied . . . *(Laughter)*

*(Robbie cues Sadat.)*

SADAT: What about the breakthroughs? The things that happened in Mississippi . . . Didn't these set the stage for other things to come, like . . . let's say, the Berlin Wall . . . things that happened right here . . . in Mississippi . . . didn't that spark . . . the rest of the nation . . . the rest of the world . . . to follow? Didn't we crack that wall?

WILLIE: Lights!

*(Sameerah and Deborah on the balcony in Berlin.)*

DEBORAH: A girl in my group, a real friend, and I were standing on the balcony of the Hotel Montgartenhauf, and standing down outside was Martin Harvey . . . Did you meet Martin Harvey yet?

SAMEERAH: No, I haven't.

DEBORAH: Come here . . .

SAMEERAH AND DEBORAH: . . . And so we went to the balcony . . . and he was standing down there . . . he was short . . . and he was reading the German morning newspaper and he had on these black-and-white oxford shoes, and blue casual pants, and blue shirt, and everything there about his character was encapsulated: punctuality—nobody else was there—liberal language, understanding, patience . . . He wasn't rushing round wondering . . . and she said there he is . . . Martin Harvey. *(Just Sameerah)* and I thought, He's short. I like tall men.

VERONICA: Back to Mississippi!

CONSCIOUS CAUCASIAN WOMAN: Kay said, "People don't like to tell war stories . . . There was a great deal to fear on everybody's part, and white people in the movement were as protected by Blacks in local communities as Black people in the movement were. It was wonderful. If I would leave a town . . . like if I was leaving Demopolis, Alabama, after a mass meeting at night to drive to Selma, some Black minister or leader in the movement would follow me to the edge of town to make sure the cops didn't stop me, and then when you got to the house where you're staying, you'd call back to where you been. I mean you felt like you were being protected as much as you could, and you always felt safe once you crossed the railroad tracks and were in the Black community."

ONA: Going from town to town as a white woman . . . I'm surprised . . . What about you made you able to do that?

CONSCIOUS CAUCASIAN WOMAN: And she said, I was lucky enough to have that early experience, to visit Boston on a church trip . . . and see things were wrong . . . and I've always been independent . . . so then to see that my freedom . . . I mean I got involved more for myself than to help anybody else . . . because my house was in danger . . . My freedoms were being abridged. Dr. King used to say, "You can't keep a person in the mud without staying in there yourself."

KAY: And then to see how hypocritical people were who had said they were your friends . . . all those relationships broken . . . and then to see all the wonderful relationships formed in the movement. The people I met in the sixties have been my lifelong friends.

SHEILA: Going through those small towns back then must have been fearful.

KENT: While there was a logic to nonviolence, in terms of strategy in the movement, and considerable nonviolence in terms of belief, most places I stayed had a shotgun propped in the corner of the room at night.

KAY: One night in south Alabama, I was staying at the home of . . . a leader of the NAACP. One thing I had to get used to in my new life was staying with a farm family that got up at six o'clock in the morning. *(Laughing)* He would've been up for an hour and a half at six. Anyway, I was in the back of the house one night when the Klan did shoot in, and my host shot back . . . not unusual in '65.

SHEILA: Oh?

KENT: But nonviolence as a way of life . . . many people, Black and white, believed in it back then. It was a scary time, but it was also a time of great strength because you believed, and it was true, that you were part of something that was really changing the world.

KAY: I feel sorry for young people your age because we kinda got baptized in the streets . . . and all my life since then, I been searching for a way to impart those values to young people . . . that service and struggle for change is a way of life . . . When

I saw the Chinese students at Tiananmen Square, I just said, "Wooow."

*(All talk about what the Businesswoman said about her husband.*

*Note: Use the following text as reference.)*

BUSINESSWOMAN: I don't know what the first move was . . . whether the buses came first . . . but let me say this on behalf of Martin Luther Harvey. He'd been arrested back in the thirties in Ohio, trying to integrate a movie theater . . . those kinda things . . . and he said, I'm working at a state university in the South . . . in Baton Rouge. He was dean of students at Southern University, and I cannot do what I used to do . . . but when the movement started in the sixties, he said, you go on and do it, but do it for both of us. I had a private business, wasn't gone lose a job, so he said, You have to do it for me, too.

ROBBIE: Sheila said that was the sort of thing the Black middle class . . . could negotiate with their families.

MOTHER AND CHORUS: Well I lived in a community that you could say was a very very poor community.

The schools had water on the floor / no paved streets.

Being poor you have to work harder / I was the sole support. / I didn't get welfare, but I could get commodities / doing hair, sewing, and other little things / helped people in the neighborhood when they needed things done / because I understood paperwork and they didn't . . . and I was pushing for change.

MOTHER: Because I knew that it had to be something better. I had three boys and three girls, and I had two beds in the room and the boys had to sleep in the room with the girls and my prayer was, Lord, I've got to get these girls out of here, you know, because girls grow up and their periods come on and all this kinda stuff, and I say, I didn't want them in the room, and he answered my prayer on down through time because I was wanting to get outta there. That was my prayer. That really was my prayer.

BRIGHT WOMAN CHILD: One of the more traumatic experiences . . . at thirteen being designated as a leader, being put in a paddy wagon, being driven to downtown put in the basement of downtown where you drive down into the city jail, left in that paddy wagon, with it running at the end of May when the weather was extremely hot, and then they turned the heat on us and it was just a godsend that just a few days before, we had been in freedom-school training where they had taught us to do rotation breathing, so we all got down on the floor and actually did rotation breathing. And what you have to remember is during that time, polyester was in. We didn't have on breathable cotton, so many of us when we got out of that paddy wagon, our clothes were sticking to us, and the texture of the fabric had actually been penetrated into our skin and we had nearly suffocated.

TOUGALOO OFFICIAL: Tougaloo College first involved with the visit of Reverend Bevel and Diane Nash of Nashville to the campus, and they asked if they could be housed there as they attempted to mobilize the community for some civil rights action. President Bittel gave permission. And as the plot thickened, more activities were generated.

BRIGHT WOMAN CHILD: I have a love for Tougaloo College right now because the then president of Tougaloo College in '63 who was white (I can't even recall his name), and there were many white instructors, and these people tutored us. Psychologists were brought in to teach us about what it meant to be isolated and what it meant to be out by ourselves and to get us to free up our emotions because you were trained to be like a poker face, show no expression when people cuss you out or they spit in your face or throw metal objects at you when you're sitting in, a class trying to learn, you were taught to keep your mind on what you're doing, keep your head straight ahead, hold your head up, don't cry. So, at some point, you had to release those emotions. So, Tougaloo College will always be a part of my life because they were there for us students who integrated.

PROFESSOR: Integrated schools? I was for it, but I'm grateful I missed it. I went to all-Black schools. There is concern and general belief that Black kids cannot learn on the part of white teachers. We were Black and poor, but those teachers instilled in us, and inspired in us, that we could and we would learn. I look at the caliber of students who came out with me. I got a classmate who is a CBS News White House correspondent. I know three people from one family of Lanier graduates, the Spinley family, who went to Harvard University Law School. Four of 'em are lawyers. One of my classmates' son is a Rhodes Scholar . . .

SAMEERAH: White schools have never been able to do what Black schools were able to do in terms of nurturing young Black minds. Jesse Jackson said Black schools tell you what you can do and white schools tell you what you can't do.

ROBBIE: Let's talk about it!

*(All talk about how this was talked about in Mississippi . . . Robbie cues Ona.)*

ONA: In the jail sequence, that's where this movement was born.

KENT: The freedom riders was here . . . and they said they wadn't go'n' leave, said they wadn't go'n' pay that bond.

SHEILA: . . . And so we in the community said we must find something to do to help them, and the idea came to me to call some churches . . . to get some money . . . said the freedom riders are here and they're gonna stay . . . and they didn't come prepared to stay . . . they didn't have clothes . . . a lot of things that they needed . . . so Mount Helm Baptist Church was the first church that reported to me . . . I was still living over the funeral home downtown . . . and at the service . . . these churches came bringing me this money . . .

VERONICA: . . . And it was quite a sum . . . It just shocked me that people were that interested and wanted to do . . . and we were able to buy things that they needed . . . and I knew people were serious because people would just slip money in my hand . . . whites and Blacks would do it . . . not just Blacks.

SHEILA: Canadians came. And then there came a movement called Wednesdays in Mississippi, and these were women that were social conscious women in northern areas who wanted to be there, and they conceived of the idea of coming down on a Tuesday, staying all day Wednesday, and then flying back out Wednesday night. And in that time we had to give them as many experiences as they could have. So that they could go back and tell the story . . .

SADAT: Sounds like to me, you had a lot of positive . . . not a lot of negative racial experiences.

ONA: Well, part of it was because I was a businessperson and I didn't have anyone to be threatened. My parents did not work in white homes.

DICK: Light change!

JAMES: The students themselves were aware of everything that was going on and when the principal assembled the students to inform them that Brenda, Hollis, and Curtis were not going to be admitted back, they organized a walkout from the school in which most of the students participated. They just cleared the classrooms and walked out. They proceeded to come toward where we were assembled. That was Masonic lodge, the only place we could meet. And we quickly organized to support them. McDew, Bob Zellner, Bob Moses . . . and others joined the students.

SADAT: I was chosen to stay out as a communication link with the rest of the world. The assemblies proceeded to go on downtown. As they approached the city hall, they were confronted not only by the police, but active members of the Klan, and began to be arrested. Bob Zellner was attempted to be pulled away from the crowd because he was a white student, and Chuck McDew and Bob Moses grabbed him and pulled him back and interjected their bodies between him and the Klan, who at this point were beginning to beat people with clubs and sticks, and they began to arrest everybody. I began to contact people I knew outside, called Harry Belafonte late that evening and he informed me of where Bob . . . Robert Kennedy, attorney general, was. I finally found him at a party out in Hollywood and began to explain to him what was going on, and he referred me to John Doar, who was the head of the Civil Division of the Justice Department at that point who lived in Arlington, Virginia, and I finally contacted Doar that evening and informed him of what was going on, and he assured me that they would come down and monitor the situation.

JAMES: Everyone was in jail but myself. And there was a warrant out for us, and they didn't know what we looked like and the police were coming around this Masonic lodge where we were.

Downstairs there was a market. After the arrest, the police came looking for Charles Jones.

SADAT: I was at the phone, which was downstairs in the back, and I put on a white jacket and came out to the meat counter, didn't let 'em see my face too much, and asked them what they wanted. I proceeded to appear to be cutting meat . . . I didn't know what the hell I was doing. *(Laughing)* I messed up about twenty dollars worth of beef . . . but anyway I told 'em, I didn't know Charles Jones . . . No, suh. I sho will tell 'em that y'all looking for 'im, and they went away.

*(Tape of witness: two actors enact the story:)*

> Later that evening I had a call from Doar, who said he was in town and was coming over, and in about a half hour, I heard this knock on the door. It was at night, 'bout ten o'clock, and I inquired, and he said it was John Doar. So this was the Justice Department. This was the United States government . . . this is the cavalry coming . . . coming to the rescue . . . this is the greatest most powerful country in the world, and its emissary was here to help us. I opened the door. He came in and said, Turn the lights out and close the door . . .
>
> He said, You know the Klan has followed me from the time I got off at the airport. He said, Those people are serious, aren't they? I'm just as scared as you are. It was at that moment, Sadat, that I lost all fantasies . . . or innocence about what we were doing and what we were about . . . When I realized . . . not only was he not there with the cavalry, but he just as scared as I was.

So we were on our own literally at that moment . . . the fear . . . being caught . . . lynched . . . But I stayed on the phone, and we made contact with several people, one of whom was James Forman, who had just come in from Chicago, who walked into the SNCC office in Atlanta, and began to function at that point, so we were able to raise enough bond money to get Bob and McDew and Zellner and most of the students out . . . and we went to Atlanta and regrouped and restrategized and came back in different forms. I then left. I went down to Albany, Georgia, with Charles Sherrod and we organized the Albany movement which . . . involved the entire Black community. At one point by that Christmas, more than twelve hundred people had joined us in jail, but that's a whole 'nother story.

DICK: The fact of what happened in Jackson, and it was originally planned to happen in New Orleans, the way it came about, seems to be something at work greater than an individual. Are there other events . . . supposed coincidences, things that happened that weren't supposed to happen, sort of illogical? . . .

SADAT: It's amazing to me that people who were in the forefront of the movement that came to Tougaloo to speak or to find a little comfort or support, it's amazing that Tougaloo never came under any danger.

TOUGALOO OFFICIAL: I've pondered that question. It was a mystery, a mysterious place . . . Very seldom would any of the officers come on campus. When the freedom riders were there, they'd line the County Line Road along the railroad track all the way back up to Hilwood . . . But they didn't come on campus. I remember a few days after Martin Luther King was assassinated, some students from up at the Madison School in Lexington up there, wanted to have a memorial service, and that was denied them. So, in protest, they walked out of the school and started walking down the road. I don't think they knew where they were going, but they were walking toward Jackson. Well, they called out the highway patrol and the highway patrol was harassing them walking down the road, and they withstood the harassment until they got down to Tougaloo. So they turned into Tougaloo and when they got to the gate, the police pulled back.

*(Robbie cues actor playing Professor.)*

PROFESSOR: I was fourteen years old that summer when Mrs. Fannie Lou Hamer and I testified on police brutality before the United States Congress, June 16, 1964. It's in the congressional record. Mrs. Hamer had been beaten while in prison in Winona, Mississippi, and I had been spat upon and had my arm twisted by police officers while I was incarcerated in jail here in Jackson.

Following that episode, Mrs. Hamer went on to Atlantic City and went down in history for her outstanding position with the Mississippi Freedom Democratic Party.

CHORUS: There were Fannie Lou Hamers all over Mississippi.

VERONICA: Another story from the movement is Carrie . . . somebody or other . . . The thing that sustained us during that period was the mass meetings at night . . . in churches . . . where you got to talk to each other about what had happened and where you got to sing your praises . . . and Carrie Lee McGee . . . don't forget that name . . . worked in a white home as a cook and so forth, and she would come back every night at the mass meeting to share her experiences . . . you know it was emotional release and all that . . .

So this particular night she said, Well, I went to work this morning . . . and the lady wanted to know what happened . . . the curiosity was, oh, tremendous . . . they were just dying to know what was happening and she say, Carrie, what went on at the meeting . . . She says, Well us done decided to boycott Jitney Jungle. And she say, Oooo . . . Carrie Lee, you telling me I can't buy no more groceries in Jitney Jungle? And she say, Miss So and So, I wouldn' tell you nothing like that, no ma'am, I wouldn't tell you nothing like that . . . *(Laughter)* What are you thinking? . . . Say, But what I is saying is . . . that if you bring anything in this house from Jitney Jungle . . . youse gon' cook it . . . So humor helped sustain me.

KENT: What was the saddest personal thing that happened?

BUSINESSWOMAN: For most of us it was Medgar Evers.

KENT: . . . Okay

SAMEERAH: I had been with him just two hours before he was assassinated. He had come late for this particular mass meeting . . . because he'd been up in the Delta . . . working . . . and we were just about finished and he didn't come into the main sanctuary . . . and we think that his assassins were in the audience . . . We often had some white persons in the audience, and we never knew whether they were friend or foe.

And I could see death on his face. I went back to the anteroom to speak with him and he say, You want me to take you home? I said, No, I have my bodyguards with me . . . In those days we were running ambulance service. I got home about a half hour . . . and like I told you, we were living above the funeral home . . . and here came three calls one after another . . . for Gwine Street. And I called a girlfriend who lived on Gwine Street . . . that's near where Medgar Evers lived . . . and I said, Has something happened to Medgar? We had three calls to come to that particular address, and I thought maybe Medgar . . . She said, It must be . . . because . . . never so much screaming . . . such loud screaming . . . have I ever heard before. She said I'll call back and let you know. Well, by the time she called back, our man had gone on down there, and we did know by that time that it was Medgar.

BRIGHT WOMAN CHILD: We didn't have police officers, we didn't have integrated eating facilities or public accommodations, we did not have desegregated schools. All these things were problems plaguing our community . . . I recall I was part of the early mass meetings with my parents, and other neighbors, to hear this man, Medgar Evers, to hear what he was talking about as the new field director of the NAACP.

SHEILA: One thing that was very clear for me was my involvement with the youth organization, and I had worked with teams that had gone out on voter registration.

We went down in South Jackson, which was then called Dudaville. First time I realized people right in my own city had outside bathrooms, and there was dire poverty. By then we had moved to Shady Oak, and that was called a more affluent area, and they had just started developing Bellaire, so those were the big-shot houses. We had been stigmatized as being those folk out in North Jackson because we not a part of the downtown or the Lanier area or the West Jackson area, so those differentiations about Black folks in the sixties were . . . kinda interesting.

VERONICA: One of the things that happened in the sixties was that we had an opportunity to put aside all those fights that folks had. When we started organizing those demonstrations, we would meet with the children from West Jackson, from Jim Hill School and there were children on the steering committee from Lanier and then the students form Jackson State and Tougaloo.

SHEILA: I shall never forget the night that Medgar died and the T-shirts he had in his arms were T-shirts we wanted for a demonstration the next day, and we actually made a big deal about going down getting those bloodstained T-shirts 'cause we wanted to wear 'em . . . all these melodramatic things that only teenagers could come up with. I felt a personal responsibility for his death having been one of the last persons to ask, Can you please have those T-shirts for us, and we knew he was going back to the office just so he could pick up those T-shirts . . . which is why we felt like he was not with the security force that he normally was from a mass meeting straight to his house because he had pretty much dismissed all those folks and he actually drove home by himself that night.

I don't think the adults realized at that time how much we internalized the whole thing, that he had died and why he had died and all, so the next few weeks were very traumatic, and we just went totally out of control as to what the adults wanted us to do. We had our own secret meetings, and had the big massive march that has been talked about, of more than a thousand children.

ROBBIE: Also, I took his remains to Washington by train from Meridian, Mississippi, and Mary Cox, who was the secretary of the NAACP, went with the remains . . . and all the way along . . . it was like that . . . the world came . . . all the Black . . . at every stop . . . and they cried . . . and Mary Cox and I had a chance to release our grief and all that . . . because we were alone there on the train.

He was the first Black person buried in Arlington cemetery . . . The others have been buried just outside the wire . . . but he is actually buried in Arlington cemetery.

ONA: So I think that I might have answered your first question: Why I might have been interested in this movement . . . And it's certainly because of the history of my grandparents, my paternal grandparents, and my aunt and her experiences . . . Oh, but this is something I must add . . . *(Story of uncle who was lynched, improvised)* . . .

I travel a lot and whenever I fly back into Mississippi, I look down and see the trees, the rich green hills, the church steeples, and I think: Oh, how beautiful . . . Oh, how beautiful . . . and then I remember the horrors.

ONA, VERONICA AND CHORUS:

We who believe in freedom cannot rest . . .
cannot rest . . .
We who believe in freedom cannot rest . . .
cannot rest.

DEBORAH: Lights.

END

# SOLO AND COLLABORATIVE SCRIPTS

# INTRODUCTION TO *INDIAN BLOOD*

*Elin Diamond*

As we take our seats for a performance of *Indian Blood* (American Festival, Cornell University, 1989), Robbie McCauley is cutting up apples and munching some. She watches us intently, her eyes scanning right to left, left to right. Three jazz musicians from Sedition Ensemble enter, flanking her with ease. She smiles slightly but she's all business. There is work to do tonight.

On the wall behind performer and musicians are three enormous projections of thousands of names of Native Americans (or, in our still-used vernacular, American Indians). From our seats we cannot read the names, but we are asked to bear witness to their presence. In the course of the evening Robbie will summon multitudes of anonymous people of color lost in the Indian Wars and other U.S. wars of domination. And woven into these summonings will be memories of the beloved and flawed men in her family, namely her grandfather who fought in the Indian Wars and with Teddy Roosevelt's Rough Riders at San Juan Hill in 1898, and her father for whom the U.S. military was a career path to patriotic service and self-respect. Robbie's mother and grandmother will provide other threads to the fabric of stories: Grandma P, who galvanized a reluctant husband to flee when the Klan showed up in their front yard, and Robbie's mother, who urged Robbie *not* to confront the difficult legacy of her fathers: "Is it correct to stir your fathers in their graves?"

It's been thirty years since I saw *Indian Blood* and I still feel the power of Robbie's response to that question.

*Indian Blood* (1986–1989) grew out of *My Father and the Wars* (1983–1986), both pieces commemorating, and trying to understand, the life of her father, who died in 1977. Family memories for Robbie are always entangled in America's long history of racism. As she puts it: "I knew from very young that I am not only the people I come from, but the world I was born into."[1] To remember her father, then, is to remember his world—the bruising contradictions of African American life through the twentieth century, particularly the lives of Black men whose dignity and pride in military service earned them not praise from a grateful country, but rather the backlash of resentment born of centuries of ingrained white supremacy.

The world of Robbie's father was dominated by his own father's service in the army's all-Black 24th Infantry of the Tenth Regiment—the famous Buffalo Soldiers—which dates back to the Civil War and which, in the decades after, patrolled Indian territories, fighting and killing Indians to protect white settlement and "manifest destiny" expansion. For Robbie, the bitter paradox of her fathers' service lies in family genealogy: "Grandma P's grandmother was a full-blooded half-blood." Eyes rolling a bit, Robbie explains, "That's what they said in the family if you had one parent full-blooded Indian and the other'n real Black . . . So everybody down the line on [my] grandmother's side they just said they was half Indian." Robbie's looks are brought into the story: "They say I have Indian blood, that I have an orange undertone to my skin, that I look good in green." Some in the audience laughed at that line, a nervous laughter, because what Robbie was layering for us is the grim truth that no American's legacy is untainted or unmarked by our country's expropriation of Indian lands and culture.

*Indian Blood* delivers harsh messages, but in a beautiful jazz-shaped structure that juxtaposes memory fragments of family history with historical data, leaving us with fleeting poetic images whose power accrues, not through a linear thought process, but incrementally over time. Music builds these images. Robbie lays her story words on top of jazz lines so that a verbal riff becomes a jazz riff that might make Robbie tremble with joy or flame out in rage. The play begins with two such images, and they establish how Robbie wants to frame her family stories.

We hear a jaunty boogie piano line on top of which Ed Montgomery's tenor sax lays down a stark minor-key melody. Robbie whisks away her apple tray and, as the music picks up, she introduces the first image: The United States as a country perpetually at war:

> I was born in 1942 when the war was very new
> and now the war is over I am four years old . . .
> I was / born / in 1952
> the war was very new
> and / now the war / is over / I am ten years old . . .
> I was born in 1962 / war was very new
> and / now the war / is over / I am twenty years old . . .
> . . .
> I was born in 2002 when the war was very new . . .

In rhythmic ten-year increments, a war begins, ends, and another one begins. Robbie's life's chronology is war's chronology and war is never done. From our perspective, it is remarkable that Robbie wrote *Indian Blood* in the late 1980s and that she ends her grim recitation in 2002, over a decade in the future. She couldn't have known about the disastrous Iraq War that began with the bombing of Baghdad on March 19, 2003. *And yet she did know.* Having educated herself in revolutionary discourse in the 1970s, Robbie had a well-honed Marxist critique of capitalism; she knew that war has always been used to pry open markets. Corporations, greedy for more market share, find ways to profit from wars supposedly fought for other reasons. "No blood for oil" was a common anti–Iraq War protest.

The second image offering a perspective on *Indian Blood* is Robbie's rap on class and caste:

> Racism is class based / is class bias
> is based on class / is caste bias
> is class is class is class is class
> is caste bias / is race based is caste bias . . .

Marx teaches us to think about class, but the toxicity of racism demands that we also look at the rigid stratification that "caste" describes. In the U.S., upward mobility is a favorite narrative, the ability to move from working class to middle class, and beyond. But that's for white people. In a caste system, people are marked as privileged or unprivileged from one generation to the next; no change is permitted. Rocking to the beat, Robbie pushes out these lines, putting stress on *class* bias and *caste* bias, until the rhythm moves inside her body. She speeds up, repeating the words, faster and faster, until April Greene, at the piano, yells, "Robbie!" A few moments later Robbie clarifies:

> Inside the relentless grappling
> With the causes of my oppression /
> Inside the class contradictions
> Of the open city / Inside my revolutionary dreams / in the
> mountains
> Among the trees, I'm African, I'm Marxist
> It helps.

It helps to know your history, and it helps to have an analysis. But as Robbie and her audience well know, the love, conflict, and heartbreak in families defy even the most righteous analysis. How can she resolve the contradiction of warrior fathers carrying out the U.S. government policy of systematically annihilating the Indians, when, with Indian blood running through the family's veins, it means practicing a form of self-annihilation?

The first war story poses the problem. Robbie carries a beat-up suitcase whose significance we haven't yet learned. April asks: "Do you have Indian blood?" and, in response, Robbie angrily kicks away the suitcase and comes to the mic:

> I told y'all about San Juan Hill like Grandfather was some
> hero.
> I said he woulda said he went up that hill and talked
> It over with his Indian brothers about taking their land
> from the Spanish to give to the Americans in order to survive
> and how Teddy Roosevelt and 'em were just pushing that
> Rough

> Rider stuff and Grandfather and 'em were just doing their job and not getting their pictures in the history books. Well, history not remembered gets told anyway. I looked again and HERE THEY ARE

Robbie turns to the back-wall projections, guiding our eyes to slides of the famous Buffalo soldiers of the army's all-Black 24th Infantry. Her grandfather's honorable service is framed by a granddaughter who sees U.S. wars in historical-political, not patriotic, terms. Robbie's resonant line, "History not remembered gets told anyway," is a touchstone for *Indian Blood*. Part of the post-1960s legacy, which the editors of this volume share with Robbie, is the realization of the deep bias in the teaching of American history. In our childhood history books, facts about slavery, Reconstruction, and Jim Crow were deliberately "not remembered." Similarly, expropriation of Indian land was folded into the story of manifest destiny instead of what it actually was, the arrogant actions of an imperial power. Three times over the course of *Indian Blood* stage lights go out and a "Teacher" (Robbie in thick 1980s glasses) comes on a video monitor, the first time to denounce "the not-so-secret war to annihilate the Indians . . ."

Perhaps more effective is when Robbie, in oversize army coat, impersonates her grandfather standing guard at the Canadian border, ready to shoot any Indian crossing into the U.S. She wields a narrow signboard on which is painted FREE THE LAND as if it were a gun. Deepening her voice to channel her ancestor, she speaks: "To be on watch here is a great opportunity for a colored man." The "gun" she holds, both an oppressor's weapon and a sign supporting freedom, states the contradiction clearly, and maybe we shouldn't be surprised when Robbie cites the writer who made contradiction an aesthetic principle: "Grandfather was a Father Courage with the paradoxes of parents who lead their tribes through the wars." If Brecht's Mother Courage profited off the war, Robbie's grandfather derived status and stability from it. As Robbie ventriloquizes him, though, the cost of valor is despair: "It was my job to kill the Indians. It was my job! It was my job! It was my *job*!"

A generation later Robbie's father inherits his father's paradoxes but African American disempowerment has become increasingly intolerable. Robbie's father "defied Moynihan," the notorious

1965 study that described African American families as pathological, with struggling mothers and absent fathers. Robbie's father does not leave. His children grow up and prosper. He follows the family tradition of military service: "Seems like my father was always in somebody's Army Navy Air Force National Guard . . . He loved uniforms and other male mythology." But honorable service makes no dent in a Jim Crow world where any white person selling a service can demean any Black person purchasing it. In class terms, Robbie's family may be "sho nuff poor" but they survive just fine in capitalist America. In the absolute terms of caste, though, they are near the bottom. Several stories in *Indian Blood* have to do with her grandfather and father negotiating insults on southern roads. Often this negotiation means referring to or actually pulling out the honorable discharge papers of father and son. On one occasion the family pulls into a gas station and young Robbie watches her father in his navy uniform ask for gas. The gas station owner cuts him off with, "Wat'chu say, Sunshine?" Usually, Robbie notes, her father would defuse such situations:

> But this time Daddy's breath turned into a tornado . . . The white dude kept saying, "Nigger Nigger Nigger Nigger Nigger," and then I closed my eyes.

Later her father told her what transpired in those moments:

> I put that joker in a hammerlock and I said, "Looka here, sucka! My papa took San Juan Hill with Teddy Roosevelt, and if it wasn't for that, you wouldn't have your manifest destiny li'l gas station on the side of this dusty South Carolina road," and then I dropped his ass to the ground. When he gave me my gas, I said, "Yes, sir!"

History not remembered gets told anyway. This is history lived in the everyday, shared in the family, felt in the body, recovered in stories. Her father's paradoxes in this sense are historical, as are his moods, which his strong-willed daughter struggles to interpret. Robbie performs the most powerful father-story to a jazz marching beat, reliving her father's anger and releasing her own:

> Do you think I do not understand the other father parts? . . . I understand why he pushed me down the stairs with a Bible in his hand . . . I know he fought their wars and they defined manhood for him . . . and when he came home [he] beat us up; beat us up with this thoughts, beat us up with his words, beat us up with his fists! I understand the violence in my life—and the contradictions . . . HE LOVED AMERICA!

She turns from the mic in disgust.

In the jazz structure of the piece, though, disgust and anger are interrupted by lyricism and softer recollections. Robbie tells a tender story about her Georgia childhood: on a quest through white people's territory in search of strawberry bubble gum, she finds herself deserted by her friends. Robbie finishes the journey alone, buys the gum, and chews it proudly all the way home. Remembering the family's migration, Robbie and April do an old-fashioned time-step dance number to Martin Aubert's banjo accompaniment about leaving Georgia for Washington, DC: "We're leaving the South today / And we ain't never coming back this way." And with theatrical brilliance Robbie brings her father's faltering body into her own. The story fragment begins with a telephone call in early February 1977, informing her of her father's death. "Daddy was only sixty-three. I wish I could have seen him one more time." She mimes his slowed down march steps—"Uh, uh, uh, uh, uh"—exhale. "Uh, uh, uh, uh, uh"—exhale. "Worn out. Exhausted. Too tired," he says, his historical burdens are as heavy as his physical ones.

At the end of *Indian Blood,* Robbie at last opens the beat-up suitcase to reveal her grandfather's and father's military discharge papers, documents that brought dignity to the family and maybe saved them from being killed on southern roads. Yet these same documents implicate them in the slaughter and forced removal of America's Indians. This paradox explodes into a final improvisation with the musicians roaring out dissonance and Robbie shouting out lines from the documents into the microphone while the Preamble to the Constitution appears on the back wall. Finally Robbie yells: "STOP," and walks to the other mic, closing the evening with these quiet words: "Somebody asked me, 'Should I stir my fathers in their graves?' . . . I can't believe they're resting yet."

And of course neither is she. The last wall projection shows the multitude of Indian names on either side of a photo of an affectionate young Robbie leaning close to her father in front of the family car. The photo is lovable. The politics of the juxtaposed images is painful. In Robbie McCauley's jaggedly beautiful theater, we learn to bear witness to such contradictions. If "history not remembered gets told anyway," we've learned how to listen to that telling. At the start of the show, we ate Robbie's apples; by the end, we've become her collaborators.

1. Robbie McCauley, "Thoughts on My Career," *Performance and Cultural Politics*, ed. Elin Diamond (London and New York: Routledge, 1996). Reprinted in this volume pages 15-36.

# INDIAN BLOOD

*Robbie McCauley*

## PRODUCTION HISTORY

*Indian Blood* was created in collaboration with Martin Aubert (guitar and banjo), April Greene (piano and vocals), and Ed Montgomery (saxophone and clarinet). It premiered in its complete form in November 1987 at The Kitchen in New York City. It toured to Hallwalls (Buffalo, NY), Painted Bride (Philadelphia, PA), American Festival at Cornell University (Ithaca, NY), and elsewhere.

## PROLOGUE

*Preset. Band enters.*

*Slide: Three panels Indian names.*

*Light on Robbie and April.*

*No music.*

ROBBIE AND APRIL *(Improvising)*:

I was born in 1942 when the war was very new
and now the war is over I am four years old . . .

I was / born / in 1952
the war was very new
and / now the war / is over / I am ten years old . . .

I was born in 1962 / war was very new
and / now the war / is over / I am twenty years old . . .

born in 1972 when the war was very new
now the war / is over / I am thirty years old . . .

1982 / the war was very new
now the war / is over I am forty / years old . . .

1992 when the war is / very new
now the war is over I am fifty years old . . .

I was born in 2002 when the war was very new . . .

*(Lights change: Robbie walks into path of light.*
*Music: Wars Intro (minimal).)*

ROBBIE: Somebody asked me . . .
APRIL: Is it correct to stir your fathers in their graves? . . .

*(Slide: Panel 1: Grandfather.)*

ROBBIE: Mother always called me the mouth.
APRIL *(As Mother)*: You ought not to be talking about dead folks behind their backs.
ROBBIE: We been killing Indians over five hundred years and most Americans are still Indian.
APRIL *(As Mother)*: Mouth almighty and tongue everlasting! . . . *(To Musicians)* Ready!

## 1. INDIAN BLOOD

*Music: Wars Intro.*

ROBBIE: Grandma P said he was on a pretty big black horse . . . She'd laugh when she told it . . . He was on this big pretty horse, she said pretty big black horse.

APRIL: Do you have Indian blood?

ROBBIE: I told y'all about San Juan Hill like Grandfather was some hero. I said he woulda said he went up that hill and talked it over with his Indian brothers about taking their land from the Spanish to give to the Americans in order to survive and how Teddy Roosevelt and 'em were just pushing that Rough Rider stuff and Grandfather and 'em were just doing their job and not getting their pictures in the history books. Well, history not remembered gets told anyway. I looked again and HERE THEY ARE!

*(Slide: Black and Indian Cavalry.)*

APRIL: Do you know what class you're in?

ROBBIE:

Somebody said I was in the class of 1967.
Somebody said Blood is red, that's all.
Somebody said America has no class.

*(Slide: Flag Salute.*
*Indian Blood Rap.*
*5/4 Class Rap.)*

APRIL WITH ROBBIE:

Racism is class based / is class bias
is based on class / is caste bias
is class is class is class is class
is caste bias / is race based in class bias
is based on class / is caste bias
is class is class is class is class.

When whites were slaves in the USA
it had to end one early day
for when they escaped
as slaves intend / they were hard to catch
they could blend / they could blend.

And somebody said a rose
is a rose is a rose is a rose
but a rose has roots, has thorns
and a stem and petals and a color and a smell
and racism is based on class / is caste bias
is class bias is race based in class bias
is class is class is class is class.

*(Refrain first verse.*
*Music fades. Robbie still rapping.)*

APRIL: Robbie!

*(Music: Dissin' It.)*

*Indian Blood*, The Kitchen, NYC, November 1987. Photo: © Vivian Selbo.

ROBBIE: Oliver North had numerous hours to sell the hysterical anti-communist right-wing ideology to people everywhere, and we didn't even ask for equal time.

APRIL: Rap on!

ROBBIE:

Inside the relentless grappling
with the causes of my oppression /
Inside the class contradictions
of the open city / Inside my revolutionary dreams /
in the mountains among the trees,
I'm African, I'm Marxist, It helps. Nobody dares
know what the last word is.

. . . am not anti-communist, have never been
antisemitic, homophobic, anti-anti-racist,
am very much anti-imperialist, and probably
antidisestablishmentarian, I don't know,
it takes so many negatives in America to
make a positive . . . I can hardly obsess
without eating.

APRIL: Food!

*(Music out. Improvisation on food and feeding the audience.)*

ROBBIE *(Improvising/feeding/eating)*: Food is a good reason and a bad excuse for anything. "You got to eat so join the army," stuff like that, eat . . . . . .

Putting food in the center of everything is one of those thoughts that go through me like music.

*(Music: April piano improvisation of Father's Anger.)*

Daddy had been a mess sergeant once, so for him to have meals on time was definitive. "You don't eat at other people's house! You got enough to eat at home! And be home for chow time, it's a matter of respect!"

His folks had been hungry between wars. You know there was never not a war we weren't fighting for them. There was my grandfather at San Juan Hill in 1898, and before that there was Crispus Attucks and so many of us fighting on both sides for them in their rebellion in the 1700s. And always the Indian wars . . .

Anyhow, Daddy and 'em had been hungry between wars. Mother and us and them had not. A drunk playwright once told me mine was a classic Black family—you know how white women marry up, well Black men marry up. The thing is I never knew we were anything class-wise because in America we're taught to dismiss it, and we lived you know in the future where things would be better and we ate and usually had a car and we knew labels. Tom Peanuts. Nehi Drinks. Columbus Linen . . .

APRIL: I thought you meant Gucci or Pucci or something.

ROBBIE: These some of the factories near where we lived down south. They'd say hard work makes a light load. They'd say do what the white people do, but don't act like 'em. And that might've been good advice if we didn't have to kill the Indians . . . but I'm getting ahead of myself.

Nehi Bottlin' Company was right up on 13th Avenue, right up from li'l 12th Avenue where the colored dentist who cracked Miz Lillie's jawbone was, which is how people described that part of 12th Avenue between 23rd and 24th Street: li'l 12th Avenue where the colored dentist who broke Miz Lillie's jawbone is. And he worked in that broke-down wood house with the dental chair and Miz Lillie would sit on her front porch on 23rd Street with her mouth broke. We used to bring her aspirin and Co' Colas from Mr. Reddick's store.

Me and my sister would take notes to Mr. Reddick and read 'em to him since he couldn't and Grandma Willie said it was just 'cause po' white folks wasn't educated. (I used to think when they got educated / wouldn't be no more prejudice, but I had no understanding then about Indian land.) I played with his daughters, Sheila and Martha Faye, when I was real small. I even taught Martha Faye how to read. But after we got to be ten, everybody knew you just said "how ya do" to the white folks, do business, or nothing.

Upsouth in DC we hardly ever saw white people. It was the most frustrating apartheid city. No signs. You just had to know where not to go. Had to hold your pee. One time they gave us a jar at the gas station and I had to squat over some weeds while Daddy stood guard in front of me looking dignified. But you could buy liquor anywhere. People said a white bar would sell you a cup of liquor at the back door.

Mother would say po' Black folks don't know how to do nothing but eat and drink. I didn't realize that according to America we were sho nuff poor. It took me years to figure out reasons for Daddy's anger.

APRIL *(On piano, singing torch song mode)*:

His anger was a never-ending well
that would blow up like a winter wind.
I knew November Tuesdays
those dull gray days
would soon be Sundays in Spring.
I thought like that all the time—
Darkness would be sunshine,
storm would be calm.

*(Music out.)*

ROBBIE: The teacher.

*(Video 1—Text: Everyone knows there was a not-so-secret war to annihilate the Indians. Not to tell it in history books for children, to kill the story like that, is a sin of omission. It was government policy to kill Indians. The history books have screwed people up. Everything is not like they say it's supposed to be. Andrew Jackson was a major annihilator. And they try to put him up there with the great presidents, with the so-called great ones, but there's a lot of, "Uh, uh, uh, we better not bring that up"—and history has a lot of "Uh, uh, uh" in it.*

*Slides: go to black. Travellin music in.)*

## 2. GRANDFATHER ON WATCH

ROBBIE: The blood was everywhere. Grandfather took a deep breath. He'd got one more Indian. And now he was alone with his thoughts and a smoking gun.

"To be on watch here is a great opportunity for a colored man."

Grandfather was a Father Courage with the paradoxes of parents who lead their tribes through the wars.

"Some of us went to Canada too / following Harriet / but we don't hardly hear tell of 'em anymore. / Reckon they did all right. / Survival is what it is. / Nothing more or less. / Not something to be bragging about. / It is my job to kill Indians. / They say if you talk and talk, no one will hear what you say."

Well, I don't know about that.

Grandma P's grandmother was a full-blooded half-blood. That's what they said in the family if you had one parent full-blooded Indian and the other'n real Black. Her grandmother had the "features"—that's what was said when you had high cheekbones. So everybody down the line on her grandmother's side they just said was half Indian because the grandmother was a full half-blood.

And Grandfather an' 'em were some African men from way back. Being in America . . . the warriors . . . wasn't the same.

Now, on my mother's side we were half white, but that wasn't nothing but some rape.

*(Slide: Silhouette.*

*Travellin music out.*

*Church music.*

*Video 2: Middle Passage.*

*Robbie and April become Church Ladies.*

*As Middle Passage tapes fade out, April becomes the Aunt, Robbie becomes the Child.*

*Slide: Paper dolls/Father and Daughter.)*

ROBBIE *(As Church Lady)*: These confessions are becoming a kind of mourning for the lost connections.

APRIL *(As Aunt coming from church)*: Plukanani! Plukanani's here to see you! Plukanani! Plukanani's here to see you!

*(Slide: Paper dolls.)*

## 3. AUNTS, CHILDREN AND GRANDMOTHER

*Music: Strawberry Bubble Gum.*

ROBBIE: One of the aunts called me from the garden. Plukanani. It was a funny name. When somebody said it was African, we laughed. Shoot, I don't know why she was here to see me, she always had her lips poked out at me, I think she thought I was some kinda chump. One time she pulled out my Shirley Temple curls soon as I got back from the hairdresser. But this day she just came by my front porch to play. I think she wanted to pull me out too.

I told her I wanted some strawberry bubble gum. She said strawberry bubble gum? I said yeah strawberry bubble gum. She waited a while. Then she said, I know some bubble gum tastes just like strawberries. You blow it up and when it bursts it turns to strawberries in your mouth and it's real juicy and the juice runs down the side of your chin.

Where is it?

Past Jordan City through St. Elmo going toward Wynton.

Let's go!

It was about five miles. And we walked and walked, past the ice house, past the Jordan City Columbus Linen store, past the bakery where they had that good cake, past the white movie where the colored had to go in the side and up to the balcony where it stank, all the way to St. Elmo where it got real quiet and weren't hardly no stores.

By now Ann Lizbet and Jean and Oscar Marshall had come wid us. Well, when we got past St. Elmo over by the Booker T. projects going toward Wynton, Oscar Marshall said he was going back 'cause li'l Wesley, who'd come wid him, had to pee. Now if we'd been over in East Highland, they'd've turned around and peed right in the dirt, but now that we was in white people's territory, everybody was getting scared. Plukanani act like she ain't never heard of no strawberry bubble gum. Ann Lizbet and Jean said, When you find it, bring us some.

Well I went on by myself through white people's territory—till I felt like I was getting lost. I headed back up through St.

Elmo by myself and walked right into a drugstore past a statue out front of a little black boy caddie wid gold clubs on his back . . . I just wanted that bubble gum. I went up to a white girl about my size. I said, You know about some bubble gum turn to strawberries in your mouth? She said, Yeah, there it is. It cost a nickel. I chewed it all the way home.

*(Music: Up 'n at 'm.*
*Slide: Slave ship.)*

Hit the deck! Up and at 'em!
Give them sheets a square corner.
'Em shoes should have a spit shine.
I ought to be able to cut my finger
on the corner of that mattress.

That's actually the way we woke up in our house / except it wasn't really a fascist household, Daddy wasn't that powerful. He just got off acting like a top sergeant. "It was his pleasure," as my Grandma Willie used to say.

*(Music: R-i-i-i-i-ng! Ring! Ring!)*

Phone calls after midnight and before six A.M. I fear always mean death.

I'm tired, sick and tired.
Can't make it no more Harriet.

Uh! Uh! Uh! Uh! Uh!

Worn out. Exhausted . . . too tired.

Africa! My Father! Memory of chains!
I remember my hair flowing in the breeze
like an American gothic movie. It was
a cover for the real fantasy. We don't
speak now of longing for freedom.

We're afraid we won't be heard. We
are in exile, and yet we are home.
Thousands of us carry the history
in our bodies, meet each other
in this wilderness and nod our rhythms.

*(Dim out.*

*Light on Robbie and Band dim. All other lights out.*

*Video 3: Dark for a few measures, then shows image of child playing ukulele . . .*

*Music: Band takes up theme from video, with variations: Grandmother Theme.*

*Slide: Grandmother.)*

She was half Indian washing clothes out back of the colonel's house, Ft. Leavenworth, Missouri, 1897. She didn't pay him no mind. Grandpa rode the horse through the clothes. She just washed the clothes again, still not paying him no mind . . . till he went and asked the colonel could he court her.

*(Slide: Grandfather.)*

Grandma P said when he came by, she was hanging up the clothes. He was on a pretty big black horse. She'd laugh when she told it. She said Grandpa used to come by and talk to her, and she'd say, How you do, fine thank you, and try to pay him no mind, but he was on this big pretty horse, said pretty big black horse, and he was trying to pin her down to go to a dance.

She said she couldn't ah he had to get permission from you see ah he had to get permission from the colonel she was working for she said that he did go and ask and the colonel gave permission for her to go. And that's when they started courting.

Her mother and father and brother had been taken by the flu epidemic, and she had to be placed. You know how they would place 'em back then.

First the church came. The church people came, and they sent her to school, and during those times among us she said when you learned to read and write you taught the others. And that was some of the things she did until they placed her with the colonel. And she said he was very nice to her. Very nice. And the colonel was the one that gave Grandfather the permission to marry her.

*(Slide: Black.)*

## 4. GAS STATION

*Video 4: Gas station.*

*Robbie on video and onstage doing gesture language with story.*

ROBBIE: So he got out of his 1950 black Buick. He was vulnerable and strong. With an incredible voice. The kind of presence that the Goetz-ian* sort of white man feared. Anyhow he walked up face to face with the dude and said, Fill 'er up. And do the windshield, please. He'd spoken first. I guess the moment was this, that the white dude was ready to strike down the threat before the strong/gentle presence of my father fully resonated in the air.

Daddy was in the navy back then. Navy blue uniform. Brown/black skin, deep-set brown/black eyes, and those incredible teath, the white sun.

So the dude had the nerve to cut off my father's direct request with, What'd chu say, Sunshine? Usually Daddy would have attempted some dialogue around this. I'd seen him do it before with Black and white dudes. He'd've lit up a cigarette, be surprisingly articulate, the way macho men be when the air is charged.

But this time Daddy's breath turned into a tornado, I couldn't tell which way the breath was going. The white dude kept saying Nigger Nigger Nigger Nigger Nigger and then I closed my eyes. Something happened real quick. It was very private.

* Bernhard Goetz, a white man, infamously shot four African American men on a New York City subway train on December 22, 1984; he claimed that he believed they were going to mug him and that he shot them in self-defense. He was convicted of criminal possession of an unlicensed handgun and found not guilty on charges of assault and attempted murder.

I don't know what kind of deal they made. Mother and 'em kept still. When I looked up the white dude was getting up off the ground. He got us our gas, but didn't do the windshield. Daddy said, Yes, sir . . . It was about a mile down the road before he lit a cigarette.

Nobody ever really told that story the way it happened, except one time Daddy told me. He said, "I put that joker in a hammerlock and I said, 'Looka here, sucka! My papa took San Juan Hill with Teddy Roosevelt and if it wasn't for that, you wouldn't have your manifest destiny li'l gas station on the side of this dusty South Carolina road,' and then I dropped his ass to the ground. When he gave me my gas, I said, 'Yes, sir!'"

Later that night, dead in the night, I do remember. Everybody else was sleep. Daddy smoked a lot. I lit his cigarettes and we saw an amazing forest fire.

*(Slide: Klan fire.)*

## 5. OPPRESSOR TANGO

*Music: Oppressor Tango.*

ROBBIE: Do you think I do not understand the other father parts? . . . I understand why he pushed me down the stairs with a Bible in his hand like some half-assed fascist, like a distorted Calvinist. I know he fought their wars and they defined manhood for him. And don't anybody tell me they know what it is. I know men tend to go in circles and women can go straight ahead; but I will not let my arrogance about the blood and the moon obscure my perception of the government. I know he fought their wars. And when he came home, beat us up; beat us up with his thoughts, beat us up with his words, beat us up with his fists! I understand the violence in my life—and the contradictions . . . HE LOVED AMERICA!

ROBBIE AND APRIL:

The oppressor is smarter than we thought—
he's made it passé to be oppressed,

out of style to be emotional about injustice,
it's absolutely boring to wish for his death.
So we pull ourselves up by fashionable boots
and try to get over with a hustle or two
in a world turning backwards,
in a world turning backwards,
in a world turning backwards . . .

*(Slide: Mother and baby.)*

ROBBIE: When I told mother I went to therapy, she said: Girl, are you crazy? . . . What did he say about me? It was a woman, I said, and it wasn't about you, it was about me.

APRIL: Girl, are you crazy? . . . What did he say about me?

ROBBIE: It was a woman, I said, and it wasn't about you, it was about me.

APRIL: Long pause. Mother driving.

ROBBIE: She said I was insecure.

APRIL: Mother hit the brakes so hard at the red light.

ROBBIE AND APRIL: This is America, what the hell you supposed to be?

APRIL: I may not have been a producer of security, but I sure as hell raised you. I did that.

ROBBIE: 1975. I'm thirty-three. Still smoking. Cracked lips. No breath. Thinking about Daddy's breath. 1975. I'm thirty-three and the thought of AA meetings makes me stop drinking. 1975. I'm thirty-three. I know Daddy won't be with us long.

*(Video 5: Teacher 2.*
*Slide: Classroom with Indians.*
*Slide: Klan hoods.)*

## 6. GEORGIA

*Music: Georgia.*

ROBBIE: In Georgia we used to get men out of town in the middle of the night. My grandmother would fry chicken. It was not a liberal time. Both men and women swallowed hard, lot's of sweating and delicate wiping. Tight necks. People knew how to act like that, with a lid on.

I decided not to talk at all unless I had the floor so to speak. I'd go to a secret garden . . .

ROBBIE AND APRIL: . . . Where roses fall gently over rivers that seem surprised, where children play, the ground hugging their little toes and the sky is like a mother, like a mother.

*(Slide: The mouth.)*

ROBBIE: When they realized I wasn't mental the aunts would try to pull me out, so I'd know how to say the right thing. 'Cause if you say the wrong thing. Don't say it like that. Say it like this. Don't say it like that. Say it like this. They do it in these high soprano Southern Belle voices to drown out the late-night dangers and the drum in our stomachs.

*(Sound: Heartbeat.*
*Slide: The Father.)*

Heart beating / chest pains / heavy breath just like my father. / That's my father telling war stories in the background. 1971. / But we can just go on. I'll just go on talking and singing and do 'cause that's the way it always was in my house, everybody doing whatever, and Daddy talking in the background, going on and on.

I'm obsessing just like my father. If Daddy could've obsessed in public, if he could've done out loud in public like me—who knows?

I remember his chest when he walked into a room / great presence. I was never quite sure if it was myself or him who judged the world so, so determined to fix it . . . But I am sure it was him. He was here first. I would have loved to have been more carefree . . .

*(Music: Unrighteous Fantasies [song].*
*Slide: New Negro.)*

Unrighteous fantasies crowd my light.
To be

other than I am.
To be like them.
I am here. They are there.
I come to avenge
avenge my father's death.
To play Medea.
Play Antigone.
Play Electra.
To play Medea, whose
father was king.

Medea, whose father was king, was considered a barbarian by the privileged Corinthians. I know Medea well.

Father like Atlas holds up image of success. Defies Moynihan. Does not leave. And the children grow up and prosper ever after to leave him silently in the grave to thank him now and again in sentimental longings.

I should get a more material perspective on this.
I'm here to hear the stories
to avenge my father's death.
Not to do art for the sake of itself alone
but to use it as a weapon.

Electra has no rage like what I know.

*(Music: Stone Mountain [song].*
*Slide: Stone Mountain.)*

Traveling up south 'long the Georgia coast
Grandfather stopped the car. He said
I want all o' you children and Grandmother too
to turn around and look at Stone Mountain.

He said I want you to look
at Robert E. Lee
chiseled in that mountain.

Everybody said their last look at Stone Mountain
was chiseled in their memory.

Everybody turned around and looked at Stone Mountain
all the brothers turned around and looked at Stone
 Mountain
Grandmother turned around and looked at Stone Mountain
Sister turned around and looked at Stone Mountain.

He said we're leavin' the South today
and we ain't never comin' back this way.

*(Slide: Ebony Steppers.*
*Time-step improv, Robbie and April.)*

Goin' from Mississippi Alabama Louisiana,
goin' to New York, Detroit, Gary Indiana.

Cornbread collard greens
black-eyed peas
when we get up north
we ain' gon' eat none of these.

We're leaving the South today
and we ain't never coming back this way!

*(Slide: Fred Astaire.*
*Robbie and April improv. Song out.*
*Jokes with rim shots after each:)*

'Course my father went back to marry Mother . . . but I can't say too much about it because Mother say if I talk about her like this when she dead she gon' come back and haunt my ass.

My mother who often speaks in italics would say, All white people are not bad.

My father who spoke in capital letters would say, A CRACKER DON'T HAFTA ACT LIKE A CRACKER.

Overseas a young joker sat cross from me, a coupla drinks . . . He say . . . Sarge, I'm scared of niggers, that's why I'm prejudice.

YOU THINK WE AIN'T SCARED OF CRACKERS?

*(Slides: Uniforms.)*

Seems like my father was always in somebody's Army Navy Air Force National Guard. He longed to be a policeman. He loved uniforms and other male mythology. He liked his cigarettes raw and whiskey straight in a shot glass. He wanted a Cadillac more than anything else in the world.

Somebody told me she didn't like Indians calling themselves "Native Americans," Because if they're Native American what does that make me? Immigrant, I said.

## 7. STORIES TOLD OVER AND OVER

ROBBIE: . . . I'm here to hear the stories . . .
There are so many Father parts.

*(Slide: Chains.)*

Traveling from southwest Georgia, 'bout 1930, my father, all the brothers, and Sister, my Grandma P, all their stuff packed in an old Studebaker. Grandfather driving. Daddy tried to jump out the car and go after a white man standing cross the way hollerin', "Look at all of them niggers stuffed up in that ol' raggedy Studebaker." Grandfather yanked him back in the car and sure enough soon as they got outta town they saw a chain gang truck.

I remember seeing chain gang trucks on 23rd Street. Black men in prison clothes huddled down. White men standing with a gun. I remember the convoy trucks too. Black men in fatigues up inside. I used to get the chain gang trucks and the convoy trucks mixed up. I used to run 'longside looking for my daddy. Everybody said he was off in somebody's war when I was born.

Anyhow, Grandfather said, "See those chain gang trucks? That's why I'm taking you boys out the South. 'Cause of the kinda boys you are. Strong manish boys. Stay down here. Y'all'll end up on the chain gang."

*(Slide: Scottsboro Boys.)*

And that's the way that story went . . . But lo and behold, there's another part to that story . . .

APRIL: Uh uh . . .

ROBBIE: See. After the Spanish-American War. You know my grandfather was in the 24th Infantry of the 10th Cavalry, all Black regiment fighting Indians for the Americans. And we were supposed to have been very proud. Anyhow after they came back from the war, most of the men in the 24th got jobs on the army bases as servants. My grandfather came back after fighting their wars and got a job as a valet to the officers at the officers' club. And the officers' club was called the Reservation.

APRIL: Hush your mouth!

ROBBIE: You could look it up . . . Anyhow, Grandfather was doing fairly well (as they say). They had a little house outside the Reservation. Grandma P was happy because they had nice furniture and good china dishes. The officers would party a lot at the Reservation. This was the late twenties, so it was still prohibition. And they asked Grandfather to go get their whiskey for them. They said, "Sergeant, we know y'all get the best corn liquor." You know it was a big thrill to have the colored people get their whiskey for them. (You know how it was in the twenties, white people would go up to Harlem to hang out.) It was juicy. A little corrupt. Thrilling. Grandfather wasn't into it. He was one of those upstanding law-abiding folks.

Grandfather just said NO . . . A coupla nights later, my Aunt Marie tells me—she was nine years old at the time—her mother, Grandma P woke her up and Aunt Marie who was nine years old looked out the window, and this is what she saw . . .

*(Slide: Klan.)*

Grandma P said, "Papa we got to go." She had a toothache and wanted to go into town the next day to get it fixed. Grandma P started wrapping dishes in cloth. Grandfather said, "O no, we gonna stay." Grandma tore off a piece of cloth and heated the water on the low-burning wood. Grandpa kept saying, "We can stay, we can fight it . . ." She squeezed the warm rag back in her jaw and hollered quiet, "Papa, the boys!" . . . And that's how they started up south.

And then there's the part about the broke-down car.

APRIL: Here we go . . .

ROBBIE: Traveling up south, they pulled into a South Carolina town, a street. A neighborhood. White people and their dogs sitting on the front porch . . . and the Studebaker broke down. Here come the white men off their porches, from behind their houses with their hands pushed back like they were protectin' their women . . . Grandfather got out the car, walked up to what looked like the head white man, pulled out his discharge papers and told him about San Juan Hill and Teddy Roosevelt and the men told their women to go get lemonade, and Grandfather and Grandmother and all the children had a drink, and the men took Grandfather to get tools to fix the car. Now this story was always given as an example of how dignity and background and self-respect and official papers could keep your ass from getting killed.

Wasn't that nice?

APRIL: Very nice . . . but I have a feeling . . . there's . . .

ROBBIE: Another part . . . It got mighty hot driving up the road. Aunt Marie remembered it was sho' nuff summer heat because Grandpa had a birthday right before the Klan came, and everybody knew he'd made his birthday the fourth of July. Grandma P had a rag in her mouth, her tooth aching, and Grandfather pulled into a filling station to get some ice. He walked right in and said, "My wife is in the car suffering from a toothache, it's hot, and could you give me a piece of ice." They said, "Nigger, get on away from here." And so Grandfather held his breath, got back in the car and went on up the road. Stopped at another filling station. Grandfather went in and told 'em about the heat and the toothache and "could you give me a piece of ice." And the folks told him to, "Get outta here Nigger." And one more time Grandfather held his breath and got back in the car. At the third gas station he pulled up the car, got out and went to the back where he had his gun. Grandma P and the children sat still. He tied his gun to one hip and his discharge papers to the other and went inside the station. Don'tchu know he came out with ice and co' colas and cheese and crackers for the children!

APRIL: Wasn't that nice?

ROBBIE: Mighty mighty nice . . . Another story told as an example of how when you got background, dignity, self-respect, official papers, *(With April, both laughing)* and a piece on your side, you can keep your ass from getting killed.

*(Teacher video.*
*Slide: Indian/Pilgrims.)*

## 8. UNTOLD STORIES

ROBBIE: First Grandfather went to Baltimore to work on the railroad. My father (who considered himself some kinda teacher too) said that Grandfather went first to Baltimore to work on the railroad. History not remembered gets told anyhow. He would say your grandfather built the railroads with the Chinese. (Well, we all know that they imported tens of thousands of Chinese people over here to build the railroads, and that they finally settled in California.) What they don't show in the pictures is there were Black men among them. From the east the Irish built the railroad and there were Black men among them. Sister would always say no matter what, if it was back-breaking work, you know there were Black people in there because that's the way they always used us—but we just never got the credit! And Daddy would say the Negroes built this country just as good as anybody else, and don't you forget it! We'd be sitting on the bed, and Daddy would be building the railroad. He said the Chinese would be coming from this way and your grandfather and the Black men would be coming from that way . . . and they'd be building . . . He didn't say nothing about the Irish, but . . . we didn't mind . . . and he'd build the railroad . . . build the railroad on the bed across the nation for us.

People in my family were about the government like some folks are about church. My heart would beat fast when the flag flew. Daddy would say "United States of America" with a low voice. Women in my family married servicemen for two generations. Except for me. By then I was about America like a jilted lover.

*(Music: Gregorian chant.)*

I used to want to be Catholic.

APRIL: Why on earth . . . ?

ROBBIE: Well you know how they cross themselves when the ambulance comes by or when they pass by a church or when a funeral passes, y'know it's something. And when they sin they can go to church and confess once a week and that's it and be forgiven until the next sin the next Friday. It's very private, not like the Southern Baptist church where you had to carry your sins like a load of sackcloth on your back or confess all out loud in the church . . . too much! And the Catholic girls in my neighborhood always were in love with the celibate white priest . . . which I thought was mysterious.

This all changed when I went to a Catholic hospital in Washington, DC, half dead of a diabetic coma. I'm slipping in and out, Daddy's driving.

I hear all this stuff: Get her out of here! Mother stepped back. Daddy, my daddy, the last surviving boy of ten children whose namesake my cousin Bobby died at seven in the hospital waiting room because they waited too long to get to him and no we didn't sue we grieved knowing that's the way it just is sometime Lord Jesus! Daddy's sister dying of diphtheria because the colored hospital was twenty miles away and the major said if I'da known it was the sergeant's baby we'da blah blah blah! Daddy held the doctor upside the wall and said you gon' do something and do it now. I half-remember Daddy's sweat smell, Mother's eyes steady. I remember the siren sound of the ambulance to the city hospital not private Catholic called Providence. At the city hospital I got out of the bed walked down the hallway the green walls toward the light coming from under the door closed at the end of the hall. I walked toward that light coming from under the door. When I got up on it, the door was open and Mama Willie who'd died in 1962 was sitting in her green rocking chair. I kept walking toward her rocking in the light, her eyes steady like her daughter's had been before, she said "get back" . . . And I came on back down the hall heard somebody say she's going to make it . . . Well, I was through with the Catholic Church, and this was years before I knew that Bishop Bartolome de las Casas and Pope Julius the Second initiated the African slave trade because the Indians couldn't/wouldn't, were dying.

*(Slide: Burning cross.*
*Music: Ring Ring Ring.*
*Slide: Father obituary.)*

Early February 1977. I got a phone call. 6:30 A.M. early in the morning. Daddy was only sixty-three. I wish I could have seen him one more time.

*(Slide: Indian men.)*

## 9. APARTHEID IN AMERICA

ROBBIE: Everything reminds me of apartheid in America. I remember the COLORED and WHITE signs. I was too young to be born into that.

There's a town in North Carolina that had the words WHITE and INDIAN on their separate bathrooms.

There's always been apartheid in the Mormon church against Black people, but the Mormons have come up with something about Indians being their long-lost brown brothers (you remember . . .) that they were to meet over here in the United States . . .

Could be like the Catholics fronting for the European colonizers in the fourteen, fifteen, sixteen and seventeenth centuries.

Could be like the Calvinists fronting for the Boers or the Anglicans fronting for the British in South Africa.

Could be like the Zionists fronting for the U.S. in Palestine, I don't know, you could look it up.

The Mormon church is the fastest growing church in America, is among the top corporations in the country. One quarter of the nation's energy resources are on Indian land. In fact, this is all Indian land!

APRIL: Indian land and African slave labor was the foundation for the industrial revolution and the rise of capitalism in the U.S. and Europe.

ROBBIE: Mormon men in suits roam reservations looking for children / cajole Indian families (some bribed with food) / to give up their children to the Mormon church / to white families / to be educated / be Americans / to come back to the tribe as leaders.

Some children who could not be won over by the Mormons come back home / have identity crises / roll to the side of their beds / hear the ghosts of ancestors calling them.

Sometimes I feel like I was kidnapped. Feel like I hear the spirits of my ancestors calling me. My neck is hot. Feel like Grandfather walking the balance between survival and freedom. They say I have Indian blood in my veins, say my skin has orange undertones, that I look good in green. Indian blood in my veins?! . . . I feel it's on my hands!

The Spanish-American War where the U.S. took for itself Puerto Rico, Cuba, Hawaii, the Virgin Islands, the Philippines, and Guam (and they'd just wrapped up the major Indian Wars), this Spanish-American War only lasted five months. The 24th Infantry, Grandfather's unit, participated in these conquests like mercenaries. It wasn't no Black people's war. What would we do wid Puerto Rico? The Klan was well established by then. We had our own war in the United States . . . but we never did form our own army . . . The thing to do in the United States was to survive, get a piece of the pie. Did I tell y'all I was diabetic? What the hell I want with some damn pie?

Anyhow, after this hundred-and-fourteen-day war that made America the biggest power in the world, Grandfather and them went back to the Philippines with John J. Pershing to take part in the "quelling of insurgents." My Filipino friend Jessica told me that some of the men in the 24th Infantry, Grandfather's unit, actually betrayed Aguinaldo. Grandfather was doing his job, in with the Black soldiers that crushed the resistance of Jessica's them folks. Of course, she said Filipinos betrayed each other too. I said we betray each other too / and then we said you have to / and then we said you don't / and we both sigh like a long scream . . .

## 10. RETIREMENT

*Slide: Retirement papers.*

*Improvisation on letters: Enlistment/Retirement/Band/Congratulations.*

*Two video screens overlaying: Robbie in graduation cap, reciting Preamble to the Constitution; Robbie in Black Panther beret, reciting Declaration of Independence.*

ROBBIE: STOP!!!
EVERYTHING OFF!

## EPILOGUE

*Light on Robbie.*

*Slides: Indian names/Father and Daughter.*

ROBBIE: Somebody asked me, "Should you stir your fathers in their graves?" . . . I can't believe they're resting yet.

*(Lights out. Slides remain.)*

END

Robbie and her father, Robert McCauley, Washington, DC, 1950s. Photo courtesy of Anita McCauley Henderson.

## SCORE FOR INDIAN BLOOD: A SAMPLE

*Ed Montgomery*

SYNTH A

& GUITAR

# TRAVELLIN'

"INTRO"

# TRAVELLIN'

"INTRO"

SYNTH B

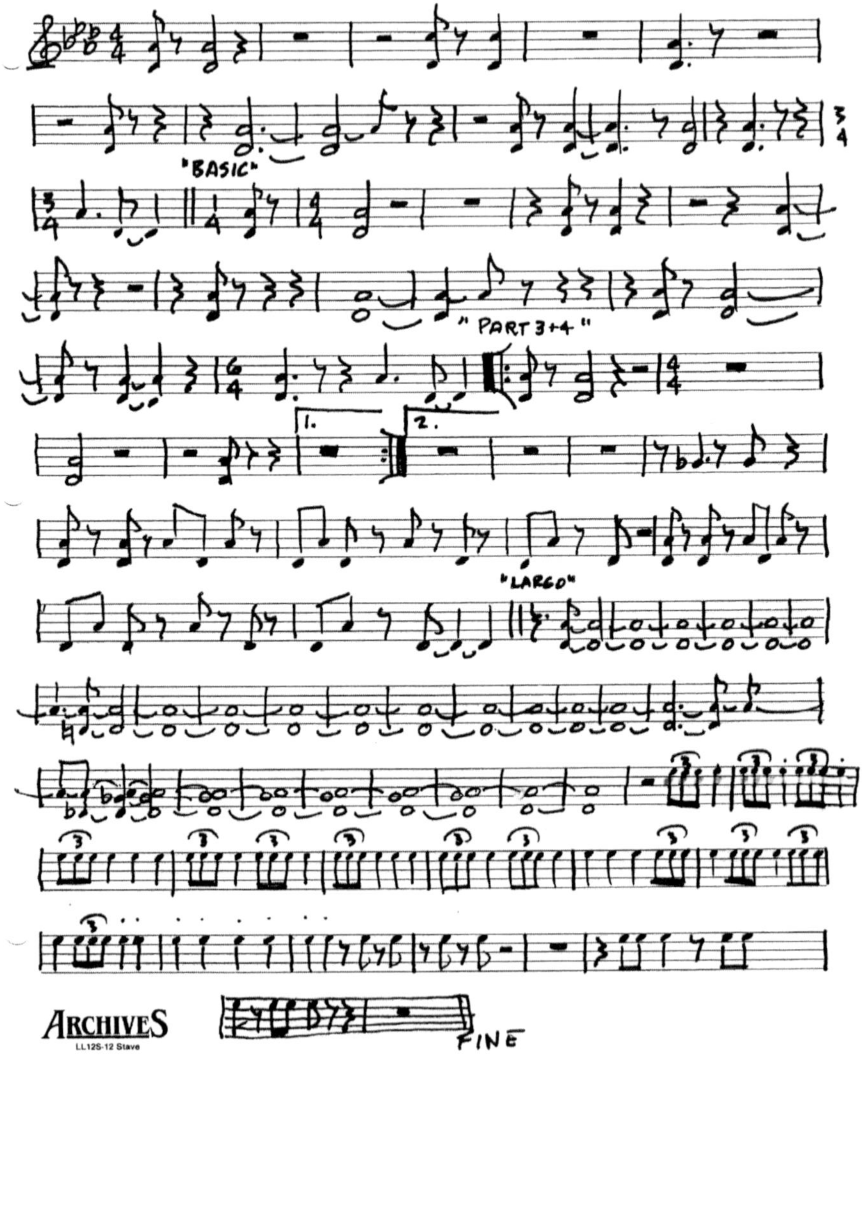

# Unrighteous Fantasies

music: E. Montgomery
lyrics: R. McCauley

21
pla-ay - ay E - lec - tra, to play Me - de - a, whose fa - ther was
king.
Fine
B
spoken:
Medea, whose father was king, was considerd a barbarian by the privileged Corinthians
29
I know Medea well. Father, like Atlas, holds up image of success,
33
defies Moynihan, does not leave, and the children grow and prosper ever after
37
to leave him silently in the grave--
to thank him now and again

41
in sentimental longings
I should get a
more material perspective
on this.
DS al fine
Chord changes for solos
45 A♭ C B♭min G♭ E♭min
49 B♭min A♭m E♭ E E♭7
53 B♭7♭5 A♭m B♭m G♭ E♭min
57 D♭7 E♭7 F B♭
61 E♭ Cm G♭ F
65 E♭min B A7 A♭

Bb 1 — UP'N'AT'M

SYNTH A — "UP'N'AT'M"

SYNTH B

# UP'N'AT'M

Bb1

# OPPRESSOR TANGO

GUITAR

# OPPRESSOR TANGO

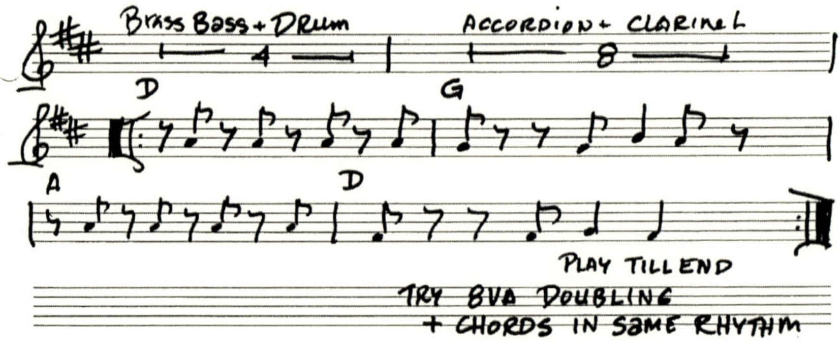


SYNTH 2
LOW BRASS

# "OPPRESSOR TANGO"

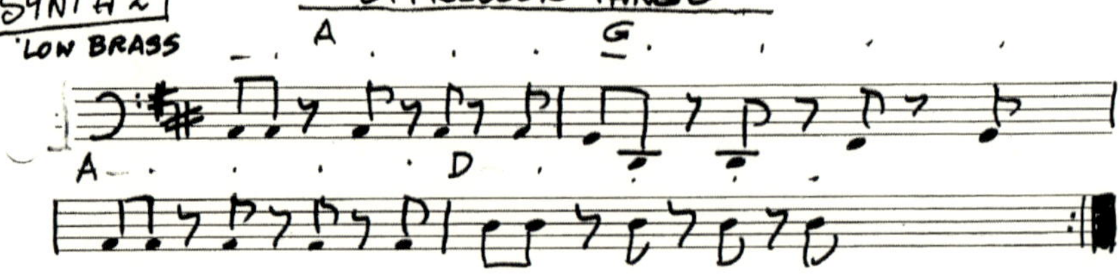

# INTRODUCTION TO *SALLY'S RAPE*

*Cynthia Carr*

In the spring of 1990, I saw an early version of *Sally's Rape* at the Studio Museum in Harlem in conjunction with "The Decade Show." Most spectators that evening had been bussed uptown from Soho's New Museum. Most were white. I can't ignore that observation in the context of *Sally's Rape*, constructed as it is to bring racial subtext to the surface. So there we were. White people. In Harlem. Bussed. Listening to Robbie McCauley talk about her great-great-grandmother Sally, who "had them chillun by the master like that was supposed to a *been* something." Which is the kind of story most white people can handle. Horrific but historic. Couldn't-happen-today. I-wasn't-there. Except that *Sally's Rape* is about the way we live now. It's about the way such stories continue to shape Black/white relationships because the past has never been dealt with.

So at the heart of *Sally's Rape* is the dialogue, the friendship, and the inexorable difference between Robbie and Jeannie Hutchins, "that white woman." In the words of a white spectator at the Harlem show: "I don't know what that white woman was doing on the stage."

Hutchins told me: "White people don't want me to be there. White people want to identify with Robbie."

I wrote the paragraphs above in 1991 and I wish enough had changed by now—after more than thirty years—to make them read like an artifact. Back in 1990 and 1991, I saw *Sally's Rape* four times in four different venues. Rereading the play now, what impresses me is the subtlety with which Robbie addresses the heaviness of racism. And forces white people to feel their whiteness.

Racism continues to thrive, in part, because people do not talk about it across racial lines. Robbie began work on *Sally's Rape* around the same time she began the community projects—all of it about "the dialogue" between Black people and white people. Ultimately, it's also about why talking to each other is so hard. For those of us who are white, usually the first thing that comes up is guilt. That is a "stuck" place. We go no further. Then there's Black bitterness and Black fear to go with white ignorance, white insensitivity, white slowness. Not ready. Not ready.

*Sally's Rape* begins by seeming to defuse all that. Robbie and Jeannie walk on stage holding teacups and saucers. We see their easiness with each other. They're friends. They're discussing comportment. But tiny cracks in their united front appear almost immediately. And it's amazing how profoundly the history of racism can come up around something as ordinary as a teacup. Robbie says that her people went from jars to cups and saucers. So she took a class in tea pouring to learn it properly. "Like my Aunt Nell said, if you do the wrong thing, you could get your ass killed." But it's a casual pronouncement, not aimed at Jeannie who replies that in her family they used mugs.

I developed a theory about the play—that the camaraderie between the characters works to get white spectators to drop their defensiveness. So when Robbie suddenly steps back into family stories about slavery—Sally's life, Sally's rape—the stories burrow in deeper because the barriers are down. And we never see real antagonism between the characters—meaning rage from Robbie, guilt from Jeannie.

They pass out cookies and apple slices. "Food eases tension," say the stage directions. And they encourage some audience participation almost from the start. Already I'm making it sound so difficult—but I don't remember experiencing difficulty (and I hate audience participation). They divide the spectators into three sections: one will speak a short sentence of agreement (like "that's right"), another will make sounds of assent (like "uh huh"), and the third will respond with dialogue (something to add, something to disagree with, etc.). "Let's practice with something from the context of the piece," Jeannie suggests.

So Robbie states, "I believe white is a condition that anyone can take in. It causes one to feel superior in order to be okay." She encourages the audience to talk about it. She may choose to talk back.

This is one element that makes *Sally's Rape* different every time it's performed. Robbie also designates a couple of sections as places where she and Jeannie will improvise their dialogue. In the first of these, they sit facing each other on two chairs and they talk about why they're angry with each other about difference. The stage directions explain: "Jeannie thinks Robbie can see through her to something she can't admit. She thinks their idealism is similar. Robbie thinks admitting the differences in their histories is more important. Jeannie is concerned that she can't win. They try to reveal something to each other as if they are alone and honest about their differences."

The dialogue they then improvise—labeled "suggested text"—goes way past the usual platitudes about race.

"What upsets me is language," says Robbie. "I can't win in your language."

Jeannie replies: "You're going to win anyway. What upsets me is there's an underlying implication that you're gonna unmask me. That you're gonna get underneath something and pull it out. That you can see it and I can't."

And it develops from there.

The text above, included in the script published in this book, was transcribed from the 1991 performance at The Kitchen in New York City. It was probably different the next night and could be different again for other Robbies and Jeannies.

Robbie did envision other actors taking this on, improvising changes in rehearsal within "the context of the written dialogue." I suppose that would not be easy. Nothing here is easy. Robbie wasn't looking for easy. What *Sally's Rape* is showing us is that, ultimately, Jeannie cannot go to that place where Robbie's been. This isn't Jeannie's fault. It's what *is*. The play also shows us that they have to stay connected.

This is illustrated later on the auction block. Robbie steps onto it naked while both she and Jeannie direct the audience to chant, "Bid 'em in!" It's a shocking confrontation with the unspeakableness that was slavery. Robbie expresses no rage. Jeannie expresses no guilt. The audience has to chant. Each time I saw this piece, the white spectators had a hard time getting the words out. During one of the shows, Jeannie barked, "Come on! You have to help her!" Black spectators would join in willingly. "They get it," Robbie told me. "White people have a problem because they don't want to be generalized as white. They don't understand that this is for all of us. We all participated." She sees it as a cleansing ritual. The stage directions call it "a moment of communion." That is, we are recognizing our shared history as Americans.

Later in the piece, Robbie tells Jeannie to get up on the auction block. It doesn't work. First of all, Jeannie objects: "I thought we weren't going to do this. It's so arty." Robbie asks the spectators to do the "bid 'em in" chant, and Jeannie takes down one strap but never disrobes. "Do you have something to say?" Robbie asks her. "No? That's something right there."

And what happened to Sally illustrates another grievous difference. Any sexual assault is horrific, but in Sally's case it was not even considered a crime. She was property and her owner could do what he wanted with her. So Robbie names it right in the title: *Rape*. Naming it is a political act. She speaks Sally's words: "Wasn't nuthin' to it. You just stay tight till they finish." While she's still on the auction block, Robbie declares, "Aunt Jessie said that's how they got their manhood on the plantation. They'd come down to the quarters and do it to us and the chickens."

As Robbie describes this dehumanizing act that wasn't even called rape during slavery time—"at night they pulled us out in the dirt" —Jeannie talks about the rape crisis center, the help you can get.

"Ain't no rape crisis center on the plantation," Robbie tells her.

"Then what do you do about it?" Jeannie asks.

There is no answer.

*Sally's Rape* is one of those pieces you carry out the door with you. While I can certainly think of many other performances that moved me and stayed with me, this one had direct impact on my life.

I had interviewed Robbie before writing about this work in 1991 and we discussed the difficulty of getting white and Black people to talk to each other about race. I believe I'm the one who observed that usually those who can't speak personally are white people. As if I wasn't one. As if I could speak personally. I felt like such a hypocrite. As we concluded, I felt compelled to confess. My grandfather had been a member of the Ku Klux Klan, and I had never told anyone. I feared that this would make Robbie angry. That just proved how much I had to learn. Among other things, she told me that hearing it was a relief "because I feel like I'm not making up something." Eventually I realized that Black people were more ready to hear about this than white people—and they were definitely less surprised. "The 'nice white people' I know all come from something," as Robbie put it. Yes. Few of us are descended from abolitionists, Underground Railroad conductors, or Freedom Riders. Many of us have stories that do not make us proud.

It took a couple more years before I was ready to write about the lynching that had happened in my father's hometown—a lynching I'd heard about as a girl. Had my grandfather been involved? Only part of the book I then wrote was a whodunit. A larger question for me was—how do we recover from these atrocities? How will Black and white people ever reconcile?

When I looked into the (admittedly incomplete) reconciliation work that went on in South Africa (after apartheid) and Chile (after Pinochet), I discovered the words of Chilean legal philosopher and activist José Zalaquett. If you have to choose between truth and justice, he said, choose truth. "Truth does not bring back the dead but releases them from silence."

In 1995, I moved to my father's Indiana hometown for fourteen months to do research. While there I attended every one of the antiracism meetings occasionally organized by some community group or church, and I found a general pattern. For Black participants (and I did hear a woman say this), it was "here we go again," while white people experienced it as a huge and frightening step. (Not ready!) Usually there was no second meeting.

In *Sally's Rape*, Robbie and Jeannie are doing the work of reconciliation. They are honest with each other, a big requirement. Robbie tells family stories: Sally "down on the ground being done it to"; the slave who "learned how the white folks do," and then taught reading writing and numbers to his son who taught Robbie's grandmother; Uncle Buck asking after the Civil War, "Massa is we free?" and Massa saying, "Yeah nigger you free," before shooting Uncle Buck dead. We never learn much at all about Jeannie. She's there to take these stories in.

In *The Fire Next Time*, James Baldwin famously called on "the relatively conscious whites and the relatively conscious Blacks" to work together to "create the consciousness of the others." I know it's painful for the relatively conscious whites to hear what Black people went through because of racism and to know that they can't fix it. But we can't go numb. We can acknowledge that it's heavy for us too. We who are white have to own our terrible histories, which means owning the pain. That's a way to get to moral accountability. As Robbie once said to me, "Racism won't be over until you have to live with it the way I have to live with it."

# NOTE FROM ROBBIE MCCAULEY*

I had a dream in which I heard Sally's voice. The line that came to me in the dream was, "I don't wanna do it." It was an interesting dream because the atmosphere was there of the town that I lived in in Georgia, and the smells were there. I was very close to the time of slavery when I lived in the South because we heard the stories, so I associated those smells that were in the dream with those stories. It was a wonderful kind of connection, the dream.

## STYLISTIC INFLUENCES

I'm influenced by Black classical music, or jazz, in that it has a clear theme and narrative, but it is also random and impulsive. It was the music that I came to knowledge in when I was a teenager. In the late 1950s, early 1960s, what was then called modern jazz—the music of Charlie Parker, John Coltrane—was popular among the teenagers that I grew up with. It's the ability to sing the hard things and make them beautiful. That's what I gravitated toward in the music at that time. The blues is also a part of that. Living in the South,

* From the publication of *Sally's Rape* in *Moon Marked & Touched by Sun*, ed. Sydné Mahone (New York: Theatre Communications Group, 1993).

the blues was just all around me. Again, it's singing the hard things beautifully. I work with music through the passion that I have for it and the ability to hear it deep down. People tend to think of music as something written; however, when one is creating, one is not thinking of what is written. It helps me as a writer to think of it in the same way that I imagine a musician's passion connected to the form.

## ARTISTIC CHALLENGES AND DISCOVERIES

Dialogue is an act. One of the comments I'm sensitive to is, "You're talking about it, but what are you doing?" In *Sally's Rape*, it released me physically to write it. From that personal dialogue, on to the dialogue between me and Jeannie Hutchins, on to the dialogues with the audiences, I found that just the nerve, the boldness to speak about the charged issues of race relations can be something right there. It is an act. It is not before or after the act. Saying the words, allowing dialogue, making dialogue happen is an act, a useful act in the moment.

This is not new, but it is something that we tend to gloss over too much. We carry in our bodies unspoken sadness and anger and resentment. It is bigger and harder to carry it than to release it. And when we release it, we find out more information about it; we help our ability to move with it. You don't get rid of it, but you're able to handle it, take it with you, and to transform.

## THE AESTHETIC

I define my aesthetic as "content as aesthetic." The way I shape work is to listen to what is going on; and of course, "listen" is a big word. I'm looking, I'm smelling, I'm tasting, I'm touching, and I value that. This is what most artists do, but I continually sensitize myself to find in it those elements that I can personalize and put in my work.

What I'm concerned with in narrative is that the stories are known. We share the story that is known. Whether people know it or not, it is as I call it, part of their collective memory. Personal stories are the same. My listeners also know my personal story because my personal story is all of our story. This is just my part in it.

The thematic thread in my work is the connection of things that have been torn apart. I don't try to make connections. I'm trying to find the connections that are there. For instance, I know about differences between races. I know about commonness between races, between men and women, and so forth. The commonness is easier to speak than the differences. I'm most interested in speaking those differences. In a strange way, speaking the differences makes the connection happen. And I'm not talking about "we shall all hug and overcome everything." It's simply that it helps us to see where we are on this whole earth—and out of that, many things can happen.

## DEFINITIONS OF HEROISM

For me, the particular story of Sally is not the rape. It is her understanding it. This comes from the fragments that I picked up about her that I do when I'm on the auction block. She asks the white man how much was the house that she wanted to buy, and then she worked for money to buy the house so that none of us ever had to do what she had to do. How many mothers does that cover? That's historic. That's heroic.

## DISTINCTIONS BETWEEN WOMEN'S AND MEN'S WRITING

I recently heard the writer Deena Metzger say that women can pay attention to the things that are immediate. To me, the immediate or so-called small things are the big things, the things that we are ignoring in our development. Sally says, "It wasn't nothin' to it," when the men came down to rape them. That's a loaded statement because it means that it was done constantly and people called it other things. They didn't call it rape. Now we know that rape has to do with power.

I'm going against the myth of the romance of the slave master and the overseers with the slave women, even Thomas Jefferson. I'm going against the myth because it was a power thing, so we call it rape. Sometimes it was actual, brutal rape; sometimes it might have been romantic. It doesn't matter. It was a rape in the sense that we know what rape is now. It's the everyday rape that happens in those power situations; and so it's "ha ha," a small thing. When

I started *Sally's Rape*, of course, Bosnia wasn't in the picture. But now that's being talked about—rape as part of domination.

This attention to small things has to do with our connection to our bodies. If you bleed every month for a large part of your life, then you are in touch with reality, with the moon, in a way that men don't have to be. The little things that we do are a part of us and are connected with the whole. I remember when I was pregnant, I said, "Oh, this is what women feel like! *This* is it!" Of course, I cried, fell down. I suddenly felt like millions of women in the world.

## THE DARKNESS AND THE LIGHT

I'm constantly reversing the images of dark and light. *Sally's Rape* might be considered a dark image, but I go to it, and there is the light. There's a line that Jeannie says in the piece, right before she says, "I wanted to be Billie Holiday." She is "looking for light in tunnels of despair." That came out onto the page out of nowhere. I was thinking, I'm writing really corny stuff here; and when she read it, it sounded really good. So that's my feeling about darkness and light.

I personally have dealt a lot in my life with depression and what is called darkness. In terms of artistic imagery, as many artists understand, the dark images are where one finds the light. Artistically and politically, I'm much more fascinated with what is difficult in beauty. When people think of the light, they think of being bright and at ease. I wish I could do that. But inside that darkness, that's what I am; I am at ease. I'm drawn to it. And here I'm using dark in the way that it's usually used, but I don't see it that way. I think it's because I'm an actor, my energy comes out of going to places that are difficult emotionally. When actors see pain, they run to it. What is personal about it is all of my baggage and heart stuff, but I've learned to find the light in that stuff. It's a hard thing to admit.

It's not like I'm trying to come out the other side. I'm trying to live in a place where that is usually what is going on—like I love to come back to New York City.

The light comes with simply exercising my mind, my sensibility, going to places full of energy and information. Pain is full of information. It exercises my mind to deal with that information.

Again, it goes back to the body, the release. What you know is something you can carry with you rather than be burdened by.

So much of this has to do with sexuality. Black women particularly struggle to deal with the image of the saint and the whore, or the church lady and the slut. It's part of the puritanism of America, but it is also part of our own issues with sexism, how we are perceived as women. The issues are also economic as well as social. There are places in extreme, places in between, there are places all around, but we get stuck in the inside of sexual images and in the way we internalize what we're supposed to do and what we're not supposed to do. Part of my struggle is around those issues of having been raped and silent about it. I know that information, I've dealt with it and I can carry it with me. But in *Sally's Rape*, I found out more information about the tightness between my thighs.

In the piece, I say, "There's a tightness between her thighs. When it lets go, she screams with terror." So there's no good sex in there. Knowing that, the discovery of that power is something you can take with you as information, and let go. Whatever you wanna do with what you let go is your business.

Robbie McCauley with Jeannie Hutchins, *Sally's Rape*, 1990. Performance: Studio Museum of Harlem, New York, 1990. Presented in conjunction with "The Decade Show: Frameworks of Identity in the 1980s," 1990. Courtesy the artist and New Museum Archives. Photo: Dona Ann McAdams.

# SALLY'S RAPE

*Robbie McCauley*

## PRODUCTION HISTORY

*Sally's Rape* began with a solo performance by Robbie McCauley for the Women & Theater Program Conference at New York University in 1989. With Jeannie Hutchins joining as a performer, early work-in-progress versions were presented in New York City at Lincoln Center, PS 122, BACA Downtown, and the Studio Museum of Harlem. The full, completed version *Sally's Rape: The Whole Story* was presented at The Kitchen in New York City in 1991. It toured to Boston; Louisville; the American Southwest; Rutgers University; St. Paul, MN; Prague, Czech Republic; and elsewhere.

*Sally's Rape*, the co-winner of the 1992 Obie Award for Best Play, is featured in two videos: Maria Beatty's *Sphinxes without Secrets* and *Conjure Women* by Demetria Royals.

## PLAYERS

ROBBIE: the one who plays the people in her and who tells all she wants to tell. She is an actor who sings and dances. She is Black.

JEANNIE: the one who plays the roles she's given and who sometimes erupts. She is a dancer who sings and acts. She is white.

AUDIENCE: those who are there, who witness and talk back.

## AUTHOR'S PRODUCTION NOTE

Some of the scripted dialogue in this piece came out of my conversations over tea with Jeannie Hutchins. Some of it emerged from improvisations during our performances. So the actors—the parts of themselves that connected with the subjects of the piece—became the characters.

The improvisational dialogue in parts 4 and 8 may change somewhat if other actors play the characters. It would be best if these changes grew out of work between the actors and director on the subject of the piece.

The stage directions are just a guide to suggest the ease with which events between the actors, and between the actors and audience, can happen.

The music for the song "Grandma Sally," which is reproduced following the text of the piece, was composed by and for a performer with some minimal knowledge of how piano notes and chords are played. The piano playing is essential to the piece. If the actor playing "Robbie" cannot read music, she should consult with a musician. If she cannot manage the playing, the music may be recorded and played while she mimes playing the piano and sings.

My thanks to Ed Montgomery for transcribing the music for "Grandma Sally," and to Esther Kaplan for transcribing one of the November 1991 performances of *Sally's Rape* at The Kitchen in New York City.

## PROLOGUE: TALKING ABOUT WHAT IT IS ABOUT

*A bench up right. A piano up left. A large, sturdy square table up center and two chairs. All are set at angles. Rocks are lying about the space. General lighting. Audience enters, sits.*

*Robbie and Jeannie enter with cups of tea on saucers. They walk to a space down left in conversation between themselves, aware of audience. Easy talk.*

ROBBIE: Somebody said it was about cups.
JEANNIE: Somebody else said it was about language.
ROBBIE: What do you think it's about?
JEANNIE: Well, that one person said it was about you and me. And I know it's not about me, but it's about you and I'm in it.
ROBBIE: It's my story, and you're in it because I put you in it.
JEANNIE: Fair enough.
ROBBIE: It *is* about cups.
JEANNIE: It's about getting culture.
ROBBIE: Cup says culture.
JEANNIE: Comportment.

ROBBIE: Commonality. Well actually, where I come from, cups and saucers were like . . . We had to learn about these things. I mean we went from jars to cups and saucers . . . nothing in between. I once went to a class in tea pouring . . . It was Japanese, but it was about containment . . . proper . . . deportment.

JEANNIE: Doing the . . . proper . . .

ROBBIE AND JEANNIE: . . . right . . . thing.

ROBBIE: Like my Aunt Nell said: If you do the wrong thing, you could get your ass killed, so it was more like a matter of life and death.

JEANNIE: You know, we had cups and saucers. I even think we had six that matched. But mostly we used mugs.

ROBBIE: Mugs?

JEANNIE: Because they hold a little more, and they have a bigger bottom, so they don't tip. The only disadvantage of a mug is after you use a spoon you have to just kind of put it on the table, and it leaves a little mark.

ROBBIE: I think sometimes we did this for the sake of itself. Cups and saucers. Charm school. White gloves.

JEANNIE: But that's South, too. I mean, that's Southern stuff. The one girl that was like that I knew . . . she had gone to charm school, she was being groomed to be a Southern Belle. She had monogrammed sweaters. She went to charm school one summer in junior high, and she learned to walk like this . . . *(Does the walk)* with a book on her head. And we all tried.

ROBBIE: We didn't worry about books on our heads. We already had this *up* thing. I guess that was the African in us before I even knew it. But we *(Walking, Jeannie following)* had to contain our hips. To keep tucked up. Slightly seductive but not too much . . . *(At the bench)* and when you sit . . . you know this part.

JEANNIE: Yeah, you touch the front of the seat with the back of the calf, and then you descend without bending at the waist.

*(They sit together; Jeannie crosses her legs.)*

ROBBIE: Now you can—no! *(Hits Jeannie's knee away)* Don't do that. *(Jeannie corrects) Now* you can drink your tea. *(They sip simultaneously)* My Aunt Nell would have *died* if she saw you—

JEANNIE: —cross my legs like that.

ROBBIE: That's it. Put your feet just so, or slightly cross at the ankle.

JEANNIE: Why was that?

## 1. CONFESSING ABOUT FAMILY AND RELIGION AND WORK IN PROGRESS

ROBBIE: Almost everybody in my mother's family was half white. But that wasn't nothing but some rape. These confessions are like a mourning for the lost connections.

*(Robbie starts singing "Wayfaring Stranger" and Jeannie joins in.)*

ROBBIE AND JEANNIE:

I'm going there to meet my mother
I'm going there no more to roam
I'm just a going over Jordan
I'm just a going over home . . .

*(Robbie continues humming like in church.)*

JEANNIE: That was the only thing that would make it worth going to church for me, to sing those songs. But I didn't really have a religion, so that's why I invented one. When I was about seven,

I invented a religion, and it was all about rocks, and trees and leaves, and nature and so forth, everything that I knew. And I tried to convert my best friend, Eileen, who was Catholic. It ended up just being mine.

ROBBIE: I envy that. To have a religion that you find where you are was something I couldn't even conceive of until Africa. Before that, of course, it was the big white God up there . . . If oppression is at the core, if there must be one at the top and others on the bottom . . . the struggle will always be . . . *(Gesture of pushing and straining)* You know, I mean, the way I dealt with religion was to be a Marxist . . .

JEANNIE AND ROBBIE: . . . another . . . big white God . . .

JEANNIE: What was it your Aunt Nell said when you said you were a Marxist?

ROBBIE: "Well, at least you're *sumpthin'*." If this . . . *(Same gesture)* kind of struggle, if oppression, is at the core, then this work will never end. It's a work in progress . . .

JEANNIE: Well, if you can dialogue, you can get rid of some of that.

ROBBIE: Well, *if* you can weed it out. *If* it's about something else, then—

JEANNIE: *Then* it's a work in progress . . .

ROBBIE: . . . a dialogue . . .

JEANNIE: Otherwise, there is no progress.

ROBBIE AND JEANNIE *(To audience, alternating the lines between them)*: And we can't have a dialogue by ourselves. So you're in it. Don't worry I won't jump in your face or down your throat. We'll feed you. *(They pass out cookies and apples, improvising about "fishes and loaves" and about how food eases tension, may help you talk)* We'll use hand signals, lead like camp directors, divide you into groups. One . . . *(One of them points out sections of the audience)* Two . . . Three. Well, it doesn't matter what section you're in, it just matters who you are, and you can change your opinion as time goes on.

Group One will be the agreeable ones. When we signal like this, *(Two fingers up)* you say, "That's right!" "Yes indeed," or "I'm telling you." Any short sentence of agreement. Let's practice. *(They lead responses with Group One)* Good! . . .

Group Two will be the bass line. You just go "uh huh," "umm humm," or "yeah, yeah." Here's your signal . . . *(One finger pointed out)* Let's try it. *(Group Two practices with sounds)* Very nice.

*(Talking fast)* Group Three is the dialogue group, people who have something to add, to disagree with, who like to talk.

ROBBIE: Don't worry, I'm in control. Your signal is two hands out flat like this . . . Dialogue?

JEANNIE: Let's practice with something from the context of the piece. Lights!

*(Lights on Robbie and Jeannie in two house aisles. Stage black.)*

## 2. STATING THE CONTEXT

ROBBIE: I believe white is a condition that anyone can take in. It causes one to feel superior in order to be okay.

*(They signal to the groups. Groups respond. In this improvisation with the audience, when Robbie feels someone makes a strong point, agreeable to her or not, she impulsively stomps her feet.*

*Stage lights up. Aisle lights off. Jeannie moves among rocks.)*

*(Walking in 6/8 time)* It's about my great-great grandmother Sally who was a young woman with children when official slavery ended. And she's in me. She was house but *field.*

My Aunt Jessie who died at the age of ninety-three—

JEANNIE: Ninety-six.

ROBBIE: She always put her age back. She said we was bad off in Harris County 'cause the white folks wasn't doing too good, and we were brought up to believe that, that our well-being depended on white people being well-off. You know how families can raise you with counterrevolutionary ideas in order to survive.

*(They call for audience response. Robbie waves off dialogue.)*

We don't hafta discuss *that.*

*(Jeannie moves among the rocks. Robbie continues in 6/8 rhythm.)*

It wasn't *fine* like the gone-with-the-wind type house-nigger mythology. Sally did the housework and the cooking, and she tended to Mistress when some really fine white folks come to visit. They say that they might not a been really rich white folks anyhow. They say Sally had them chillun by the master like that was supposed to a been something. They say Massa was mean and nasty. You know how white folks gets when they ain't doin' good. Word was freedom was coming, everybody know what happen on that day freedom come when we follow Uncle Buck—I believe that was his name—

JEANNIE: Yeah, Uncle Buck.

ROBBIE: —up to the massa porch. *(Sudden anger)* But back up in *heah* 'fore freedom they say po' citter white folks was buying us ignorant! No telling what woulda happen! *(Pauses)*

## 3. TRYING TO TRANSFORM

ROBBIE *(Upset, she moves over left)*: I I I become others inside me, standing at the bus stop with my socks rolled down screaming things I shoulda said, "Just because people are crazy don't mean they can't think straight!" Hollering periodically at white men: "YOU RAPED ME! GODDAMN MOTHERFUCKA! YOU RAPED ME!" *(Reaching out, gathering air)* Sometimes I'll gather and push away the wall of vibrations that make walls between us . . . *(Throws air to Jeannie)* Black

JEANNIE *(Catching, molding the bunch of air)*: Black

ROBBIE: Women

JEANNIE: Women

ROBBIE: Get

JEANNIE: Get

ROBBIE AND JEANNIE: Bitter.

JEANNIE: Black women get bitter. Scared somebody gonna look at them, run and search for the wind, look at them go to the bottom of the pain and sadness, looking for breezes. You know how Black folks gets when they ain't doing good.

ROBBIE: It's a journey of chains.

JEANNIE: I latched on, crawled in like a spider clinging to the walls, looking for light in tunnels of despair. I wanted to go deeper, darker, never to remember the empty days. I wanted to be . . . Billie Holiday.

ROBBIE: I wanted to be Rosa Luxemburg!

JEANNIE: Rosa Luxemburg?

ROBBIE: Poland.

JEANNIE: That's so idealistic.

ROBBIE *(Aside)*: So was Billie Holiday.

JEANNIE *(Responding to aside)*: I didn't have to know that to want to be her.

ROBBIE *(Does dance kicks)*: Poland. She liked Poland. Communism wasn't even a word back then. The main deity in Poland is a black madonna. In Eastern Europe women were more revered, more venerated.

JEANNIE: Do you have proof? Who told you that?

ROBBIE: A woman from Eastern Europe.

JEANNIE: Well, a woman from Turkey told me there was no racism in Turkey.

ROBBIE: Well, from her point of view, there probably wasn't.

JEANNIE: Why are you so understanding, so generous toward people in another part of the world?

ROBBIE: I was listening to a woman who had pride in her ancestors and that turned me on.

JEANNIE: That's very nice.

ROBBIE: Socialism goes way back. Way back women gathered in groups to pick. And Africa. Let's do 1964.

*(Light change: a pool of light center. They stand in it. Other areas dim.)*

In 1964 at the library job a U.S. history major who'd graduated from Smith College said—

JEANNIE: "I never knew white men did anything with colored women on plantations."

ROBBIE: I said, "It was rape." Her eyes turned red. She choked on her sandwich and quit the job.

JEANNIE *(Pointing at each audience group in turn)*: Was the Smith College graduate denying . . . ? Lying? . . . Or dumb? *(Audience response)* Yeah she was dumb. I keep telling you that.

*(They cross past each other. Light change.)*

ROBBIE: Why do I feel like crying . . . because she went to Smith College . . . I think of the dumb educated bourgeois thing in me . . .

JEANNIE: You have this thing that an Ivy League education could prevent her dumbness about that, and there's nothing that can prevent that.

ROBBIE: Right, I do have a thing that an Ivy League education oughta prevent that. I mean, look, okay. I wanted to go to Barnard, and they didn't let me in . . . a rejection letter . . .

JEANNIE: And you're bitter.

ROBBIE: Bitterness about Barnard I admit. But when I'm sitting around my grandmother's breakfast table, and she's telling me something that this woman who went to Smith College didn't know, a U.S. history major—

JEANNIE *(Overlap)*: Well, aren't you more fortunate then, that you learned so much more through your grandmother?

ROBBIE: The point is that Smith College, all those colleges, are places that people should go to learn things that help the world. All right? And if she went there and studied U.S. history and comes out sounding dumb about what went on during slavery time, I don't understand. I can't give her no credit for just being dumb. I mean my grandmother would also teach us that . . . You know, we lived in a neighborhood back then down south that had Black people and white people, back when they had signs that said WHITE and COLORED to separate bathrooms and stuff. Well, back then there were white people who lived down the street from us because that was where they had to live. And we played together till we were about ten. After ten back then we couldn't speak to each other. Even back then my grandmother taught us that white people were not genetically evil or anything, they were just dumb, and when they learned something, they would be smarter about us . . .

*(Jeannie starts to do folk-dance steps in 3/4 time. Robbie joins in.)*

. . . and we could get together and change the world.

JEANNIE: Rosa Luxemburg had no patience for bourgeois women who didn't work. She called them—

ROBBIE: Co-consumptive.

JEANNIE: More parasitic than the parasites. She was a small, powerful woman.

ROBBIE: Zaftig.

JEANNIE: When she talked, people listened. I believe she would have marched with us.

ROBBIE AND JEANNIE *(They stop dancing)*: She was murdered by men who would later be Nazis.

ROBBIE *(Turning, kicking, squatting)*: Dancing in half circles. Trying to connect. She was internationalist—so far ahead of her time—we haven't begun to get there yet—

JEANNIE *(Overlap)*: —as opposed to nationalist.

ROBBIE *(Dancing)*: In Pennsylvania a town with the black madonna and the little brown Jesus. A Polish town. In Eastern Europe way back . . . women more venerated . . .

JEANNIE: There's one in Texas too. I sent you the postcard. The shrine to Our Lady of Czestochowa.

ROBBIE: Not long ago in Poland a pilgrimage to her.

JEANNIE: But you've never explained why in Poland there'd be a black madonna.

*(Pause.)*

ROBBIE: Socialism goes way back.

JEANNIE: But a burned statue or anything, there's no explanation for it?

ROBBIE: Way back, way back! Women gathered in groups to pick and hunt.

JEANNIE: Did they really hunt? That's unsubstantiated.

*(Pause.)*

ROBBIE *(Stops dancing)*: Of *course* they hunted. And of course it's unsubstantiated. And Africa.

JEANNIE: Old memories. Ancient stuff. We all come from one African woman. Dancing in circles, pushing walls. I was underneath him in the dirt too—he doesn't want to hear this, he thinks he civilized the world! I sold slaves when I worked at the Welfare Department. Did you put them on the ship?

*(Jeannie puts her hands on Robbie's hair. Pause. Robbie lifts them off.)*

## 4. MOMENT IN THE CHAIRS

*They set up the two chairs. Light changes. One bright circle. Other areas dark. They sit in the light, face each other, hold hands and move their arms to and fro, as if giving and receiving dialogue.*

*They improvise on why they are angry with each other. The differences go deep. Jeannie thinks Robbie can see through her to something she can't admit. She thinks their idealism is similar. Robbie thinks admitting the differences in their histories is more important. Jeannie is concerned that she can't win. They try to reveal something to each other as if they are alone and honest about their differences. The following is an example of the dialogue that has resulted in performance.*

JEANNIE: Your hands are like ice.

ROBBIE: What upsets me is language. I can't win in your language.

JEANNIE: You're going to win anyway. What upsets me is there's an underlying implication that you're gonna unmask me. That you're gonna get underneath something and pull it out. That you can see it and I can't.

ROBBIE: What do you think it is? I mean, it's better if you say it.

JEANNIE: Some kind of delusion, self-deception.

ROBBIE: About what? I mean, what's the content of it?

JEANNIE: About my idealism. I have some idea of . . . humanism, something that we share, more important than our differences. Of greater . . . Of greater value.

ROBBIE: Let me see if I can use the language to say what I feel about your idealism. I think it covers over something in your history that makes your idealism still a whim. It angers me that even though your ancestors might have been slaves—because they did have white slaves . . . only made Black slavery mandatory for economic reasons, so they could catch us when we ran away—that history has given you the ability to forget your shame about being oppressed by being ignorant, mean, or idealistic . . . which makes it dangerous for me. *(Stands)*

JEANNIE: I have the same thing about education you were talking about. I mean I believed that through education, if I could change my thinking, that anything would be possible. And it just sounds so stupid.

*(Robbie may use this moment to say something more to audience. Jeannie takes chairs away, joins Robbie facing audience. Beat. They go stand in front of bench, pick up cups and drink tea.)*

## 5. SALLY'S RAPE

ROBBIE:

Do you think Thomas
took his Sally to European tearooms?
And what did she wear?
And what do you think Mrs. J thought?

ROBBIE AND JEANNIE: That musta been some business, huh?

*(They take their cups to piano. Jeannie first sings with Robbie, then becomes Mrs. J and does the dance of the frail white lady.)*

ROBBIE *(Plays piano and sings)*:

Grandma Sally had two children
by the master. One of 'em
was my Grandma Alice, my mother's
grandmother, where my mother got her name.

*(Robbie continues to play. Mrs. J speaks, conscious of the music.)*

JEANNIE:

In the woods . . .
I immediately become Harriet
in the woods.
Swamps are my memory.

ROBBIE *(Coaching)*: Shoot.

JEANNIE:

Shoot, how you gonna be scared of freedom?
Some teachers don't know nothing.

ROBBIE: Once.

JEANNIE:

Once somebody I almost married
said I was too scared of dogs.
I said I'm scared of slavery.
I wanted to be . . . darker . . . deeper.
These are dreams but the wounds remain
and there are no meetings of ourselves
at the crossroads.

*(Lights change. The auction block. Jeannie moves bench center to be the auction block, but then improvises with Robbie, deciding to move big table there instead. Jeannie takes bench down left. Robbie steps onto auction block, takes off her sack dress, drops it on the block. She is naked. Jeannie starts to chant, "Bid 'em in," coaxing the audience, taking time to thank them for joining in. It should be a moment of communion.)*

ROBBIE:

On the auction block. With my socks rolled down,
I take off my sack dress. Mistress? Come on.
This is what they brought us here for.
On the auction block. They put their hands all down our bodies
to sell you, for folks to measure you, smeltcha . . .
They say in Ecuador where forty percent of the population is African,
that Jesuits heaped us into huts by the hundreds
and listened while we bred.

JEANNIE: That's what they brought us here for.

*(Auction block light is blue. Jeannie circles down near audience, leading the chant, and back to dim light up right.)*

ROBBIE *(Still naked)*: Aunt Jessie said that's how they got their manhood on the plantations. They'd come down to the quarters and do it to us and the chickens.

A TIGHTNESS BETWEEN HER THIGHS. WHEN IT LETS GO SHE SCREAMS WITH TERROR. AND THEN TIGHTENS AGAIN. WHY DOES SHE KEEP COMING TO ME IN THESE NIGHTMARES? THEY SAY SALLY WAS TOUGH. BOUGHT A HOUSE AFTER SLAVERY TIME. TAUGHT HER DAUGHTERS TO BE LADIES. ASKED THE WHITE MAN, HOW MUCH WAS THE HOUSE ON 23RD STREET. HE TOLD HER AND LAUGHED. LIVING IN ONE OF THE RED HOUSES, PAYING BY THE MONTH, TOOK IN WASHING, CLEANED UP THEIR HOUSES FOR MONEY. SHE ALWAYS SAID FOR MONEY. TOOK SEVEN HUNDRED AND FIFTY DOLLARS TO THE BANK, WHICH IS WHERE THE COLORED HAD TO GO TO GET THE PAPER FOR PROPERTY. SAID SHE DID ALL THAT AND NONE OF US EVER HAD TO BE WHORES.

*(Jeannie ends chant, signaling with her hands like a conductor. Robbie asks the light board operator to bring up the lights as she picks up the sack dress and holds it in front of her.)*

*(To audience)* I wanted to do this—stand naked in public on the auction block. I thought somehow it could help free us from *this*. *(Refers to her naked body)* Any old socialist knows, one can't be free till all are free.

*(Lights back to auction-block blue. Robbie curls down onto block.)*

In the dream I. I am Sally being *(An involuntary sound of pain)* b'ah. Bein' bein' I . . . I being bound down I didn't I didn't wanna be in the dream, bound down in the dream I am I am Sally being done it to I am down on the ground being done it to bound down didn't wanna be bound down on the ground.

In the dream I am Sally down on the ground being done it to. In the dream I am Sally being done it to bound down on the ground.

*(Jeannie moves auction block back, places chairs down right and crosses past Robbie to bench. Robbie, carrying dress, goes to Jeannie's light.)*

## 6. IN A RAPE CRISIS CENTER

ROBBIE *(Putting on dress)*: Before they changed the Bill of Rights/ Constitution/Articles of Confederation—whatever it was for white men before they changed it—it said they all had a right to land, cattle, Negroes, and other livestock . . . pigs . . . dogs . . .

JEANNIE *(Curled up on bench)*:

To be raped is not to scream
but to whimper and lock and never to remember
but feel the closing in the thighs
between the legs locking up everything
biting lips, the teeth bleed.

ROBBIE:

On the plantation you hafta stay tough and tight
no matter how many times they come down there.
Sally stayed down there with us in the quarters
and at night they pulled us out in the dirt.

*(Jeannie crosses to chairs, stands. Robbie crosses to bench, sits.)*

Wasn't nothing to it. You just stay tight till they finish. Sally worked in the house, but she stayed down in the quarters with us. He took Sally out on the ground.

JEANNIE: In a rape crisis center, your wounds are fresh. They can put warm cloths on you, tell you it's not your fault.

ROBBIE:

Wadn't nuthin' to it. The others watched.
Sometimes they did it too.

*(Pause. She crosses and stands down left of Jeannie.)*

They say Sally had
dem chillun by the massa like it was supposed
to a been something. Shit, Thomas's Sally was just as
much a slave as our grandma and it was just as much a rape.
One Sally's rape by the massa no gooder 'n an n'othern.

JEANNIE: All anyone would have to do is keep you warm.

ROBBIE: After slaverytime, say Sally married Gilford, a Black man, and they had two boys. And nobody, not even them two chillun she had by the massa—which is what everybody called 'em like that was supposed to a been something—nobody ever blamed Sally for calling them two *boys* her real chillun.

JEANNIE: There's no reason to feel that cold all the time.

ROBBIE: COLD. VERY COLD. VERY VERY VERY COLD.

JEANNIE: Someone would give you a cup of tea. Hot chocolate. Warm milk.

ROBBIE: These new ones with the alligators act like they wadn't born with no memory. I don't know what all went on underneath those houses of women and silent men.

JEANNIE: Herb tea.

ROBBIE: You . . . let the cabs roll by . . . let shit roll off your back . . . *stay* . . . ain't no rape crisis center on the plantation.

JEANNIE: Then what do you do about it?

## 7. TALKING ABOUT DIFFERENT SCHOOLS, AND HOW TO DO

*Pause. Robbie crosses over to chairs. They both sit.*

ROBBIE: My Ma Willie and my Aunt Jessie had a school. It was called—well, their school, I don't remember what it was called. But they had gone to Mr. Pierce's school. Now, Mr. Pierce's father or grandfather was—

JEANNIE: I think it was his grandfather.

ROBBIE: But Mr. Pierce himself had taught my grandmother and them, so it must have been his father who had been a slave and had worked in the big house and looked in and learned how the white folks do. So his son had a school called Mr. Pierce's School where the girls, and I reckon some of the boys, went to learn how to do. Now when my Ma Willie and Aunt Jessie opened their school it wasn't just for how to do. It was for reading, writing, and numbers, and Aunt—

JEANNIE: Tell them about the motto.

ROBBIE: Jeannie likes this. Back then they said, "Each one teach one." And that's how the learning was transmitted. My Aunt Jessie could name the capital and the river it was on of every state in the United States.

JEANNIE: Alphabetically.

ROBBIE: Alphabetically. One of the first words they learned was *garage*. It was a new word back then. Garage—a building in which you place an automobile.

JEANNIE: What about rhetoric?

ROBBIE: Oh yes, they learned rhetoric. My mother said rhetoric was learning to tell the truth over and over.

JEANNIE: You know we had classes in a garage too. But I think they were opposite. The whole idea was wild abandon. This was about a year before I invented the religion. But the whole thing was nature. My teacher had a long red ponytail and a drum under her arm, and we'd go running across the room. We were about six years old, all girls. Some forest . . . some beast . . . some storm . . . you know the whole thing—wild, free, running!

*(Robbie runs across the space and back.)*

Yeah, we were freer than that.

ROBBIE *(In her own world)*:

What difference it a been, it a been by the master?
They all come down there. They all do it to you.
And do it to the chickens too.
What difference it a been?

JEANNIE: What do you do about it? See, this section to me is where everything is clear. The difference in weight. I say the word "free," and what do you think of? A feather, or a butterfly. You say the word "free," it's totally different. It's light . . . substantial, flimsy . . . weighty . . .

ROBBIE: Come, let's do this.

*(Robbie and Jeannie get the auction block.)*

JEANNIE: I thought we weren't going to do this. It's so . . . arty.

ROBBIE: Get up there. *(To light board operator)* Put the auction block lights on, please. *(To Jeannie)* Take off your dress. *(To audience)* Let's do it for her, please . . . Bid 'em in. Bid 'em in.

*(Jeannie takes down one strap.)*

*(To Jeannie)* Do you have something to say? *(Jeannie shakes her head no)* That's something right there.

*(Jeannie gets down and moves block back.)*

## 8. THE LANGUAGE LESSON

*Robbie holds Jeannie by her shoulders from behind.*

ROBBIE: Everybody know how on the day freedom come, we followed Uncle Buck up to the massa porch. And Uncle Buck said,

JEANNIE: "Massa is we free?"

ROBBIE: And that white man took out his shotgun, and said, "Yeah, nigger, you free," and shot Uncle Buck dead.

JEANNIE: Massa is we free?

ROBBIE: Shot Uncle Buck dead.

JEANNIE: Massa is we free?

ROBBIE: Say it again.

JEANNIE: Is we free?

ROBBIE *(To audience)*: They say Massa was mean and nasty. He was all dressed up, and the ladies too, and they all came back to the kitchen. And one of the uncles took the blame for stealing the bucket of fatback and greens that Sally was gon' bring down to the quarters for us. And they made him eat the whole bucket of fatback and greens, until he commenced to rolling on the floor and passing gas, and they laughed and laughed . . . and the ladies too.

JEANNIE: Is that it?

ROBBIE *(Aside)*: They say that day might not a been really rich white folks anyhow. *(To audience)* On the day the really rich white folks came, they dressed up Sally and one of the uncles like staff, like house staff, so Massa and them would seem richer than they were and so we'd seem more profitable. They were figna sell us! Figna sell us further down south Georgia! If the war hadn't a come, no telling what woulda happened. *(Pause)* I reckon we'd a never been here to tell y'all this.

*(They call for audience response. Robbie waves off dialogue. Jeannie sits on bench.)*

JEANNIE: But you were already in south Georgia. How much farther down could you go?

ROBBIE *(Sits next to Jeannie)*: They say Sally had them children by the master to save us. How come they thought she had a choice? Survival is luck. Or unlucky.

*(They improvise. The following is an example of the dialogue that has resulted in performance.)*

You wanna try the language lesson?

JEANNIE: Okay . . . They was from south o' Albany way down Seminole or Decatur.

ROBBIE: That's sort of—

JEANNIE: Jimmy Carter.

ROBBIE: Sort of a bad imitation of a white southerner.

JEANNIE: I'm not trying . . .

ROBBIE: As I've said before, try to know, like actors do, what you're talking about.

JEANNIE: Farther south?

ROBBIE: Where slaves were sent, couldn't get back from, way away from their loved ones. It resonated dread. See it, know it, feel the dread when you say where that place was. *(Doing it)* They's from souf a Allbeny way down Semino o' De kaytuh.

*Sally's Rape*, The Kitchen, NYC, 1991. Jeannie Hutchins and Robbie. Photo: © Joyce George.

JEANNIE: They's from south o' Albany way down Semino o' Decatur.
ROBBIE: Better. When we learned the English language, we had to learn the English culture. I only learned later that iambic pentameter was street language . . . like rap . . . "To be or not to be, that is the question." Deep ambivalence. I could play Hamlet.
JEANNIE: If they let you.
ROBBIE: If I wanted to.

*(They sit quiet. Lights out. Applause.)*

## EPILOGUE: LEAVING THE AUDIENCE TALKING

*Lights up. Jeannie and Robbie get their cups of tea.*

JEANNIE: There's a part we sort of want to do to involve the audience, but we get more involved . . .

ROBBIE: It has to do with talking to people, even if you already know 'em, and especially if you don't, how a lot of people in different cultures greet each other. I know some Native American cultures do: "Who are you and who are your people?" And where I come from, African American folk be like, "Who children you?"

JEANNIE: So our idea was that you were going to turn to somebody else and find out something.

ROBBIE: Which you can do.

*(Robbie and Jeannie walk off.)*

# GRANDMA SALLY

WORDS AND MUSIC BY ROBBIE MCCAULEY

# INTRODUCTION TO *SUGAR*

*Maureen Shea*

One day in 2006, when I was chair of the Department of Performing Arts at Emerson College, where Robbie was a professor, I approved expenses for her professional travel, as I did for all faculty members. She'd gone to Ohio State University and then to the University of Texas at Austin, she said, to teach and perform a fragment of a work in progress she was calling *Sugar*—about her diabetes, she told me, about race, about her life.

I asked her why she was traveling so far away to try out the piece when she could be developing *Sugar* as a full-length play and production at home, at Emerson, in Boston.

I'd known Robbie then for more than a decade, having met her in the early 1990s through the renowned voice teacher Kristin Linklater, then saw *Turf*, a remarkable piece she developed with residents of the "Southie" and Roxbury communities from their stories about the Boston school busing crisis of the 1970s and, finally, in 2001, recruited her to found and lead a graduate-level program in Theatre and Community at Emerson, where she taught until 2013. Having been a long-time admirer of her courageous and important work, I had always wanted to collaborate with Robbie. Our friendship—long, meandering talks about family, politics, and relationships over the years—only deepened that desire. In 2010, we pitched *Sugar* to Rob Orchard, then executive director of his newly founded presenting organization, ArtsEmerson. Having read a proposal and just a few pages of the piece, and based on his deep respect for Robbie's impressive body of work, he offered us a February 2012 slot in his season, in the Paramount Center's Jackie Liebergott Black Box Theatre.

Robbie and I then asked the installation artist/designer Mirta Tocci to collaborate on the project with us, designing scenery, projections, and props. She'd worked with Robbie many times previously on theater productions Robbie had directed for Emerson Stage, The Theater Offensive, and Roxbury Repertory Theater. They spoke the same artistic language.

Next, we invited the pianist/composer Chauncey Moore to join us. Robbie and I met Chauncey when I directed her in a staged reading of a new play in which she played an old man, a jazz pianist noodling on his piano in the Ninth Ward as Hurricane Katrina raged outside. Like *Sugar*, that piece was also a memory play. One evening, Chauncey arrived at rehearsal to accompany another actor/singer also in the play, and from the wings, he saw Robbie performing a monologue onstage, faking playing jazz as she spoke. There was an upright piano stored backstage, next to where Chauncey was watching her. All of a sudden, we heard music. Chauncey was improvising, underscoring Robbie's monologue, playing the notes he imagined Robbie was playing from seeing the way the music in her mind lived in her body, watching her hands move over an imaginary keyboard. Yes—we needed Chauncey.

Valued lighting, costume, and sound designers joined our artistic team later, closer to opening, but for almost a year, it was Robbie, Mirta, Chauncey, and I working together on *Sugar*. Here are some of my notes from that remarkable time.

*Sugar* is Robbie's story, and more. "Life is bigger than biography," she writes, "sugar, more than sweet."

This is the story of Robbie's life as a diabetic from childhood to the present, a series of events and relationships punctuated by unpredictable and often violent diabetic episodes. But it is also a story about love and race (as is true of all of Robbie's plays), the Black Arts Movement, and the legacy of slavery in America.

*Sugar* is a memory play. Robbie is its narrator and protagonist. Robbie asks, "How do I look back, go forward, and be here at the same time?" She speaks to the future when she writes about her daughter, Jessie.

She speaks to the past in her relationships with Mother and Daddy, big sister 'Nita, cousins, aunts, Grandma Sally, lovers, husbands, beloved fellow theater artists, now gone. And the thinkers that affected her most—especially Karl Marx and his blessed contradictions . . .

I'm thinking about Susan Sontag's *Illness as Metaphor*, "sugar" as "sweet" metaphor for the insidious disease that attacks her body. Just as racism attacks the body politic.

We start in an empty rehearsal room. Robbie stands there; Chauncey sits at his keyboard. Robbie asks, "What now?" Chauncey echoes, "What now?" There are some folding chairs in the room. I ask Robbie to start moving them as she talks with us, helping her create minimal locales she can then settle into, sit down in—her kitchen table, a church pew, a movie theater, a seat in her classroom. She has begun. I ask Chauncey to play whatever he feels as Robbie works. He waits several weeks until he sees her move, tunes in to what she's saying. Then a line about being in the garden as a little girl, in Georgia. Chauncey plays a fragment from the Gospel hymn "In the Garden" as Robbie speaks. He has begun. We have begun.

Chauncey will underscore Robbie from an upright piano onstage. The music, although scored, should feel improvisational. He's Robbie's silent scene partner, her confidante. Listening. Laughing. Singing with her. Helping her.

Mirta proposes an acting platform twenty-five feet long, only eight feet deep, and just a foot high. It will be painted red, "like an artery," she says. Three wooden folding chairs will be painted black lacquer. In the pre-show, Robbie is seated, with a beating heart on the full-stage projection screen behind her, animated. Whenever Robbie has a diabetic spell, we'll see huge projections of microscopic blood cells. Overwhelming. Tangled. Twisted. Beautiful. Blood cells. Carriers of life and death. We'll see the interior landscape of Robbie's physical body as she reveals her "interior" life to us.

Robbie and I have lunch in my home in the summer of 2011, talking *Sugar*. The grilled cheese sandwiches and iced tea get us talking about childhood comfort food. And family gatherings. Robbie was raised eating southern comfort food with her mother's family in rural Georgia—homemade food that was central to her culture and community, essential to family rituals around meals. I'm struck by the irony that for the undiagnosed juvenile diabetic she was, this comfort food might also have been poison that could kill. I suggest that she write about it. She comes back with an aria to food, material food made metaphor and irony. Whole days as a child spent preparing food and eating it: breakfast, lunch, and dinner. Robbie quotes her mother, "Food is everything. That's all we do." "Food in the family was love," she says. We end up placing this aria at the beginning of the piece. The irony will unfold.

Watching Robbie in rehearsal, Joseph Chaikin's *The Presence of the Actor* comes to mind. This is one of Robbie's great gifts: PRESENCE. She is always miraculously, magically PRESENT. The most present actor I've ever worked with.

But then Robbie herself is always present. She never "small talks" (even though it may seem so). She always talks "big." Her warm, friendly, intimate conversation invites and disarms, preparing you to face the hard truths embedded in seeming "chat." You are ready and willing to embrace these truths because they come from this quiet, unassuming, dignified woman who sees and knows you.

Her language is prose, but highly poetic prose. No meter, *per se*, but cadence. Robbie's a certified Linklater teacher, and it shows in her writing. The marriage of voice and text lives here as in Linklater's *Freeing Shakespeare's Voice*. Image, metaphor, irony, assonance, antithesis—so many rhythms and figures of speech—embodied by her in performance. In rehearsals, we use Linklater's vocabulary, as if Robbie were performing Shakespeare.

Made by Robbie the actor, the text on the page by Robbie the writer is like a seashell. We "read" the text as we might study a shell, seeing its curves and striations as trace evidence of the living organism that made it. As she performs her own words now, you know she performed as she wrote. The body and embodied voice, mind, and memory are the living organism. The text, the marks they make.

"Sugar" is a loaded image that Robbie unpacks in every way possible. Her opening line: "Sugar is complicated, like love, full of pleasure and pain." As a child, sucking on sugarcane with "Red Shirley," "laughing like the end of the world." Sugarcane as commodity—the cause of the triangular slave trade. Profit from sugarcane "feeds" slavery. Slaves on sugar plantations—dying for the "white."

Sugar is "sweet." Sugar is sex. And then there's Mick Jagger's "Brown Sugar"—the racialized bodies of Black women.

Mirta wants to place a six-foot-long bundle of sugarcane stalks lying flat on the stage floor on the diagonal down right, balancing the mass of Chauncey's piano down left. She wants Robbie to pick it up at some point and carry it on her back. "Really?" I say, thinking about how charged the image is. "Yes," she says. She has already discussed it with Robbie, she tells me. Robbie likes it. "When?" I ask. "When do you think she should do it?" "Whenever you decide . . ."

Robbie tells us how "sugar" disrupted her life as a professional actor, her diabetes causing her to miss not just single performances but major career opportunities.

She tells us how racism disrupted her public and personal life, her sense of self. "Sugar carries shame," she writes, the shame of diabetes intersects in my mind with the shame of the Fanonian moment: "Look, a Negro!"*

Robbie chronicles hard-fought struggles and hard-won victories over her illness and in her society. She writes about "being at war" with her body. Robbie is "battle scarred" from her war with sugar. But she is not "battle weary." There is more to overcome on both fronts.

Robbie speaks to disparities in health care, medical research, the lack of healthy food in poor neighborhoods. All still going on.

Robbie speaks to war, the current wars in the world. All still going on.

* While attending medical school in France, the Martiniquais psychiatrist and theorist, Franz Fanon, encountered a white child who screamed to his father, "Look, a Negro!" The incident left Fanon feeling enraged and deeply alienated, like "an object among objects." He compared such psychic violence to the experience of African peoples under colonialism. (Franz Fanon, *Black Skin, White Masks,* trans. Richard Philcox. New York: Grove Press, 1952, p. 89.)

"You know, I suppose to a been dead," she tells us. Her illness is as visible on stage as her race is. The neuropathy in her feet and hands: She talks about it. We see it. But she overcomes these physical obstacles with every move of a chair, with every step. Every movement. Every word. She hurls chairs in frustration. She moves through and throughout her diabetic "episodes." She sings and dances wildly, drunkenly, to "Brown Sugar." Performing this one-woman show, holding the stage alone for more than ninety minutes—at her age and still with "sugar"—she's fragile, but she's strong. Robbie is living proof of overcoming.

I need to stage this play in such a way that Robbie can sit at times and drink water throughout the performance. She's already written a remarkable beat near the end of the play where she sits down, chats with us, and checks her blood glucose. If needed, (and most often it is), she gives herself a shot of insulin on stage, balancing the paraphernalia on her lap. It's a many-times-a-day, lifelong, everyday activity for her. But in the hushed theater, it's mesmerizing, infused with the force and sacral symbolism of ritual.

It would be ill advised in most instances to have an actor sit down for twenty minutes this far into a performance. When Robbie does so here, she's acting as if she's in her seat on the Fung Wah bus, a four-hour trip she took many times from Chinatown, Manhattan, to Chinatown, Boston. She's seated alone, but we feel as if we're sitting next to her with time to kill as she seemingly rambles from subject to subject, from why it should be okay to inject insulin in public, "just like nursin' babies," to childhood candy-bar wars with her sister. We're ready for this intimacy, especially after the presentational energy of a reenacted spoken-word performance in the previous beat. We know what's coming, but when she lifts her sweater, swabs the injection site, and finally gives herself the shot, Robbie jolts us into a realization of what Diderot called the "paradox of acting," i.e., how an actor can be oneself and someone else (even if that "someone else" is a performance of self) at the same time. This is *her* body. As in *Sally's Rape*, Robbie was "playing" Sally, but it was *her* naked body on the auction block.

Never direct Robbie's movement. These aren't acting choices. There is no "brain" here—no cognition—it's kinesthetic intelligence, Howard Gardner's Multiple Intelligences, his "bodily-kinesthetic intelligence." She often can't remember the lines *she* wrote because there is no "head" involved. No "memorization" involved. It's all experiential. As an actor, these words are new to her body. The words of the playwright are made strange by the actor, now to be embodied. How she moves is how she moves. Leave it alone. It's wonderful and always "right."

Mirta comes to rehearsal and sees Robbie moving the folding chairs to create different locales. She wants to engineer sticks of white chalk attached to the bottom back legs of each chair; when Robbie moves them, they'll leave what Mirta calls "scars" on the red floor, "a map of memory," she says, the marks increasing in size, shape, and complexity. Robbie writes, "I have slave memory in my body." At one point, she shows us a scar on her wrist. Have Robbie try to erase the chalk marks with a rag. They won't go away.

The suffering is there, but Robbie also celebrates her illness, her art, her culture, her race. They come together around empathy. We empathize with her vulnerability, her physical suffering. Theater is the art of empathy. The only real solution to racism? Perhaps empathy is how we begin?

In rehearsal, we reach the end. The large sheaf of sugarcane is still there. Robbie begins to exit. "Here," I think. *Finally.* See it. Put your bag down. Pick up the bundle. Try to put it on your back. It's a coda. A musical coda. Robbie grapples with the cane. She struggles and it begins to fall. Chauncey gets up from his keyboard and comes over to help her. I say, "Let's leave that in." "Wait," Chauncey says. "I'm a young Black man helping her carry sugarcane on her back?? What does *that* mean? Can we *do* this?" And Robbie says emphatically, "YES."

Chauncey tenderly places the cane on Robbie's back, silently asking if she's okay before he goes back to his piano. Robbie then carries the bundle of cane on her back across the stage. As she bears the burden of diabetes every day of her life. As she bears the burden of racism every day of her life. As she carries her ancestors, carries cane *with* her ancestors, like her ancestors. As she relieves them of their burden by taking it on herself to relieve others' burdens. She is bent but unbowed by the weight of history.

Robbie says she has a poem she thinks would work to say here. At the next rehearsal:

> White racism, as I've said before, is a condition . . . like
> diabetes.
> You may be born with a tendency for it, but you don't have
> to die of it.
> It can be managed.
> The symptoms come from excessive privilege,
> which is a metaphor for sugar.
> So, balance . . .
> balance the intake of privilege,
> and exercise the reality that white is not "all that."

The motifs in *Sugar* twist and turn, overlap, loop back on each other, like jazz. Like jazz, *Sugar* unfolds in a continuous present.

# SUGAR

*Robbie McCauley*

## PRODUCTION HISTORY

The first complete production of *Sugar* was presented in January 2012 at ArtsEmerson, Boston, MA, directed by Maureen Shea, with musical accompaniment by Chauncey Moore; sets and projections designed by Mirta Tocci; lighting designed by Kevin Semagin; costumes designed by Rafeal Jaen; sound design by Darby Smotherman. It was produced by ArtsEmerson at the Jackie Liebergott Black Box Theatre in collaboration with the Performing Arts Department at Paramount Center Emerson College. The production toured to New York Live Arts, New York City, and elsewhere.

## 1. BODY MEMORY

*The stage is a platform fifteen inches high by thirty feet long by ten feet deep, painted glossy blood red. Upright black piano is stage left.*

*Three bound sheaves of raw sugarcane on the floor stage right.*

*Two industrial-sized bags of sugar, one stenciled* WHITE SUGAR, *the other* BROWN SUGAR, *thigh high, are upstage at the side of piano.*

*Three black wooden folding chairs are stage center, randomly placed, the back legs rigged to make lines, "scars" on the floor when they slide.*

*Projections in various scenes, largely images of the interior of the body, veins, cells, etc.*

*Robbie and Chauncey enter during house announcement. Robbie carries her bag, sits in chair downstage center. Chauncey continues crossing to stage left, sits at piano. Lights up on Robbie sitting in chair downstage center, unwrapping a bar of candy.*

*Excruciatingly slowly, having difficulty with the plastic wrapper, Robbie takes a bite of the candy, chews and finally speaks:*

ROBBIE: You know I suppose to a been dead.

Sugar is complicated, like love, full of pleasure and pain.

It's complicated. *(Shows candy to audience)* Gives you energy, and can eat you up from the inside out.

*(Robbie crosses to piano with her bag.)*

The Negro folks that raised me, much as I was cared for and much as I was loved, the ignorance and despair coulda cut me up. *(Plops bag on floor by piano)*

Not love nor diabetes has killed me . . . yet.

*(Puts candy in bag.*

*Crosses upstage. The chairs leave marks on the stage every time she moves them, as if making "scars" on the floor.)*

Sugar is sweet. We want it, crave it . . . the children's treat. We call't all the babies sugar pie.

My mother's daddy was called Tugg, short for Shugg short for Sugar, sweet man. Too much grown folks business for me.

How do I look back, go forward, and be here at the same time?

Mother, a child herself, licked the baby, then put sugar on her face to make her sweeter . . . poor baby had flies all over 'er. *(Laughs)*

*(Ritual memory)* Food is everything, Mother said, that's all we do.

*(Chauncey plays "Come to the Garden.")*

I remember Jesus coming to me as a little girl in the garden. In Georgia. The backyard—with chickens, the fig tree and pecans.

*(Image: brick wall as the side of the house.)*

Down the street sugarcane grew round the side of the red house and peanuts too. Behind the red house, me and Red Shirley sucking sugarcane and laughing like the end of the world! . . .

In our yard we had a pecan tree and plums, a peach tree,
Okra, corn and tomatoes—succotash in our yard!
Honeysuckle and mint. Ma Willie cooked like God.

*(Music stops.*
*Turns to face a stovetop/oven.)*

Big pretty-skinned women with loud laughter lived in our house.

*(The following punctuated by chords, crescendo.)*

We woke up to the smell of thick bacon baking in the oven cast-iron frying pan, flaky biscuits baked with lard, and during the war ate with oleo and homemade muscadine jelly, fresh eggs I went wit Ma Willie to get from the chicken house early in the morning, grits stirred in perfect timing to meet on the plate with flawless fried eggs, with just enough salt and re-e-e-e-al butter.

*(Music stops.)*

Dinner start being cooked soon after.

*(New upbeat music starts.*
*Crosses to chair center, sits, as if it's where Robbie and Sister sat cleaning and snapping.)*

Me and Sister helped clean greens, shell peas, and snap beans; or cut cabbage, peel potatoes for salad, and help pluck feathers off the poor chicken whose neck Ma Willie had cracked.

Sometimes there was rice, and gravy that seemed to be stirred and spiced all afternoon. Only on Sunday or special days did we make rolls.

And cakes—Ma Willie, chocolate, Aunt Jessie coconut, and Aunt Nell a pound cake so good make you want to slap somebody.

Mother used to tell how when their baby cousin Alice Josephine came to live with them . . .

Any day—the best cornbread in the world made in the cast-iron pan.

At night we had supper.

*(Chauncey begins slow "Amazing Grace.")*

. . . Syrup and biscuits with leftover sausage and ham.

On Saturday we had Aunt T's family secret chili hot dogs.

And on special occasions, she barbecued ribs over a tin tub in the backyard with a sauce—she took to heaven with her.

*(Music out.)*

The smells and tastes stay with me.

*(Makes chair downstage into church hall bench.)*

Every once in a while we talked about white folks, who Ma Willie and Aunt Jessie said were just ignorant.

Jesus was white, and gentle, so I pretended the backyard was the garden we sang about in church, knew in my life he'd fix white folks.

Ma Willie's Grandma Sally, who'd been a slave, was one of the founders of First African Baptist Church.

*(Music starts.)*

Grown folks talked about "back in slavery time"—how the white man on the plantation got Grandma Sally pregnant, and how she didn't take no money from him after freedom, but worked cleaning white people's houses to buy her own house and became a fine citizen.

She'd sit those two light-skinned daughters on the porch in organza dresses.

*(Music out.)*

What I liked about church was the show of it, the way people dressed, the hats, and the choir.

*(Music.)*

And the cooking— Lots of cakes, just as good as ours at home. Down home we called ourselves poor people like folks did who'd been in the Depression. I thought we were rich 'cause o' how we ate, and our Sunday clothes. First Baptist was uppity . . .

*(Music out.)*

. . . not sanctified

*(Cues Chauncey to play Sanctified riff and dances downstage.)*

. . . like the church me and Sister would sneak to on Monday nights and slump down in the back and watch the people play music on washboards and dance. *(Harmonica riff)* Somebody even played harmonica. *(Harmonica riff)* It scared Sister. *(Harmonica riff)* I liked it.

*(Music shifts, darker: "Soon It Will Be Done," Mahalia Jackson.)*

Although segregated by white people, we had no interest in doing anything with them. We talked with pride about the colored swimming pool, the library . . .

*(Church changes into a movie theater. Film chase music/ Western. Clicking sound of projector.)*

. . . and the Liberty Movie Show!

We hated going to the white movie where you had to pay in the front and then take your tickets to the back and up the stairs to the colored section where it stank!

Change for us was getting better things for us.

*(Gets out water bottle, takes a sip.)*

White folks water fountains were clean. Aunt Jessie told us to never drink from the Colored one which was usually broke and filthy.

*(Puts cap on bottle, notices thumb.)*

Grandpa Tugg put his thumb in a machine at the mill where he was "Foreman-for-the-Colored" and got five hundred dollars to start the café business they had before the Depression.

When the Depression hit, he upped and died; and Ma Willie put on a uniform and went to work for white folks.

When we were little she did that on the side. Once she took me for company for a little white girl, like babysitting. Sometimes the white people brought their sheets and pillowcases to our house and Ma Willie boiled 'em outside in a pot and pressed 'em with a big, heavy iron.

She sewed for old white women, too. One came, she said, "Because Miss Willie knows how to fit the hump in our backs."

Everybody knew none of us would ever work that hard for white folks again.

We knew Ma Willie to be a teacher. She'd finished Mr. Pierce's School for Colored Girls and became a teacher herself. Outside the family, even white people, called my grandmother Miss Willie.

Like everyone born in the middle of a story, I've got memory in my body. Back then old folks knew so much from way back.

When Miss Fannie told me I had "a l'il bit o' sugar" . . .

*(Chord. Robbie listens/hears it.)*

Sounded serious.

*(Chord. Robbie moves in abstract way—"slave memory"—freezes.)*

Like slavery.

*(Chord. Robbie moves to another position, holds, then stands upright, hiding the pain.)*

I didn't tell nobody.

*(Expansive now, crosses downstage.)*

Miss Fannie lived in the Marshall house, a big brick house her brother had built.

Full of his wife and children, the house, wearingdown by then . . .

*("Pick-Up Sticks" music.)*

. . . was where me and Sister went to play.

I used to sneak in the house in the day, hide under the covers, and go to sleep.

*(Music fades. Robbie stands, awake.)*

Miss Fannie had grace and spoke well. I liked listening to 'er.

She let me in her room, the best one in the house, with starched curtains.

I remember sitting, picking on a scab. She gave me a piece of toilet paper, said: "Your sores take a long time to heal."

"You play hard and quit quick."

"You must have a l'il bit of sugar" . . .

*(Turns to see Miss Fannie. Chord.)*

Wasn't it something that she said that way back then?

Late '40s and '50s down south, everything segregated.

Dr. Thomas H. Brewer used to come to our house. A cultivated, sociable, and handsome, man who "fought for the race."

Once Dr. Brewer came for my stomachache. I didn't tell 'im how many johnnycakes I'd ate. Me and Sister weren't suppose to be listening, 'bout him trying to help Negroes vote. We suppose to a been sleep.

Everybody knew it was the Klan killed him later. No one was punished. I cried.

Other times he'd just visit, sit and talk and have peach cobbler with Ma Willie 'n 'em.

Except for Dr. Brewer we didn't see too many doctors, took care of ourselves. Even when the cute Marshall boy I usta rub up against chased me with a firecracker and I burst through their glass door.

*(Chord. Sharp turn. Wringing injured hand.)*

Miss Fannie said they'd fix the window if Aunt Nell fixed my bloody wrist. They just got rid of the door—people kept coming in and out—and I still have the scar.

*(Rises and angrily throws chairs. Chauncey doubles with crashing music.)*

How do you continue to dance contradictions with crashing doors?

*(Crosses through field of fallen chairs.)*

Down south, up south
  Summer, winter.
  Mother's world, Daddy's world.
  1953.
  DC.
  I played hard got tired quick up there too.

*(Picks up chairs to create diagonal table.)*

In DC there were no COLORED and WHITE signs like in Georgia—you just had to know where not to go.

In DC were lots of sa-ditty Negroes, who put much status in who you knew.

I sneaked after school to the library and read fairy tales. My world.

In DC I knew our family drank a lot, never embarrassingly, except for one uncle.

Way back when I drank, I barely remember what happened. Drunken blackouts in the middle of insulin shocks were the worst. Where's the research on diabetes and drinking? Ever' body knows I went to AA and heard the way to cure alcoholism was to stop drinking. Am I alcoholic? I don't know. I always say I stopped drinking 'cause of the sugar. I really stopped drinking 'cause I couldn't stand to go to meetings. The meetings confused me . . . me being a professional confessional . . . type a performer. As a toddler I took sips of beer . . . *(She takes a sip of water)* . . . everybody thought I was cute.

Anyway, my sister was a good big sister, we both loved words and history. She'd teach me. She took care of me because Mother worked and Daddy was in and out of the army. Like many working people we talked politics at the table.

*(Sitting at head of the imaginary table.)*

In DC Daddy dominated the conversation talking about *Senator Kefauver* and how *Senator McCarthy* was going *too far* even though Daddy didn't like communists himself. He took a lot of time teaching me 'n Sister how to say "Kefauver." It's like "Kef-offa-the-grass." He used his oratory voice telling us to learn to *compromise* like *Truman*.

Me, I liked how communism sounded and asked what was so wrong with it.

Daddy got mad trying to explain.

And Mother said, "Can't we talk about something else at the table?"

In junior high, after chores on Saturday, I'd go by myself to the movie on Benning Road and Minnesota Avenue where the colored could go. *(Sits)* . . . Eat popcorn and Goobers . . . and go to sleep.

*(Chord. Falls asleep. Chord. Adjusts to a more comfortable position.)*

In DC nobody talked about what went on in their houses.

## 2. TIMES A CHANGING

*Music riff. Robbie sits up wide awake and happy.*

ROBBIE: 1959.

Berry Gordy started Motown, *Raisin in the Sun* was on Broadway, and I graduated high school at the edge of the age of denial about race.

White kids were sneaking Black music and Black kids were sneaking Black books.

*(Music shifts to jazz riff.)*

In high school I was in love with a boy in the Contemporary Jazz Society, a club. They wore turquoise and black hats. He had a hi-fi. Once we saw Ahmad Jamal. On every date he brought me a Mr. Goodbar.

*(Music stops and resumes as R&B "Dirty Dog" riff.)*

When I found out he had two babies by a girl in New Jersey I was so sad, I stopped eating candy bars of any kind. Painful luck. *(Music out)*

The three D's of diabetes: depression, denial, and drink.

College was sad until I found the stage. First I found history, sex and civil rights, *(Freedom march riff)* went to parties, meetings and marches.

Hard to finish things.

I was too tired to go on the freedom rides. Scared of the burning bus.

Mother said, "We took y'all out of Georgia, ain't going back to die."

Dumb luck. *(Music out)*

Between men and work I have suffered depression, but worse with high blood sugar.

Has it been defined as clinical with diabetes? Have denial and drink? I wonder.

I learned a lot about history from Karl Marx, the binary images of master/slave, lords 'n serfs, capitalists and workers, the context and contradictions of history. I wonder if he had a l'il bit o' sugar. *(Miss Fannie Sugar Chord)* Him . . . the poor bourgeois intellectual . . . Marx had carbuncles. He called England "the land of carbuncles" because it was, according to him, "essentially a proletarian illness."

Told Sister I was quitting college . . . tired, going to New York to act.

She told me she would kick my narrow ass. I finished.

*(Moves chairs to set up Welfare Department cubicle.)*

*(Factory riff)* On a government job that felt like a factory, the day President Kennedy is killed, I know life has to have more, and quit. *(Music out)*

Daddy said:

"Make sure you get another job."

I do—reading books for the library. I make enough to find out why I'm so damn tired.

Back before in college I drank a lot and got skinny, smoked cigarettes, and—you know. A dental student I spent the night with told me I was too skinny. I weighed eighty-nine pounds.

*(Angry.)*

Every doctor I went to before took one test—because of the irritating itch down there I had to mention—blood test for syphilis. When I found out, each time, that I didn't have it, and wasn't pregnant (the worst shame back then) . . .

*(Crosses to Chauncey, each symptom punctuated by a chord:)*

I forgot to mention the thirst, the other itching, the constant eating, and tiredness.

Putting on a white voice, I get an appointment at a fancy private clinic I'd heard some people at work talking about. At this clinic, I was given pills for juvenile diabetes, which everybody knew most often you needed insulin for. My blood sugar so high, I'm so weak and dizzy, I called my father.

*(Acts out the story:)*

A mean-looking woman trussed up in a stiff white uniform said, "Get out of here." I remember her. "This is a private hospital," she said. I heard my father's rage break through. Mother, who'd come too, kept quiet. Willfully quiet. The whole world felt like it was coming apart, till I heard Daddy say, "My child." *(Beat)* They took me to DC General, the public hospital, the first of many times cold in the ambulance. I overhear a nice doctor saying, "They should have given her a shot, we don't like to give hypodermic needles to Negroes but *these* seem okay." *(Shares a look with Chauncey)*

He hadn't seen Daddy get mad.

*(Puts heavy bag on shoulder)* Tired of everybody, I find my first husband, a beautiful actor.

And my deepest love—the stage.

We move to New York. He gets into design school.

I work where so many college grads coming to the city did. *(Drops bag)* —The Welfare Department.

I audition, between case visits, and find work, acting.

No way for a thousand reasons is this marriage going to work.

*(Music.)*

Oh what a time it was, the sixties in New York, living in the Village! *(Takes out and puts on lipstick)* The Black Arts Movement, hippies, all kinds of change. I was acting and learning, and drinking and smoking . . . Like everybody in New York back then.

I had background though, so stayed on the edge, never fell off. Had good friends and famous acquaintances. And the beautiful men!

I studied and worked at the Negro Ensemble Company.

Looked in the Five Spot window at Thelonious Monk.

Brothers outside of Gem Spa at St. Mark's and Second Avenue selling the *Black Panther Party Newspaper* and *Muhammad Speaks*.

Jimi Hendrix up the block at the Electric Circus.

And Janis Joplin at the Fillmore East with silver shoes on.

Was at La MaMa when the musical *Hair* was in workshop. Went with Garrett Morris for a minute . . . he lived near me around there. What is La MaMa? . . . Look it up, under Ellen Stewart.

Acting at cafés directed by Marshall Mason in a Lanford Wilson play.

Nobody from where I came from knew any of these folks but I didn't care.

*(Music shifts to "tired" chords.*
*Exhausted, puts bag down at piano.)*

Still in private still I called on God.

*(Music out. Beat.)*

Met my best friend, Laurie Carlos, in Lloyd Richards' acting class at the Negro Ensemble Company. Before I knew her, Laurie got them to give me my first understudy job.

*(Chord. Robbie goes still.)*

I had my first insulin shock I remember in New York that day.

*(Chord. Robbie grows dizzy.*
*Chord. Robbie teeters in place.*
*Chord. Robbie steps back.*
*Chord. Robbie steps back.*
*Chord. Robbie turns profile stage right and reaches to find upstage column.*
*Chord. Robbie reaches column and balances herself.*
*Chord. Robbie looks at Chauncey and recovers through final chord.)*

Called in, said I needed more time with the script. Nobody knew.

Worked with the late beloved beautiful Gilbert Moses and Joseph Chaikin and Omar Shapli.

*(Music.)*

And knew people who people know, or ought to know:

*(Walks slowly downstage across stage from stage left to stage right, timing names with steps:)*

Like Antonio Fargas; Robert Hooks; Richard Roundtree; Adolph Cesar; Moses Gunn; Robert Christian; Obba Babatundé; Hattie Winston; Marcella Lowery; the gorgeous, talented Denise

Nicholas; Tony nominee, Beatrice Winde; Cynthia Belgrave; the stupendous Rosalind Cash; and the astounding Gloria Foster.

*(Music out.)*

Debbie Allen, Ntozake Shange, Anna Deavere Smith, and Denzel Washington came later, after we were kind of famous ourselves.

Went with and worked with Bill Duke for a minute. And worked with—only worked with—Samuel L. Jackson. So there.

I quit the Welfare Department and "seized the time" to study how to teach with the fabulous Kristin Linklater, whether anybody I knew knew her or not.

Acting at The Public Theater in New York City on Adrienne Kennedy's wonderful play, *Movie Star*, directed by wonderful Joseph Chaikin.

With Ray Barry, Frank Adu, Charlie Heyward, Gloria Foster.

And more. Very experimental . . . No understudies . . .

One night the theater was packed with all kinds of hip people. Peter Bogdanovich, the film director, was there.

Living uptown then, I ate a yogurt and took a nap.

*(Lies down, bag as pillow. Chord to sleep. Chord to wake up. Robbie wakes up horrified, looking around.)*

The next thing I know, three actors from the play in my apartment with my super . . . then the cold ambulance.

*(Sits up.)*

A canceled show. I feel awful. The artists understand. The play continues, it's a short run. But Peter Bogdanovich did not return.

Acting and teaching. Can you do both well? I wondered.

*(Stands.)*

*for colored girls who have considered suicide/when the rainbow is enuf* by Ntozake Shange. I was offered the main role, the "Lady in Red."

But . . . I'd already promised playwright Ed Bullins . . . and my students at NYU . . .

"Okay," I told myself, "everything would last forever."

*(Tired chord.)*

So tired a lot. Trying to do and finish everything. *colored girls* went to Broadway without me.

And Trazana Beverley who did the role got a Tony Award! I screamed with everyone else, but felt sad too.

Was taking care of the diabetes with different doctors here and there, always taking my shots, peeing on bits of paper, checking colors. This was before checking blood came along.

When Traz left the show I got the role—on Broadway, good enough for me. *(Tired chord)* So tired . . . a lot. *(Tired chord)* More tired than I should've been, but how good I was.

*(Music: sax riff, "My Favorite Things.")*

The cool white sax player with groovy brown eyes came to see me.

The '70s . . .

*(Music.)*

I'm having my own cultural revolution living in the Lower East Side.

The Nuyorican Poets Café was on Avenue A back then. Poetry was everything.

I took my insulin shots—one long-acting and two short-acting a day, but stayed silent, as silent as possible about the diabetes. The plastic syringes were in by then, no more boiling glass needles like I had to do in DC.

Like most Americans I felt if you pay your dues you ought to get benefits.

Ratners on Second Avenue, the Jewish dairy restaurant where I'd sneak by myself late at night.

The older waiters, knowing I was an actress with my whatever script out on the table, would bring lots of free bread with mushroom barley soup to die for, and silently, end of the day fresh strawberry shortcake that was so good it couldna been bad. Take your medicine, you ought to be free I felt.

*(Music out.)*

I was wild with sex, but not dangerous.

Back then friends with benefits were regular.

I did cross some lines I had no business, 'n like everybody said:

What goes around comes around.

*(Crosses to the piano to get a drink of water.)*

Forgetting how even Marx said two steps forward and one back—thesis, antithesis—but did synthesis ever come? 1980. The Reagan Revolution? A rip-off of the civil rights and cultural revolutions all I could say. We were at both sides of the continent now, tipping off the edges while the middle of America was puffing up. Me in the '80s puffing up too. When we got pregnant, crazy diabetes seemed to go away. It was my happiest time. I got younger, and had the best baby girl in the world. She slept through the night. Cool sax player is cool dad too. He led the band.

We tour around as family—do theater, politics and music . . . Preach to the choir about imperialism. I go to Nicaragua with some great New Yorkers—people, people ought to know.

What a time underground, middle ground, and above!

*(Chord.)*

Diabetes more brittle.

*(Chord.)*

More shocks.

*(Steps back.)*

Everything comes from sugar in me . . . People don't talk about pain, how your immunity's affected . . . How diabetes hurts . . . how it hurts your you-know-what as a woman . . . and legs of course, and your head . . . That night in the Ohio hotel . . . On tour . . . That night when I woke up in hell . . .

*(Hotel lights. Robbie's speech below is recorded. Movement improv with music. The first major diabetic shock in the Ohio hotel room.)*

. . . Didn't know who I was or what . . . Know I had to pee, but didn't quite know what pee was . . . Didn't know what I was, now wasn't just me who identified all these levels of consciousness, I just knew the walls what looked like abstractions in space and something that felt like breath and fear (me, I guess) . . . The silver slivers of light I kept trying to touch, walking into hardness and falling back . . . I kicked, felt no pain, felt liquid on my leg . . . try to walk fast to keep . . . to not fall out . . . walking fast to keep walking . . . Later the diabetes counselor said it was adrenaline that kept me walking, hitting walls, falling down and getting back up. I found the little light in the bathroom . . . the adrenaline connected to consciousness . . . I'd left the little light on . . . the orange juice bottle there.

*(Recovering now.)*

I drank . . . and breathed hard . . . scared, felt the shaking, the cold, the mind, the tiredness. Ate crackers and cheese, checked sugar, went to bed . . . woke up so hard, I couldn't walk . . .

Had a show the next night, had to go to the hospital, was scared, felt I'd been through hell, and hitting myself so hard broke open the rheumatoid arthritis I was told later. All from sugar.

Jazz is hard. Rock is easier . . . . . .

*(Recorded bar music: The Rolling Stones' "Brown Sugar."*

*Robbie starts dancing with back to the audience, then turns around.*

*Dances to piano as if a bar, gets bottle of water.*

*Chauncey begins singing with Mick Jagger.*

*Robbie continues dancing, joins in on chorus, beginning with "Gold Coast Slave Ship Bound for Cotton Fields," singing to audience.)*

## 3. SWEET AND SOUR

*Lights change. Robbie plays this with water bottle in hand, as if drunk.*

ROBBIE: Laurie, my best friend, our deep dark brother poet friend and me argued all night at the Orchidia (9th Street and Second Avenue early '70s Lower East Side) about Mick Jagger's song—us saying we'd take public praise of our magic beauty from whomever! . . . But that was way back . . . when me and Laurie would have nothing to do with who owned who as people to love, before Zake had us considering suicide, before our consciousness came of Columbus bumping into Santo Domingo looking for sugar in India and the rape of Black women . . . understood as the rape of land for sweet, sweet.

*(Cues Chauncey, he plays. Robbie sings, drunk.)*

O-ooo Baby baby . . .

*(Music out.)*

Brown sugar, raped away from our lives, which became more than a metaphor which is what the brother, who later became my deep dark brown sugar daddy (whose poems I lost in the Colonnade the night I danced out loud on the table), was talking about.

*(Robbie, sober now, puts cap back on bottle.)*

Up south with Black poets in late night bars. Down south Black people busy, "Couldn't git no satisfaction"—Otis Redding . . .

The three Ds of diabetes . . . depression, denial, drink . . .

Threes again. The triangular slave trade everybody knows about, right?

*(Crosses to piano, grabs top of a bag of industrial sugar, drags it from upstage of piano to center stage.)*

Slaves in the Caribbean grow sugar for Europe and New England to make molasses, rum, and cash . . .

*Sugar*, ArtsEmerson, Boston, MA, 2012. Photo: © Mirta Tocci.

*(Crosses back to piano, takes second bag of sugar, drags it to center stage.)*

. . . back to Africa to buy people to enslave again . . . to take back to the Caribbean . . . to grow more sugar.

*(Robbie stands between the bags of sugar and opens them.)*

Life is bigger than biography. Sugar more than sweet.

*(Robbie dips each hand into bag of sugar, letting the brown and white sugar fall through her fingers.)*

The politics of sugar—the seduction of nations, of women, weddings of chocolate, sugar, sex, with Africa, the Americas . . . and Europe.

*(Wipes hands, steps out. Lights up on audience.)*

I need four people in the audience to participate, four different sections.

*(Robbie improvises with audience.)*

Answer this question with one word without using the word "good" or "bad." I'll repeat that instruction: Answer this question with one word without using the word "good" or "bad."

*(Improvises clarifying instructions, explaining that this is not a riddle, but that participants should speak the word from their guts.)*

Okay, here's the question: What do you think of the American war with Afghanistan?

*(Audience members give her four words, e.g., "indecent," "tragic," "frightening," "brutal.")*

All my life has been war *(Beat)* with sugar. War against my body from the inside-out.

My heart and soul are in the line of attack. Like any war it's *(Using the audience's words) indecent, tragic, frightening, brutal.*

Thank you.

*(Lights change to club atmosphere. Spoken-word performance now.)*

CHAUNCEY: At the Colonnade!

ROBBIE:

At the Colonnade
I was a terrible drunk no romance at all
except for the night in the Colonnade when I
lectured on the table, lost his poems, and took off my top.
After, like all the others, he said he loved me best then,
like all the others insisting I open something never closed.
Wishing I'd give I'd give away my bits of freedom . . .
All the violations I participated in . . . ?
He and I knew we were killing each other.
His poems.
My life.

His mother, the angel, fed me homemade cake, told me to get away while I could. And my blood sugar didn' eem rise.

The men love drama, opera, tears. The first husband banged on my door so hard I called the police on a Black man . . . he laid on me after. I trusted myself. They did not kill him. He went away forever of course. What did he expect . . . with all the unspoken storms in my father's house?

I was only intellectual. A bang in the body, and thrusting like horses,
all I needed and rage released.
Sex is kinder than love I always knew.
And shame more difficult than guilt.

Sugar carries shame.

The second husband, free and white, needed late-night doughnuts from New York delis and my morning sugar'd be thick enough to suck out my teeth.

His extra women, who had no shame, gave me earrings, advice, and other gifts as if we were in some other country.

Doctors who'd never

*(Mimics walking on swinging ropes.)*

walked the swinging ropes
kept pushing me on balance. What were they thinking
as I found my way between mountains over deep waters?
No longer able to be rescued, I took charge, oddly inspired
by one of the extras who said to my face, "Diabetics sure sleep a lot."

## 4. THINKING OUT LOUD

*Chauncey begins playing "Dance of the Flowers" in high key, single notes, simulating a music-box sound. Robbie gets into ballet position and poses like a ballerina.*

ROBBIE: Cousin loved "Dance of the Flowers." It was on her music box and she danced to it with her gorgeous legs, no scars from childhood like me.

I knew my cousin way before she was born . . . born pretty like the women in Mother's family.

She loved to eat—but things weren't like they used to be when food in the family was love.

The garden and the chickens were gone.

Dr. Brewer and all the heroes gone too.

Industries of food and drugs full of addictions grew, a different place and time from me and Sister. We lived in a time of gentler drugs and righteous rage.

Cousin and 'em lived in a time of crack cocaine and anger without cause.

Like regular colored people after World War II, we worked, married, and kept steady.

*(Crosses to sugar bags, drags one sugar bag to downstage of piano.)*

Since Sally'd bought the house after slavery time, Mother 'n 'em'd been a family of women who married working men, or got rid of 'em if they didn't.

*(Crosses to second bag of sugar, drags it to sit next to other one.)*

Aunt Nell and Aunt T changed the big family house for two side by side in the first colored suburb. Aunt T's husband, the cousins' daddy, acted the fool. To tell the truth, after she got rid of him, she lost her fun-loving self and drank herself to death. Her two daughters never hardly got out of town. The younger one, fun-loving like her mother, stayed steady enough to get rid of a triflin' man and raise her children.

*(Gets cloth out of her bag.)*

Cousin, the older one, who liked to dance, got late onset diabetes first.

*(Tries with difficulty to lean over and wipe chalk scars off floor.)*

Food can help soothe hard memories, memories still more resonate in the South.

*(Places cloth on floor and starts to wipe floor with foot on cloth, growing angry as she speaks.)*

After losing her first leg, she got addicted to Krispy Kreme doughnuts.

*(Rage breaking)* K-c-r -r-is-p-y fucking Kreme! The stores—have you seen them?—with sugar and grease pouring into hot boiling containers.

Have you seen them? All the fast food crap they put in poor neighborhoods! How in the hell is someone who has slave memory in her body, who has indigestible sugar in her veins . . . and health disparities in her society?

*(Grows weak from the rage)* Raised all her beautiful children . . . Her sister went soon after. I never knew how tired . . . sick and tired . . . I should have been there.

*(Looks around at scars and realizes she can never erase them, picks up the cloth, holds it like a white flag of surrender overhead, defeated.*

*Light change.)*

## 5. OTHER PLACES AND TIMES

*Robbie falls across the stage. Images of blood cells and the human heart are projected behind her. Loud music. Robbie screams through the music. Desperate, reaching for orange juice in her bag.*

ROBBIE: Falling down in somebody's living room in Prague, I'm desperate for food, desperate for sugar.

Sirens . . . sirens in foreign cities.
Grateful for fish sticks and soup . . .
Sleeping only in dreams, backstage o' wars.
Horses pounding in dreams
Boats and drowning musicians.
My heart pumps . . .

*(Sits up abruptly, eyes frightfully wide open.)*

breathe awake full of horror.
Fearing God no solution. Where is love?

*(Gets orange juice out of bag.)*

Angels call, children fall. Guns everywhere. Forgive me, Jesus.

People rush through alleys; call up at windows, "Keys, Lord, keys to salvation!"

*Sugar*, ArtsEmerson, Boston, MA, 2012. Photo: © Mirta Tocci.

Trucks and couches and books . . . broken pianos move in the night.

Still I hear the trucks, they come in the night. Who's in charge?

*(She drinks.)*

I swallow hard back in America.

The end of the century, shifting like the end of time.

*(She drinks.)*

In a famous working-class city, no longer black with the soot that helped people pay bills, now full of unemployed people, Black and white, down by the river asking me if my father had worked in the ovens. In the war, I said.

*(She drinks.)*

And poets suck beer outside cafés hoping for somebody to listen again.

*(Puts orange juice back in her bag.)*

How I live through the brittle brutality is beyond me.

Now me, I'm not so much for religion. I prefer common decency. But like lots of people in emergencies, I can't help calling Jesus. Even my father who had no truck with churches said, "Ain't no atheists in foxholes."

Marx talked about religion as the opiate of the people, which in context is pretty positive about religion and people. It's wrapped in images of the sigh, the heart, and the soul.

*(Puts on cap.)*

Wonder if he took opium for his body miseries.

At thirty-nine, pregnant, I asked God to let me live long enough for my daughter to get grown.

The day I told Daddy I had diabetes was the day he tore up the mimeographed Marxist flyers I'd brought home. I saw the righteous rage of an American patriot. Picking up the bits of paper, I looked in his face and said, "I went to a clinic today and they told me I had diabetes." He said, "YOU AIN'T GOT NO DIABETES!" And he never mentioned it again.

I shouldn't be here. I'm older than all the wars.

The reason I keep living is my stubbornness.

I get that from my mother.

On the bus one day, 2000-somethin', going to Boston, the Fung Wah bus, fifteen dollars from New York at one P.M., had no business standing, but I had to get to the bathroom, we're just crossing the Manhattan Bridge but I had to use the bathroom. It's a great bus. I had on my fake ghetto cap, still not dressing my age. No matter where I am I act like I'm at home, and the driver—people call it the Chinatown bus because it goes from Chinatown to Chinatown, Boston and New York. (I am just as racist as anyone.) It's quite an enterprise. The driver, like the thrillingly rebellious underground working-class speed demon I have no business still fantasizing about, hit the brakes on the bridge, and I hit the floor on my back.

*(Slams back against the wall, palms against wall. Light change.)*

The first thing I heard was: "Your back!" "My arms," I hollered. A clean-cut white guy with earrings all over his face and two young women who'd been speaking Spanish stood weaving on the bumpy bus and pulled my arms. Bless their hearts, hurt so bad I wanted to die. "You alright?" someone say. "I'm a dancer," I said. "You better dance yourself to court," brother say. Sister wit him say, "I know what you talking 'bout."

Thank God I'd made a sandwich.

*(Resumes standing as before.)*

The cowboy/Chinese bus driver . . . who I wasn't liking no more . . . pulled over . . . hit the brakes way softer off the bridge, said, "You alright?" At least he's speaking English, I thought. "I'm a dancer," I said, still delirious. He drove a little more slowly.

I did Alexander Technique, thinking through my body. By the time my back started to feel longer and wider, my brain *(Takes off cap, puts in bag, takes out smaller insulin bag)* was back and I checked my blood sugar, which was ninety . . . put my thumb on my pulse, figured vitals were okay. Time for me to eat, I shot up.

"You're cool," one of the girls said, "my aunt's a diabetic."

That's when I wept.

*(Light change, pulls out paraphernalia, checks blood sugar with meter, prepares insulin, shoots up during this story. Real time.)*

When my friend Nikos first met me, he thought I was a junkie. I remember us flirtin' with each other. It was back in the '80s and we were on a bus out of New York to march in Washington against the war in Nicaragua. It was my last big march until appearing with a candle in Boston against Iraq. Now he's a good friend, someone I couldna got through a lot of wars without. He told me later I pulled out my needle on the bus, holding it up to the light . . . like this . . . to see the numbers. He didn't tell me till later he thought I was a junkie. I didn't tell him till later I thought he was straight. Doctors tell you you should use the needles no more than twice, because of the germs, but I know a lot of people who live a long time with a lot of germs. I think people should just do it discreetly when they have to, and it should be accepted, like nursing babies.

Do people know about women and diabetes, women's sexual dys-funk-tion? . . . And do they care? You lose feeling down there. Women can lose husbands and lovers and wives because of it. Although sometimes you lose 'em because of those saxophone hands . . . but that's another story.

When I mention it to doctors, they never gave a straight answer, even women doctors. One said, "It happens." "Try women," another said in a whisper—like I could just jump across the river like that!

And how absolutely incorrect is that in so many ways? I didn't say a thing. How silent are we women about sex after a certain age!

## 6. ENDURANCE

ROBBIE: Ever since I can remember, I wanted to eat just salad. I wanted raw green things to clean out my body, which was slimy dark green and red mud inside. Instead I ate hot brown food, even the greens were too wet and full of fat white meat. Chocolate cake, chocolate ice cream, peaches and figs, dark bird legs. Wet bitter red drippings later in New York seemed to be the be-all, but I was looking for greens, dry and clean.

I got old overnight one day, woke up the next morning didn't feel like being light on my feet. The feet lose feeling. It's so hard to not eat the wrong thing, but I'm pretty good. It's better to be perfect. If you stop eating bad food, good food tastes better. Diabetics with bad diets are likely to get heart attacks, kidney disease, blindness, amputations, and itchy skin.

In our community, didn't nobody want to hear nothing 'bout sick children who may die, just let it happen and blame on the Lord's clock. Just work till "one day she came home, sat down, and died." I had it a long time, but my mother fed us good—three squares a day, even though I sneaked peanut butter and jelly sandwiches on Wonder Bread, and slept.

Sister doesn't like avocado. She don't even like eggs!

My sister liked Almond Joy candy bars and I liked Mounds.

I'd unwrap mine and eat it up fast. She'd eat one little piece real slow, then fold the wrapper 'round it, then take it out later and eat in front of me real slow, said I should learn the word, "parsimonious."

I learned to find where she tucked her candy, and gobble it up. *(Laughs)*

I found it—I found IT, everybody! *The New England Journal of Medicine* told it, say the medical profession all those decades treated us different! Well, duh! But I'm glad it's on paper, because when I have to go for care now, people look at me, check my age, sometimes call other folk to look at me. *A six-ni . . . almo . . . sev-ty-year-o-*Black woman with diabetes and heart disease!

Daddy's heart it seems came down to me, with all its trouble. He didn't take care of his, but my pressure's always been good. When I say that to the doctors, they look at me askance, 'cause Black people and high blood goes together in their minds.

It is pretty amazing how they have ways of looking at us. But the ways they've had of not looking at us is what I want to talk about.

*(Music chords. Robbie slowly crosses to sugarcane, puts bag on floor. Music out. Robbie stands sugarcane up, struggles to hold it, tries several ways, and eventually figures out a way that she can carry it. She starts speaking. Music begins: "Come to the Garden" again, as in the beginning of the play. Robbie takes slow steps toward center as she speaks.)*

My body is a city. I have stalked sidewalks with long white lovers, with panic and l'il deaths. Black cops harassed us just as well.

*(Robbie loses control of sugarcane and drops it. She tries again, unsuccessfully, to pick up the sugarcane.*

*Finishes packing up insulin bag, puts it in larger bag, takes out avocado and proceeds throughout speech to cut it and eat it, still chatting with audience.)*

I love avocado. I once lost a boyfriend over avocado 'cause he couldn't stand it. Kept asking me was it a fruit or a vegetable.

*(Finally, Chauncey stops playing, comes out from behind piano, crosses to help Robbie. They look at each other as Robbie visually suggests that the sugarcane go on her back. Chauncey places it tenderly on her back and returns to piano. Robbie starts speech over from the beginning and resumes her steps. Chauncey resumes "Come to the Garden.")*

My body is a city. I have stalked sidewalks with long white lovers, with panic and l'il deaths. Black cops harassed us just as well. The empirical fear of us has become an embodied phenomenon.

*(Robbie turns upstage and carries the sheaves of sugarcane to stand against wall upstage center, talking over her shoulder to audience:)*

White racism as I've said before is a condition . . . like diabetes. You may be born with a tendency for it, but you don't have to die of it. It can be managed. The symptoms come from excessive privilege, which is a metaphor for sugar. So, balance . . .

*Sugar*, ArtsEmerson, Boston, MA, 2012. Photo: © Kirk J. Miller.

*(Places sugar on upstage center platform.)*

. . . balance the intake of privilege . . . and exercise the reality that white is not all that. Do metaphors have to be logical?

My daughter is like someone who came from another time. In 2002, I felt awful one day teaching. Students insisted I leave work, got a cab home . . . awkward nausea and weakness. I climbed to my then fourth-floor apartment, walked in to hear the phone ring. My daughter, then twenty, was calling she said for no reason, but said she didn't like the way I sounded, told me to call 911. Resistant as always to ambulances, I said: "No." Then there they were. She'd called Boston 911 from New York.

The next morning she was at my side—she'd taken the Fung Wah bus—when a doctor came in and told me I'd had a heart attack and needed a stent to keep the valve upright. Later she told me, "That's when I realized I have a sick mother."

I told her later to "leave me alone."

I told her I always have, always gonna, come back. She's a good daughter.

Don't worry, I'm not gon' tell everything.

Daddy, toward the end of his life, didn't like people, and didn't want to go outside the house. Once since Daddy died he appeared to me in a dream. Very dark like me in life, he came white like a skeleton and with the friendliest disposition I'd ever seen. We laughed and danced. I've heard that people change in the afterlife—like a kind of therapy.

Daddy coming back to let me know he was okay.

Mother, I think, went straight up to glory. Goodness knows she'd had enough hell down here.

*(Light change. Robbie picks up bag.)*

My story keeps going. There are so many products now. My doctor is asking me to consider the insulin pump.

I want a cure!

Diabetes makes me tired, but not that tired . . .

And yes I'm older. Everybody breathing gets older.

But, shoot, I AIN'T DEAD! Yet.

*(Cues Chauncey to play. Chauncey plays riff on Otis Redding's "I Can't Get No Satisfaction."*

*Robbie dances off as lights fade to black.)*

END

# INTRODUCTION TO *JAZZ 'N CLASS*

*Charlotte Meehan*

I hold the great honor of ushering Robbie McCauley's first performance of *Jazz 'n Class* into being through the kind of organic process that happens when art and friendship come first. Lucky me to have met Robbie in the utopic setting of "Third Bohemia," a convening of artists organized by Todd London and P. Carl in November 2012 at Emerson College (Boston). Although I don't remember exactly when Robbie and I began talking that weekend, I cannot forget the first moment of being in her presence. That powerful glow of light surrounding her speaks to a life led decidedly on her own terms—an aura of wisdom, knowledge, and intuition fueled by a singular vision of the world. I came to call Robbie a theater shaman, to which she responded, somewhat quizzically with a chuckle, "Oh, okay."

In early 2014, I asked Robbie if she would consider writing and performing a new piece in conjunction with works by Kate Snodgrass and Magdalena Gómez for a trio my company, Sleeping Weazel, would premiere in Boston and that I wanted to call *Badass*.[1] My intent with this show was to highlight these distinctive, powerful women artists' voices by placing them in conversation with each other. To my delight, Robbie agreed and set about writing *Jazz 'n Class*, which she first described as a piece about her relationship with her daughter and their respective relationships to different kinds of music—Robbie's to jazz and Jessie's to classical. In the end, that relationship plays its chord side by side with pieces of African history, the slavery aspect of American history (and its continued racism), a lesson on jazz musicians and poets, and other stories of African American life woven into a fine tapestry of experience handmade and performed by this jazz artist of words, body, soul, mind.

From the first lines of the piece, we are brought into the mother-daughter relationship of two strong women, as subjects, and time moves seamlessly from the preschool daughter Jessie Montgomery, setting straight an inquisitive stranger about the fact of her race, to the ongoing, gentle argument mother Robbie initiates on the importance of jazz to daughter Jessie's insistent taste for classical music. This narrative anchors a piece that addresses, among other things, the aging process *and* coming close to death, in a storytelling style whose sometimes hallucinatory quality pierces each non-sequiturial moment with a strange clarity—as if this is the way stories have always been told, the way they rise up from the ground, like wild flowers, before the development of the novel and without regard for the homogenization of commercial theater. Robbie's work both returns to ritual and moves forward to the deconstruction of narrative without any pretense, adherence to fashion, or desire to confound. Her intent, above all, was to communicate the many things on her mind, to bring us into her truth, and by doing so to share *the truth* of how we perceive and what we have the potential to learn together through opening our senses to her work.

The communal breathing that can exist between performer and audience is fully alive in the world of *Jazz 'n Class*, even on the page, as we breathe with Robbie, through an invitation she makes into sublime presence. How is this possible as she intermittently tells stories from the past? The presence of the past lives again through Robbie's embodiment, not only in physical performance but in her masterful text replete with time slips setting us squarely *inside* each moment with her, as if all time were moving simultaneously, no gaps between. This can happen only when the past lingers, as it does for those remembering, and re-remembering, the roots and the perpetuation of harm done to them. Robbie's memory of "a woman [from childhood] with her head wrapped holding a basket on it and singing, 'Buy any green peas, tomato, okra?'" speaks to a joyful assertion of existence just as, for example, her recalling of Amiri Baraka's "Reparations now," which she adds, "had to be close to the last words [he] spoke," asserts outrage. These memories, essential to both survival and sanity, confirm the truth of racism as the persisting outcome of slavery. This history can only be comfortably forgotten by descendants of the oppressors or, as Robbie matter-of-factly says, ". . . too many white people think they're born with no memory. They like the word 'forget.'" Robbie, who studied history at Howard University, spent a lifetime continuing her study, and this history's deeper truths flowed through her veins like dance and music and air as she lived daily with racism that underscores the realities of what it means to have ancestors who arrived to this country in bondage.

Perhaps most extraordinary is *Jazz 'n Class*'s sweeping presentation of America's original sin wrapped in the vulnerability of life itself—Robbie's life—as she begins and ends with a mother's love while alluding to the disorientation/hyper focus of teetering on the edge of death. In the context of the larger story, her heart attack becomes a metaphor for all the brokenhearted victims of racism and the wounded psyches of those who perpetrate it and/or do nothing to end it. *Jazz 'n Class* marks a culminating example of Robbie's aesthetic maxim: "the personal bigger," which she describes as her idea of setting the individual life inside the macrocosm, and thus zooming in on the intimate through an aerial view that can absorb the larger picture too. Her [real] heart attack, the highest personal drama one can experience (perhaps aside from childbirth!), which brings the music and the beloved daughter into sync, happens in Casablanca, of all places, and ends in the laughter and joy of healing, and lets the jazz free into that air. The longing for Africa, a place perhaps of lost identity, remains. But the music, always provoking the possibility of movement, plants the last image in sight and sound.

1. *Badass*, which premiered at Boston Playwrights' Theatre (March 2015), received unanimous critical acclaim. *Jazz 'n Class* was nominated for Elliot Norton and IRNE Awards in the Best Solo Performance category.

*Jazz 'n Class*, Sleeping Weazel's BADASS Festival, Boston, MA, 2015. Photos: © David S. Marshall.

# JAZZ ’N CLASS

## A Performance Meditation

*Robbie McCauley*

## PRODUCTION HISTORY

*Jazz 'n Class*, created in collaboration with Jessie Montgomery, was commissioned by Sleeping Weazel for its "Badass" Festival (also featuring Magdalena Gómez and Kate Snodgrass), and first presented in March 2015, in Boston, MA.

Musical accompaniment included excerpts from several of Jessie Montgomery's classical pieces and samples of Lower East Side jazz musicians mentioned in the text. A discography follows at the end.

Projected images were selected and designed by Mirta Tocci.

*Lights. "Aqua" by Jessie Montgomery swells, then fades under:*

ROBBIE *(Assuming meditative posture)*: Blood and love runs through it all. She be more annoyed with white people than I be. Once just one step up from toddling, she heard someone ask me if she was part Hispanic. Before I could catch my breath, she answered, "I'm one-hundred-percent Black. My father's white and you better not mess wif him 'cause he family."

Living on the Lower East Side (which nobody who lived there called Alphabet City), she'd heard enough to give such a badass reply.

Soon after she sees a kid her size with a violin, tells her father, who plays tenor sax, to get her one. (He told me he'd take it back if she couldn't play.) They went to the 3rd Street Music School (on 11th Street, which is a whole other story). And off she went into so-called classical music. But jazz—also referred to as classical—was always in her blood.

Me, I don't play anything except my life—and percussions in my heart—but the jazz blood in her is more mine than his. Which is what I came to talk about.

Way back in Africa, before this country was claimed to be white, a group of people came from the East and settled all the way west in Africa. Though different from ours, their journey compares to our journey through ourselves to where we are now. Everybody is more colored than white.

*(Music: "Strum" by Jessie Montgomery swells and fades under:)*

*(Intermittently moving to music)* Do you know Billy Bang, I ask her?

She said, "Yes, you know I knew him, the violinist . . . the jazz violinist who lived in the nabe."

I said, "You know you're not there yet."

"Mom," she said, "Billy Bang was Billy Bang. I'm not jazz."

"But . . ." I started.

Cutting me off, she said, "I know your jazz thing. Everything to you is jazz. Me, I'm classical."

"I know, Daughter Dear, I just—"

"—want me to get in touch with my internal jazz," she sighed. "Gotta go," she said, 'n hung up.

*(Strum fades out. Light change. Robbie standing with yoga mat talking to herself.)*

My butt still works.

*Plastiques*. A process I learned long ago, a way to think inside and move from deep inside body parts. Now I know it as breaking—all jazz.

Finding it hard to walk of late, I thought into my butt. Thinking released my legs, my pelvis, my mind.

*(Lights. Music: "Reflections" by Billy Bang.)*

In the middle of that night, reading the word "malevolence," I see "male violence." I'm driven to write. My arthritic hand hurts but I write anyway.

*(Moving through the writing, she reads:)*

People learn a lot from lore. My hands hurt so bad braiding her hair, her father took over, did it more gentle. She sees the world through different eyes, tells me she's most attracted to Black men. Me too, I tell her. But she has never lived up close to the threatening storm. Her father, a neighbor once said, is "really white." He's a romance addict, I say to myself, bringing flowers full of lies. (I hate flowers. They're suspect.) No longer married we remain attached. Nothing untoward. I think we were related in a past life. I don't try to be rational all the time. (Once I went to therapy, it helped.) My story is crusty old, but something bigger than age lives in it. Jazz is older than time.

*(Music: "Reflections" refrain up and out.)*

*(Placing yoga mat. Music by Craig Harris under)* Sekou Sundiata put down a rug on the floor and with trombonist, Craig Harris 'n 'em, did *The Circle Unbroken Is a Hard Bop*. Sekou once came to me to be taught, called me professor before I had credentials. I learned so much. He told me question stories like the cab driver in Kenya who asked him where was the *land* of Africa America, stories and questions that continue to sustain me, such as: "Who were *we* to sell ourselves to slave traders?" When Sekou's picture flashed on my phone at the hospital in Casablanca, Laurie Carlos—however I heard her—let me know Sekou's spirit was with me. I don't know if I'm coming or going. Laurie tells me to be quiet, say she wasn't ready for me to go any damn where. Spirits no matter how young surround me. I thank goodness. The doctors'd opened me up in a different language. Another artery collapsing, my heart weak. I'm scared, can hardly speak, think I'm dying in Venice—or in some other book—not home. Yes, Daughter Girl Child . . . you call . . . say you have a plane ticket.

One day when you were at about ten months old, I picked you up. You held me tighter, put your cheek to mine, then looked at me and smiled. Every day after I stood over your crib, your playpen, your stroller, and chanted, "You are beautiful, you are smart, you are free."

*(Music: a medley of jazz. Robbie dancing to it.)*

You were born into jazz the underground of it,
jazz didn't nobody know unless they were around—
or aficionados of—it. You came into the world into it.

Billy Bang's wife was having their little girl down the hall from you being born—into it. Henry Threadgill's daughter, no slacker musician now herself, babysat you; you playdated the sons of Jemeel Moondoc and Butch Morris in it. If people don't know them, they oughta. You saw, heard or heard of C. Sharpe and countless others in the *(Imitatively)* "nabe" . . . in and out of The University of the Streets headed by Muhammad Salahuddeen, who I'd pay homage to when he'd be seen at 7th and A, me carrying you. Not to mention the grace of Wilber Morris, bass; Ornette Coleman on almost everything, including violin; Cecil Taylor playin' the keys off the piano; music people well known or not . . . well, mainly guys . . . but that's how it was, still is, 'n that's a complaint . . . though if Edwina Lee Tyler ain' jazz ain' nobody. You crawled around people in your father's band, includin' Richard Fairfax alto sax, Ben Bierman trumpet, Bern Nix and Ayodele Maakheru awesome guitarists, Bob DeMeo on traps . . . Miguel Rodriguez on congas 'n your dad himself . . . on tenor sax—'n the poets . . . . *(To audience)* Look up Nuyorican Poets Café for that, the poets who're as much jazz as anybody.

*(Sits on mat, circling arms to include audience. Music: "Songbird" and "Smoke" by Jessie Montgomery under.)*

So far back goes this circle that entertains and . . . complains . . . this rhythm section. Al-Halq, an ancient form of performance still in Morocco. It is form and content remembered improvised and woven together . . . sometimes banal, other times elite, sacred and profane of a people grounded in tradition while free enough to have open secrets, like us.

*(Music fades.)*

Way back down south I remember a sound that sound like Africa. A woman with her head wrapped holding a basket on it and singing, "Buy any green peas, tomato, okra? . . ."

Way back, wagon shows came to our neighborhood in Georgia where there'd be a woman singing in a fancy dress, a man playing a horn and sometimes a banjo 'n somebody selling medicine which wadn't nothin' but whiskey 'n sometime selling watermelon slices. We wadn't s'pose to go look but we sneaked 'n did. When I asked my mother about Ma Rainey, she looked disapproving at me. "She wadn't our kinda people," Mother said.

I loved being the darkest girl in the family though they always said Cousin Lillie who'd died young was dark—but pretty. I liked looking in the mirror seeing me dark—and pretty. Funny about color, Daughter thought my color was the favored one. Electra-like she saw her father choosing me. (Yeah, I went to therapy once.) The Lower East Side and our places were full of people and families with all kinda colors and . . . HAIR!

Malcolm X said, "Revolution is based on land." That's what makes people mad with each other—how they deal with land, with ownership. We still carry plantation thoughts inside us, thinking light skinned people get more from the massa.

"Please, Mom," she says. "Can we not go all the time back to the plantation?"

It's hard to get out, especially because too many white people think they're born with no memory. They like the word forget. If they forget about slavery long enough they think who we are will disappear. Still genocide. They have to remember so we all can move.

Ma Rainey publicly called ugly—looked a little like me and I know I ain' ugly—was born in my mother's Georgia home city. We were First African Baptist Negroes, church right near Gertrude Pridgett's/Ma Rainey's house—now with historical status. For years it just sat there, falling apart. After the movement they fixed it up.

My family who I loved so much I had to get away from 'em, were wannabe uppity but were working-middle-class Black people—woulda been middle if they weren't working—all the women and men—teachers, clerks, nurses, truck drivers, and armed forces. Mother said she just wanted me to be normal. I woulda been if I coulda. Instead, I was moody, dreamy, acted different, read when I could (Aunt Jessie say you read too much you be crazy)—and I wadn't scared of the blues.

You were a surprise I knew I wanted as soon as I knew you were coming. You were the reason I knew I was here for. Your eyes were open when you were born 'n you looked at me with curiosity, 'n I said through my tears, "You are perfect." Later your father held you sitting across from me. Barely able to talk, he said, "She looks like you." I said, "She's got your hands." They called it a bonding moment.

*("The Poet" by Jessie Montgomery fades in and out. Doing tai chi–like movements:)*

Jazz is like air
It nourishes us whether or not we know all the complicated stuff of it.
We know the sources of it live in our souls.
Whether we feel it or not, we look for it to lean into.
Soul in this country is Black.
We breathe here from a source of Blackness and all its contradictions
Jazz is . . . air.

*(Doing plastiques, pulling thoughts from the air:)*

Poet Sekou Sundiata said collaboration is working with people you like.

Director Joseph Chaikin mentioned inside eyes. I like tuning in to all the senses inside. Chaikin said jazz is everything.

We don't know who was the first real of anybody. From California I talked over electric air with women in Morocco. They talked of freedom change hope tradition and property. We understood each other speaking different languages.

Would not been no jazz without the blues. In Black language there is no bad grammar. Another thing we added to this country. Amiri Baraka's *Blues People* should be basic text for everyone.

Revolution now, I think, is based on air, learning how to move 'n talk through air from the inside out, how to shape breath/

sound 'n how to, you know, let it go. Everybody should read Margaret Walker's *Jubilee.*

*(Trying lotus position, speaking from inner movement:)*

"What's the point?" Daughter asked.

I had you when I was thirty-nine. My mother fed you my breast milk wif a bottle.

She said, "You a better mother than me."

Still drowsy from birthing you I comforted her. "You were younger," I said.

*(Music: "Banner" by Jessie Montgomery way under building.)*

The point, Daughter Dear, is that you called me back after hanging up having to go. You called deep in tears. I thought it something personal, some guy thing, which I have no expertise in, so I was just ready to say "poor thing," but it was deeper. You needed me to teach you Laurie Carlos who said "keep your rage intact." You called me having found your rage, your natural Blackness, whether people want to admit it or not. It nourishes and of course can destroy us if not kept intact, which is the beauty of Laurie's lesson.

Frederick Douglass, you said, was asked in 1855 to speak honoring the 4th of July, and he found it hard to honor something that didn't honor him. You, commissioned to compose a piece about the flag, identified. Lucky to be a hardworking lucky artist, you heard me.

So yes, Daughter Dear, the point is your tears came from knowledge you were born into, born classy as most Black people are, 'n with a sense of class, 'n yes, hard to talk about once we buy in to it to keep our hair looking good. "Reparations now" had to be close to the last words of Amiri Baraka, our Africa America land's deepest jazz aficionado.

You living conscious of contradictions finished your composition about the flag. All I could do was grin, my chest up to my chin—your music, an orchestra, Carnegie Hall. The work was called diverse and inclusive. I thought it more . . . personal, political, smart, beautiful, and free, which is who you are, and how I'd hoped you'd be.

And I'll never forget how when I'm sick overseas you come to Casablanca—leave your work, cross the ocean to comfort me. You are descendant alive and delightful to ancestors. And we laugh close over there . . . mother/daughter/sister/friend close . . . speaking bad French . . . to each other. *(Laughter)*

*("Banner" briefly swells and fades.)*

"My rage, Mom," she said, "is full of energy . . . images . . . feelings."

*("Banner" swells up . . . and out.)*

## CODA

Yes, I said, you helped heal my heart, Baby Girl, in Morocco . . . as far into Africa as I'm ever likely to be.

*(Image: Ma Rainey's House fades into Jessie hugging Bach's statue.)*

END

Top: Robbie with daughter Jessie Montgomery, NYC, c. 1985. Photo courtesy of Marliss Momber. Bottom: Robbie composed this lullaby for Jessie when she was a baby; the Spanish translation was made when Robbie traveled to Nicaragua in 1983 with a delegation of U.S. theater workers. © Robbie McCauley, 1983.

**JAZZ 'N CLASS TRACKS** (Selected and sequenced by Oliver Seagle)*

1. "Aqua," Jessie Montgomery, recorded on Bob Stewart's *Connections—Mind The Gap*, Sunnyside Records, 2014.
2. "Strum," Jessie Montgomery on *Strum: Music for Strings*, Azica Records, 2015.
3. "Reconciliation 2," Billy Bang on *Vietnam: Reflections*, Justin Time, 2005.
4. From a concert given in 1983, no track name listed, Craig Harris, 1983.
5. Recorded during Third Muzyka z Mózgu Festival in Bydgoszcz, Poland, November 25, 2007, Billy Bang and William Parker, 2007.
6. "All the Way Light Touch," Henry Threadgill on Roulette TV, 2009.
7. "One for Monk & Trane," Jemeel Moondoc, *The Zookeeper's House*, Relative Pitch Records, 2014.
8. "Conduction #188," Butch Morris at http://associazioneroveroni.it/images/_documentiRoveroni/AchilleSucci_cv.pdf, 2009.
9. "Gaza Strip," Lee Morgan feat. C. Sharpe on *Indeed!*, Blue Note, 1957.
10. "Wilber Force," Wilber Morris, DIW Records, 1983.
11. "Lonely Woman," at Jazz a Vienne 2008, Ornette Coleman, 2008.
12. From a Master Class at NYU, Cecil Taylor.
13. "Dear Poppy," Edwina Lee Tyler, *Drum Drama!*, Percussion Piquant, Inc, 1988.
14. "Regeneration Report," Sedition Ensemble, *Sedition Ensemble*, Context Music, 1981.
15. "Songbird, Smoke," Jessie Montgomery on Strum: *Music for Strings*, Azica Records, 2015.
16. "The Poet," Jessie Montgomery, recorded on Bob Stewart's *Connections—Mind the Gap*, Sunnyside Records, 2014.
17. "Banner," Jessie Montgomery on *Strum: Music for Strings*, Azica Records, 2015.
18. "Regeneration Report," Sedition Ensemble (For Bow) on *Sedition Ensemble*, Context Music, 1981.

*This is the music used in the original production of *Jazz 'n Class*, sometimes vaguely specified in the script with phrases like "jazz medley." Some came from Robbie's personal archive of recordings; the rest is available as indicated.

# LEGACIES

# DEAR ROBBIE MCCAULEY

*Daniel Alexander Jones*

Watching you and Laurie Carlos perform your long-form improvisation *Persimmon Peel* at The National Black Theatre Festival in 1993 was an instantaneous initiation, one of the key "before and after" encounters of my life. Something like what I've read of acolytes receiving a sudden, immediate imbuing of grace, insight, and direction. You and Laurie were deliciously contradictory in your embodiments, your rhetoric, your tones. You were a generative binary star system—swirling, sparking, and summarily upgrading the collective consciousness of the room. *That's how you two rolled.* The stage was littered with books, doll babies, teacups, lace doilies, record albums, political posters, kitchen gear, and a stepladder—all tangible markers of quotidian practices—which, aggregated, made an altar of world-building. Therein, y'all enacted sacred, everyday rites. I remember in particular your gripping performance of the National Anthem at the end of the piece. As y'all sang, chewed, spat, caressed, and peeled the words of the song, you demonstrated that the work of everyday survival is also, contradictorily, the work of transcendence. *And that's how you two* always *rolled.*

Months later, you directed me in Shay Youngblood's *Talking Bones* at Penumbra Theatre in Minnesota. I often refer to the moment you called me to the lip of the stage. I had been "acting" up a storm, using all of what I believed to be my technique, all my little gestures and poetic vocal stylings, and you pretty much said, *hush*. Then, pointedly asked: "What are you afraid of?" I felt all the feelings in a rush: the fear fluttering in the belly of my character Oz. The fear I held of failing people I respected. The fear I felt about my own future. The fear I felt about the precarity of our collective sanity, sketched so beautifully in Shay Youngblood's play, and the concurrent fear of betraying the ancestors through indecision or weakness. And, and, and . . . I took an involuntary, sudden breath and like a hawk you swooped in: "NOW! NOW! ON THAT BREATH, PLAY THE SCENE!" And I did. And it was alive, and free, and chock-full of all the questions, all the *contradictions*, in the moment. "That. That's where you work, every time." Initiation. Destination. Pathway. All the things. All at once. All the time.

Watching you perform *Sally's Rape* with Jeannie Hutchins was a master class in your edict: "Always seek to house your contradictions, not to resolve them." You played, simultaneously, in the text of the piece, in the charged spaces between and around it, in the dynamic relationship with Jeannie (reflecting a wholly different set of revelations than your duets with Laurie, or trios with Laurie and Jessica), and in the energetic discursive field with your audiences (who rode a riptide current of ingratiation, fascination, outrage, disgust, implication, deep discomfort, and true exposure). It was also a master class in form; its dynamic, pulsing structure drew its materiality from a shifting relationship with its own contradictory content. Bone-china cups and chains. Decorum and resistance. Witness and warrior stance on the auction block. I watched it again and again. No two performances were the same. They couldn't have been and been true. You are always true. And by true I mean clear. And by true I mean that you have gravity. Gravity of a planet. Gravity of a coherent intention. Gravity of a commitment to explore with eyes wide open. Gravity of a person who knows in her bones that "I shall not be moved."

I remember standing by your side at Goddard College in Vermont where we'd invited you to be in residence in the MFAIA program [Master of Fine Arts in Interdisciplinary Arts], shortly before the audience entered. Your delicate earrings. Your scarf. Your impeccable posture. Your eyes clear. Still. Every cell in your body listening. You turned to me and said, matter-of-factly, "I keep getting better. Now, I can enter the space, and I see the text like a waterfall all around me. I can just reach out and use what I need. It's all there." I thought about the rigor of the music they call jazz, which you so often cite: the hard edges of late 'Trane and the interstellar contemplations of Alice and the atom-splitting blade edge of Ayler's soundings; and I thought of the artistic forbears whose work threaded its way through your own—Gloria Foster, Joe Chaikin, Adrienne Kennedy, among them. I noted your inexorable movement away from comportment with performances of doubt and from the saccharine habits of shape and *toward* expression fueled by the inimitable expansion and fluctuation of both material and metaphysical realities. If you do the work, you get better. And by better I mean bolder. And by bolder I mean unconcerned with calling the conditionings of empire anything other than what they are. With eyes wide open, perfect posture, and what I must call grace.

You are the smartest person in the room. Every time. I've wondered about that. How you carry the atomic weight of that state of being. I have written time and again of the palpable intellectual matrix that fills the space when you perform. It relieves us of our need to pretend we don't know what we know. Your mind shimmers with chords of political theory, redolent memory, gossip, interrogation, deep historical and cultural reference, good food, music and dance, and regular old laughter borne of insight. I've observed time and time again the insults to your intelligence, the vitriolic assaults upon it and upon you from suspects usual and unusual (with their isms and fragilities dangling in your face). You are dangerous to them. You are dangerous to them because you expose the fallacy of the foundations of their constructed identities simply by being yourself in action. You are dangerous to them because you are smarter than them. Every time. You have nothing to prove. You are the proof.

There's a pained look I see flash across your face sometimes. Not disappointment, although you have the right to be disappointed. Not rage, although you are entitled to and have successfully voiced yours (and theirs, and ours). But that look is something on the knife's edge between annoyance and frustration. It's a bad idea, the look says. Nothing good comes of a bad idea. We know this already, the look says. We know how it turns out. We've seen this before, again and again, and yet here we are uttering these words again, reinscribing the blueprints of our cages in this way, *why*, exactly? The look asks, wouldn't you rather excel? Wouldn't you rather transform? Wouldn't you rather breathe freely involuntarily? And so, time and again, you have come back to the work. And when you come back you prepare, quietly and deliberately, calling the litany of names, of the infinite number who were smarter than them but have not survived. And then you turn your face toward the burning stage lights and you open your mouth wide and stride into the space and you tell the stories, loud.

"Daniel, You make the continuance we hope for a reality. So much love, Robbie." The sentence inscribed in 1994 on the title page of your play in my now-scuffed and dog-eared copy of Sydné Mahone's volume of plays by Black Women, *Moon Marked & Touched by Sun*, is written in your measured cursive handwriting and has the feeling of a teacher's note: considered, deliberate, instructional. In the eyes of my then twenty-four-year-old self, it read as an assessment of my being. I felt seen and valued and named as a part of a community. Twenty-five years later, I understand it for what it really was—a command, a work order, a certainty. And so, when I consider your influence on my work, I understand it as connected to that work which came before you and through you and to me and through me. I consider the gift of the dozens of your performances I have witnessed, of the ways, as a director, an actor, and a peerless dramaturgical questioner, you have shaped my work. And the hundreds of sprawling conversations that weave among the politics of the day, high theory, history lesson, and always, always, the rich, loamy, challenging questions at the end that you leave me to contemplate. When I consider your work I come to the contradictions, the import of gravity, the work of clarity, the sense of direction, and the necessity of extending the full measure of our beings. Yes. All of that. All the time. But, your greatest influence on my work has been to make clear that it is not my work at all. It is all of ours. Together *we* make its continuance a reality.

# THE MCCAULEY SCHOOL: A WORK-IN-PROGRESS

*Omi Osun Joni L. Jones*

Robbie McCauley encouraged the double entendre of the phrase, "work-in-progress," and she was dedicated to its multiple meanings. The most obvious understanding is of a work that is not finished, is still being shaped. Indeed, this meaning seems to characterize much of Robbie's approach, and identifies one of the greatest gifts she offers those of us able to do what she prized—listening and feeling. But there's also an alternative and somewhat cheeky understanding that Robbie offers as ". . . the phrase I've been using forever to say artists have to work in progress, not backwardness, as well as that I'm studying while I work all the time."[1]

The work-in-progress that she created for decades provides an opportunity for everyone to consider the courage of trying, the impudence of boldly telling one's truths, knowing that this moment is precious but the work need not be final, the work can progress in another iteration, and the work can make a step toward the progress of humanity. These are the precepts of Robbie's well-honed school of thought—a way of being an artist, a human, a co-creator of life's possibilities. Robbie's art is driven by progress.

## LESSON ONE: THE BODY

> Look oppression in the face and dance.[2]
>
> —Robbie McCauley

Robbie defies oppression with daring and the deepest understanding of the power and vulnerability of the body. When she commands us to dance, this could be understood as the discursive and political wrangling that the U.S. has been embroiled in for centuries—a tragically familiar dance full of stubbed toes and skipped beats—but Robbie's work has not been interested in emulating worn models. Instead, she invents the models she feels are needed for justice, and she implores us to do the same. More than a metaphor, Robbie's dance is about bodies in space working it out, eye-to-eye, flinging sweat, offering up visceral challenges and truths.

Dance scholar Jasmine Johnson and I attended Robbie's performance of *Jazz 'n Class* presented by Sleeping Weazel at the Boston Playwrights' Theatre in March of 2015. The evening was a triple bill of legendary feminist performers, strutting their stuff with the audacity it takes to assert an elder female presence in a world that does not value either.

Johnson noted Robbie's sensuous agility as Robbie strode across the floor, flung her leg over a chair, sat spread-legged, scooped the air with a graceful hand, and undulated her spine with a suppleness that was erotic and transgressive.

In writing about Black Women's dancing bodies, Johnson articulates her concept "flesh dance," which "italicizes a tension that Black social dance has always embodied: It both polices Black intimacy and gender while extending a vehicle through which individual and communal pleasure might be instantiated."[3] This so clearly names Robbie's declaration of the body—fully aware of the ways that Black Women's bodies were/are used to affirm patriarchy, and flaunting those misogynoir distortions with a self-naming that teases the audience/witnesses politically into what a Free Black Woman might actually be, *and* sexually into potential playfulness and arousal. This "tension" as Johnson calls it, is exactly where the work in The McCauley School is enacted. It is in the tension that new possibilities emerge.

Robbie's body in motion confronted the limitations associated with age, limitations that her famed performances of *Sugar* explicitly discussed. In *Sugar* Robbie told us of the psychic and physical pains of aging—of how diabetes makes vaginas less willing, of how sexual intimacy must be negotiated in ever imaginative ways.

In the excerpt of *Sally's Rape* included in the documentary *Conjure Women*, I remember the awe and fear, the embarrassment and nascent courage I felt as I saw Robbie's body—naked though obscured by dim lighting—on the auction block. Dark skin screaming, the age in the folds, the round and slack, the un-young. Her body was not a phantasm. She made us look, insisted that we absorb present-day physical truth along with historical narrated truth. The recognition of actual flesh is needed for whatever is next.

## LESSON TWO: DIALOGUE

> The oppression stays on you unless you dialogue about it.[4]
>
> —Robbie McCauley

Robbie's brand of dialogue is a sturdy pillar in her positioning art as a strategy for justice, humility, love, and freedom. This is perhaps most obvious in *Sally's Rape*, in which Robbie and white actor Jeannie Hutchins work out their histories and understandings in a series of conversations born from an improvisational rehearsal process. But the alchemical potential that dialogue holds for Robbie has manifested in a host of artistic forms:

The Sedition Ensemble forged with Ed Montgomery creating jazz-inflected, politically grounded live performances and recordings in the early 1980s.

The legendary Thought Music trio with Laurie Carlos and Jessica Hagedorn that solidified a place for women of color in the development of performance art in the late 1980s with *Teenytown*, *The Food Show*, and *Heat*.

The expansive community collaborations, which included *The Buffalo Project* (the Buffalo riots of 1967), *The Mississippi Project* (voter registration), *Turf* (Boston desegregation in 1993), *The Other Weapon* (Los Angeles stories of the Black Panther Party in 1994), and workshops developed with Czech and Romany artists in Prague in 1995.

Ongoing individual mutually invigorating private/public collaborations such as that with artist/scholar Daniel Alexander Jones (*Talking Bones*, *Phoenix Fabrik*, *Bel Canto*), and photographer/producer Marie Cieri ("Primary Sources," "Participatory Theatre: 'Creating a Source for Staging an Example' in the USA").

Engagements with audience/witnesses that Robbie includes in performances so that "the audience is involved if by no more than eating with me or . . . by giving them moments to talk . . . it allows me to create an event for the audience to come into . . ."[5]

Each of these aesthetic innovations becomes a model for imagining what an artistically generated democracy might be—not solely what its rhetoric is but also how its *praxis* lives—improvisational of necessity, provisional since always born of specific contexts, and cross-cultural to prompt fertile exploration.

In her work to redress the omission of Black Women from the history of improvisational performance, ethnographic scholar/artist Lisa Biggs notes the survival implications of improvisation for Black people generally, and the role of improvisation as "sacred play to affirm Black Women's rights to respect and to a future."[6] Robbie's improvisational dialogue is an exemplar of this freedom-inducing sacred play. Robbie and Jeannie Hutchins verbally and literally dancing in *Sally's Rape* reveals the sacred because it is an act of inner expansion, and is an act of play where spontaneous negotiations occur. The important sense of sacred play is also clear in Robbie's solo work as she talks to the audience/witnesses while checking her blood glucose levels in *Sugar*, and spontaneously creates dance movements during *Jazz 'n Class*. Experiencing Robbie's work live was to see the truth in Biggs's assertion that "Undergirding Black feminist improvisation is an explicit determination to use performance to undo inequality and produce a more inclusive society. This is the fundamental work of the Black feminist improviser."[7]

## LESSON THREE: PEDAGOGY

> Go toward the thing you are most resistant to.[8]
>
> —Robbie McCauley

As one of a handful of Black Women full professors of theater in the U.S., Robbie mapped a distinctive pedagogical path from years of learned experimentation. Robbie's impulse was to expose, to wilt facades, to make a road for truth to enter the room. There was an urgency in her teaching that betrayed the stresses of our time. In a discussion about teaching with the University of Texas Black Studies communities, Robbie noted the etymology of the word *confusion* which derives from the Latin *confundere*—to mingle together. For her, this confusion was the basis for a productive working-together in which "clarity is not always the outcome I am looking for."[9]

I participated in many workshops with her at the helm, leveling piercing questions as if they were arrows seeking the psychic mark that would make the participants more present, more honest, more available to the now. Because it is the attention to now that is needed. Robbie's pedagogy seems to rest on the premise that making personal change inevitably ripples into larger vibrations of justice and love. Her questions are arresting for their precision and their momentarily diversionary simplicity:

> "Who do you think you are?"
> "What are you *not* saying?"
> "Who is in the room?"
> "What is the world around you now?"[10]

Such a tactic is not likely to engender the kind of fandom found in workshops where some participants hide themselves through acts of praising the facilitator. But Robbie is clear that "trusting me is not the point."[11] And then she offers a revelation for a lifetime of reflection: ". . . the process of learning is trustworthy."[12] This, along with her maxims—"learning how to learn is core" and "life is bigger than biography"—can leave one pondering how these enigmatic statements might open one to a more authentic and richly satisfying life.

About her teaching, Robbie would declare, "I teach from the air!"[13] I've witnessed her improvising her way through a workshop, responding deftly to the shifts of energy, alliances, and masking that take place moment-to-moment. She walked in with a plan supported by years of knowing, listening, and feeling—in this way, the "air" Robbie drew on was saturated with insights.

During the spring of 2017, I taught an undergraduate course that centered on the work of Pulitzer Prize–winning author Gwendolyn Brooks. The students were of varied racial, gendered, classed, and national identifications—and all were encouraged to explore Brooks's characters across these identity markers. Some of the students, of various racial backgrounds, objected to white students performing Black characters. They saw this as another white power move that silenced Black people—or, equally damning, that had white people speaking for Black people even when Black people were present and could speak for themselves. I told the students that one of the objectives of the course was to explore the politics and performance of race by offering up multiple racialized and gendered possibilities for the scenes they created. The cross-identity casting could be a way to investigate aspects of identity that are unspoken when bodies are cast in socially predictable ways. The students weren't having it. I turned to Robbie for guidance. I had seen her 2005 production of *A Streetcar Named Desire* at Roxbury Community College in which she cast a Black actor as Stanley with white actors playing Blanche and Stella. Here, she "switched roles around, not for blind casting but for conscious casting."[14] The production raised powerful questions about the limits of audience expectations, the political utility of charged performance choices, and the ethics of "distorting" Tennessee Williams's "intention" for the play. Surely Robbie could help me imagine a way forward with my students.

Robbie offered this email meditation as her response:

> Whenever I have experimented with cross-cultural casting, I charge the actors to talk to each other about the choice to do so. Try this as an awareness exercise: Have the white actor play a charged moment of the work (with others in the piece). Have her re-create the moment adding an awareness of herself as a white person in playing the scene. Have

> her concentrate on WHAT she is saying, not on HOW she is saying it.
>
> You may share that I learned—while innovating my Playing the Other course at Emerson—that my grad students concluded that key to playing "the other" is finding more of "the self." The best Black actors who are cast in so-called white roles do this. Denzel Washington's Richard III was an excellent example.
>
> Have her, the other actors, and the audience comment on what they saw/learned in that exercise.
>
> Thank everyone for exploring this aspect that is so important at this time in history wherein identity is a core concern for people everywhere.
>
> —*Robbie*[15]

This is sage advice, and I looked forward to trying it with my current classes. Unfortunately, this email exchange occurred so late in the semester that I was not able to apply Robbie's exercise, but I was able to share the message with those students, and our understandings had more layers because of Robbie's contributions. What's important here is the knowledge accumulated from years of measured experimentation that yielded carefully mapped processes for having everyone collectively dig deeper into who they are, and who they believe others to be.

## LESSON FOUR: BLACK

> Is we free? Massa, is we free?[16]
>
> —ROBBIE MCCAULEY

In an extended interview with scholar Vivian Patraka, Robbie spoke of many things that wrapped around the nature of freedom. She told Patraka: "I want to find a way to move the audience to have to say, 'Is we free? Massa, is we free?'" This minstrel-esque phrase appears in *Sally's Rape*, spoken by the white actor, Jeannie Hutchins, as she plays the Black character Uncle Buck. No predictable choices here, but choices that prompt generative controversy suggesting that freedom comes from effort, from contestation. Robbie's commitment to freedom is rooted in Blackness. She tells us that when she makes performances, Black people are "always the audience I imagine, no matter who is in the room."[17] The McCauley School is working for freedom—absolutely the freedom of everyone—with the firm understanding that if Black people are not free, no one can be.

The Blackness that Robbie honors is not a romanticized mangling of who Black people are. Instead, she proffers the same exacting standards for Black people as she does white supremacists, and indeed, for all of humankind. In this way, she rails against the violent patriarchal home practices that some Black people have wielded against family members. As a Howard University undergrad, she spent a semester as an exchange student at Whittier College in Whittier, California. Although she was beset with a host of indignities at Whittier, she writes that she "felt freer than ever there without a discernible menace of violence."[18] This violence was embedded in the social norms of the Columbus, Georgia, of her youth, and materialized in her father's "storms" that left her feeling "little terrors were always with me."[19] For Robbie, Black people—no matter what horrors we have endured—are not absolved from decency. The absence of the macro-aggressions at home made the micro-aggressions at Whittier a space of freedom. Freedom is relative. Is feeling free the same as being free?

The experience of freedom requires an acknowledgment of the "unfree"[20]—and Black people have been encased in the unfree position for centuries. Blackness, in its social abjection, is the very evidence of the existence of freedom. The pervasive anti-Black violence (much of it State-sanctioned) are spectacular displays of what unfree is. Black oppression allows for the illusion of others' freedoms. Actor Beah Richards in *A Black Woman Speaks* incisively reveals how any unfree condition necessitates the unfreeness of those who believe they are free. Richards speaks of the "pink slavery" that allows some white women to ignore the myriad oppressions endured by Black Women. She tells us that white women and Black Women are enslaved—"the difference is degree."[21]

In considering the role Black people occupy in the U.S.'s understanding of freedom, Angela Y. Davis puts it simply: "Slavery continues to haunt us."[22] The McCauley School presents physical connection, dialogue, critical pedagogy, and Black freedom as tools for—at least—tempering the haunting.

Robbie checks her glucose in *Sugar*, ArtsEmerson, Boston, MA, 2012. Photo: © Paul Marotta.

## LESSON FIVE: JAZZ

> I make pieces to articulate and transmit stuff from the energy of the scream.[23]
>
> —Robbie McCauley

It may be already understood by readers of and students in The McCauley School, but to make it plain: This practice is submerged in jazz. Jazz is the ever-present air that is so *here* it might be invisible to those unfamiliar with its markings. In conversation with graduate students at the University of Texas, Robbie declared that jazz is "an entity, a source, a metaphor for Black culture . . . a theme with variations in terms of [Black] identities . . . the source means it was there from the beginning . . . the heartbeat was in the body—drums . . . the heartbeat is the heart of jazz."[24] Jazz is the breath that animates each lesson. Jazz is *the* lesson.

## THE CODA

There is much to learn from The McCauley School—an institution unfettered by brick-and-mortar requirements, crushing tuition, or perpetual committee meetings—an institution that exists as a series of experiments and practices, an institution that must be built again and again in body-to-body processes. It offers us ways forward, ways to progress—not singular prescriptions but varied methods that suit the moments at hand. Robbie lays open a vista that is daunting and tantalizing when she tells us: "The future is over. The prescribed future is over. There is an empty space for us to continue."[25] This is now our work. To take up these lessons and many others offered by a Beacon—steady and guiding; an Elder—brimming with authority and sagacity: an *Àjé*—in Yoruba, a revered mature woman who is the very embodiment of wisdom, power, and cunning. As if speaking to us today, Robbie wrote in 1993: "All over the country!—people are exhausted, people don't remember or talk about history or make connections between then and now. In Mississippi people asked, Why bring it up again? But our kind of theater makes everyone part of that specific history and cuts against the anti-historical nature of American society. Artists have to do this. It looks like no one else will."[26]

1. Robbie McCauley, quoted in *Experiments in a Jazz Aesthetic: Art, Activism, Academia, and the Austin Project*, eds. Omi Osun Joni L. Jones, Lisa L. Moore, and Sharon Bridgforth (Austin, TX: University of Texas Press, 2010), 254.

2. Robbie McCauley, "Obsessing in Public: An Interview with Vivian Patraka," *A Sourcebook of Feminist Theatre and Performance*, ed. Carol Martin (London and New York: Routledge, 1996), 206.

3. Jasmine Johnson, "Flesh Dance: Black Women from Behind," *Futures of Dance Studies*, eds. Susan Manning, Janice Ross, and Rebecca Schneider (Madison, WI: University of Wisconsin Press, 2019).

4. McCauley, "Obsessing in Public," 207.

5. McCauley, "Obsessing in Public," 207.

6. Linda Biggs, "Art Saves Lives," *Black Acting Methods*, eds. Sharrell D. Luckett and Tia M. Shaffer (London and New York: Routledge, 2016), 73.

7. Biggs, "Art Saves Lives," 84.

8. Robbie McCauley, conversation in Dr. Lisa Thompson's graduate seminar Performing Blackness, University of Texas at Austin, October 12, 2016.

9. Robbie McCauley, "Jam Session with Robbie McCauley!," University of Texas at Austin, October 11, 2016.

10. McCauley, "Jam Session with Robbie McCauley!"

11. Robbie McCauley, *Agnostic Confessions: Possible Title and more text in need of shaping and editing—passages that are starting to "drop in"—a concept I'll develop as "the book" continues to explore narrative, memoir, and pedagogy*, unpublished, 11.

12. McCauley, *Agnostic Confessions*, 24.

13. Robbie McCauley, "Some Thoughts on Teaching," *Essays in Progress*, unpublished, 2016.

14. Robbie McCauley, quoted in "Interview with Robbie McCauley" by E. Patrick Johnson in *solo/black/woman: scripts, interviews, and essays*, eds. E. Patrick Johnson and Ramón H. Rivera-Servera (Evanston, IL: Northwestern University Press, 2014), 23.

15. Robbie McCauley, email to Omi Jones, December 6, 2017.

16. McCauley, "Obsessing in Public," 208.

17. McCauley, *Experiments in a Jazz Aesthetic*, 254.

18. Robbie McCauley, email to Omi Jones, "Feeling Free," December 1, 2017.

19. McCauley, "Feeling Free," December 1, 2017.

20. McCauley, "Jam Session with Robbie McCauley!"

21. Beah Richards, *A Black Woman Speaks*, in *9 Plays by Black Women*, ed. Margaret B. Wilkerson (New York: Penguin Books, 1986), 36.

22. Angela Y. Davis, *The Meaning of Freedom* (San Francisco: City Lights Books, 2012), 145.

23. McCauley, *Experiments in a Jazz Aesthetic*, 253.

24. McCauley, conversation with Dr. Lisa Thompson's graduate seminar Performing Blackness, University of Texas at Austin, October 12, 2016.

25. McCauley, conversation with Dr. Lisa Thompson's graduate seminar Performing Blackness, University of Texas at Austin, October 12, 2016.

26. Robbie McCauley, "Mississippi Freedom: South and North," *Theater* 24, no. 2 (Summer 1993): 88–98.

# I CAN'T WIN IN *YOUR* LANGUAGE: ROBBIE MCCAULEY'S PRACTICUM FOR SELF-DISCOVERY

*Carl Hancock Rux*

> What are the words you do not yet have? . . . What are the tyrannies you swallow day by day and attempt to make your own, until you will sicken and die of them, still in silence? . . . We have been socialized to respect fear more than our own need for language.[1]
>
> —Audre Lorde

In writing about her own experience as a writer, theater practitioner, actor, and academic, Robbie McCauley brilliantly asserted: "I learned that to teach is to learn and to teach is to teach how to learn and that acting itself is like teaching, that the voice is breath inside and outside and that articulation . . . is 'clear thinking.'"[2] The truth of that statement was born out in my first encounter with Robbie, which offered the beginning of a certain kind of articulation crucial to the beginning of self. Though I cannot recall the exact moment that I met her, the first thing that I said to her, or she to me, I do recall seeing her work at a clarifying moment, when I had stopped identifying my maleness with a certain phallocentric ideology based on my perceived gender and/or race.

It was 1991, at The Kitchen performance space in New York City. Seated in the round amid many other spectators, I watched Robbie enter the theater, a teacup positioned in the palm of her hand, posing a series of questions (or rather, decrying with her co-performer, Jeannie Hutchins, what the questions should *not be*), and later, at the most climactic moment of that performance, publicly disrobing, standing naked on an auction block, and encouraging the audience to bid on her body while she described the sale and repeated sexual abuse of her great-great-grandmother who had been a slave. As Ann E. Nymann writes, *Sally's Rape* was "a social experiment, in which Robbie McCauley . . . performed the Black female subject out of victimization," drawing from a tradition of Black performance "both politically and mimetically sophisticated . . . expanding it to express the often obscured experience of gender."[3]

I sat in the theater that night, self-identified as an African American cisgender male born in Harlem with a complex (though all too common) history of oppression. I'd spent my early childhood years in the New York City foster care system. Eventually adopted by a couple more than half a century older than I, I was able to attend university, become a multidisciplinary artist, and work as an academic at several esteemed institutions of higher learning. Somewhere along the way, I was forced to reckon not only with the matrix that was my own personal history, but also with the complexity of my own American history. Perhaps the singer and civil rights activist Odetta said it best when she wrote, "You're walking down life's road, society's foot is on your throat, every which way you turn you can't get from under that foot. And you reach a fork in the road and you can either lie down and die or insist upon your life."[4] This journey is a familiar process of self-discovery, akin to Robbie's idea of locating one's personal story within what she calls the "bigger story." It is a bodily process as much as an intellectual and spiritual one. And it is a quest for a tongue, a language, a means of articulation that leads to the discovery of one's most cognizant self.

Seeing *Sally's Rape*—like my years as a student at Columbia College, the University of Ghana at Legon, the American University of Paris, and my early participation in the downtown experimental theater scene—was a crystallizing moment of self-discovery. In fundamental ways, that experience challenged my sense of history and of my perceived self within it. It showed me, perhaps for the first time, a subjective and scholarly complement to my instinct for self-preservation. It challenged me to perceive the roles of power, sex, and violence in the psychological construction of my identity. It was, in fact, an interactive process that demanded I participate in a deconstruction of race and sexuality and that required me to think anew about the language of social relations, and thus in more nuanced ways, to reflect about myself.

There had been moments in my life when I was emotionally excited by music, a film, a play, or even a euphoric explosion in the African American church. But until that moment when I was witnessing Robbie's performance in *Sally's Rape*, I had not experienced (to the same degree) the radical stimulus and paradoxical enlightenment that sound, breath, gesture, and placement, could bring forth. Robbie demonstrated nothing less than theater as an integrative and applied practicum, a means of identifying intersections of personal experience with contemporary and recurring problems in society. Without (explicitly) subscribing to a feminist theory, she revealed how a contemporary woman-centered theater could clarify the links among gender, human behavior, political institutions, and oppression, along with reflecting on how these factors operate in one's own life. This was my first encounter with a radical intersection of methodology and theory rooted in real experience and artistic practice. It inspired and challenged me.

What had become clear to me, all those years ago at the Kitchen, was that there was a deeper introspection of self and the world than perhaps the artistic realm would always be prepared to engage in, but if it was going to occur, it would have to occur as Robbie had enacted her introspection of race and self: without fear, without embarrassment, with an agenda to shatter the silences. What I had discovered was not so much a feminist ideology or feminist theory in Robbie's work (and that of other writers who, like her, dared traverse the realm of nightmare and epiphany), but rather the tools for an ongoing discussion of her/history and of Eurocentric American ideologies. How could one implement the lessons of this work, whether aesthetically or in relation to life's practical problems, or both?

I brought those questions with me, some years later, when I taught an undergraduate playwriting seminar called Radical Women Playwrights at a liberal arts college in New York City. Emphasizing dramatists—from the Middle Ages to the contemporary moment—whose works engage issues of race, sex, gender, and politics, of course I included Robbie on the syllabus. Part of what her work brought to our wider discussion of new dramatic genres and forms, questions about aesthetics, and the politics of representation, among other issues, was the way theater can propose a practicum for self-discovery.

The tools of this work involve language, which is always ideological: Language is the implementation of thought into action (praxis) and all language *choices* tell a story. To ever truly understand how language as an ideological tool helped tell the story of African American experience and, more importantly, of the Black female body, you'd have to read everything from Claude Lévi-Strauss's "Structural Analysis in Linguistics and Anthropology" to Mina Loy's "Feminist Manifesto." Or you could take in a remark Robbie once made—one of her offhand comments that seem casual, but carry great profundity: "You have to make your own language if you aren't seen or heard."

For the spoken language of the stage, playwrights must tune their ears to how people actually speak and delve into the language of dreams. Robbie's language belongs to a tradition of the poetry of dreams and the poetry of didacticism, explored by other African American women writers, among them, Adrienne Kennedy, Audre Lorde, Sonia Sanchez, Laurie Carlos, bell hooks, Gayl Jones, Toni Morrison, Bernice Johnson Reagon, and Ntozake Shange. The work of these writers delves into the diversity of identity politics, testimony, histories, marginalized historical and contemporary struggles, social justice, human rights, and gender-power inequalities. What they prove is that understanding Black female experiences from various cultural perspectives can, in fact, affect one's understanding of self in relation to the other. Recognizing and analyzing the ways social institutions and power structures within a patriarchal society impact the material realities of women's and men's lives differently, is key to theoretically informed civic engagement around gender, race, sexuality, and social justice. The result is more than a self-indulgent promotion of one's own personal awareness, but rather, a challenge to the other to participate in shattering—and re-scripting—an existent narrative that has historically marginalized Black female identity and, all too often, ignored it altogether. As the theater practitioner, Barbara Ann Teer, once stated, "Each of us is our own author, director, producer, and star. In each moment, we have the power, the unalienable right to alter our actions and reinterpret the circumstances of our lives. In each moment, we have the freedom to speak, write, and invent our own scripts."[5]

While Teer offers an upbeat version of self-transformation, Robbie's work poses an even more demanding challenge to those of us who wish to launch a counterattack against sexist/racist/homophobic writing, thinking, and practices and to rebuke the long-lasting and ongoing insults to our souls: Each of us, like Robbie, must stand on the auction block and retrieve our marginalized ancestral memory and protest an existing discourse that continues to enslave us. It is the only way to perform ourselves out of victimization. If we are to win, the language must be our own because as Robbie so astutely insisted in *Sally's Rape*, "I can't win in *your* language."

1. Audre Lorde, *The Cancer Journals* (San Francisco: Aunt Lute Books, 1997).

2. Robbie McCauley, "Swirling and Connecting Since the '60s," FEED (online magazine)/Soho Rep. October 20, 2016.

3. Ann E. Nymann, "Sally's Rape: Robbie McCauley's Survival Art," *African American Review* 33, no. 4 (Winter 1999): 572.

4. Tim Weiner, "Odetta, Voice of the Civil Rights Movement, Dies at 77," *New York Times*, December 3, 2008.

5. Barbara Ann Teer, "Reinvention of a People," *New York Amsterdam News*, August 13, 1997.

## UPRISING

*Pamela Sneed*

Sixteen years old
from the suburbs, Boston
I'd go into the city shopping
with my cousin and friends
we'd venture into Boston Commons, the Park.
There were hustlers there, I didn't know then
with a set-up table.
They played some sort of game with shells
hid money under a shell or a plastic cup
moved their hands real quick
made it purposefully look so easy
naive sixteen years old, I bet
fifty dollars, a lot of money for me then.
They made it look so easy.
You just had to pick the right one.
Of course, it was rigged
I lost
felt dizzy,
sick to my stomach
lost my gaze.

On Tuesday night after the election I felt the same way
heisted in a shell game.
Walking outside on Wednesday, in my neighborhood
a white woman who barely ever speaks was crying
asked, "What do we do?"
I answered earnestly, a teacher, an artist, professor
who always tries, "I don't know."
Later, I walked up the street, a white man in an SUV
with the window down drove by.
He wore an expensive business suit
had a big brown cigar
like when babies are born
expensive like in gangsta films
like *Goodfellas*
or on
*The Sopranos* after a kill.
He looked happy, smug,
that's when I realized the Trump Presidency is a hustler's game
Ballers club
Players only
Pimp paradise
Wives with teased hair and lots of plastic surgery
on the white BET.
They made it all look so easy
like a choice
Who knew
The American Dream was a side hustle for big businessmen
with all their ugly red white blue striped flag merchandising
available at Walmart and Target, I'll never buy into again
Who knew
Freedom was a marketing idea/consumer product
Hallucinatory drug cooked up in some Rove-ian as in Karl type of
laboratory sweatshop
Maintained by the architects of apartheid
Freedom like air if you're white and male and rich enough
to keep breathing
Today, I started to cry as I wrote
to my students
knowing that in everything so far, I've tried to protect them

and realizing there are places in this world
even my maternal hands can't reach.
In Poland, the Warsaw ghetto against a Nazi fascist regime
On Southern Plantations, in fields, in Haiti
On shores of Africa
Uprising
The '60s
The streets
James
Nina
Bayard
Miriam
June
Nikki
Lorraine
Audre
Pat
Malcom
Martin
Betty
Sekou
The Unnamed
Artists
Poets
Teachers
Always
Uprising.

# EPILOGUE

Robbie McCauley. Denniston Hill, NY, 2019. Photo: © Claudia Mandlik.

# THE STORIES LIVE

## A conversation between Robbie McCauley and the Editors

*New York City: June 24, 2019; July 18, 2019; July 9, 2020*

**EDITORS:** This volume is reflective. It looks back over the body of your work over some fifty years. And some of your recent work, like *Sugar*, has also been reflective. For this last section, we thought we'd ask you to look forward, to talk about what's animating you now, what work you're thinking about for the future. You recently won the Distinguished Performance Artist award from Denniston Hill in upstate New York and will have a residency there soon. You are bringing two younger people with you—your interns, Tina Ruan and Eric Rasmussen—and working with them on a new project. Tell us about it.

**ROBBIE:** We are looking at texts by myself and the two of them and finding out what we can learn from each other through our stories—through our conversations about our uniqueness and sameness, asking how our thoughts and stories affect each other. I'm most interested in something I'm calling orthodox agnosticism. And I call it that because it's exactly what I feel in terms of who I am.

**EDITORS:** Agnostic in a theological sense or just like uncertain about everything?

**ROBBIE:** No. I'm pretty certain about some things! In the theological sense. It's kind of Pascalian. I guess. Now that I'm older I want to be safe. *(Laughs)* I guess this is what happens at this point in life: I'm just fascinated with human beings and how close we are to being perfect. And how we miss it all the time.

**EDITORS:** "How close we are to being perfect"???

**ROBBIE:** I mean, look at these things. *(Gesturing toward the small digital device recording our conversation)* The things that people can make from nothing, from *nothing*. And we should be able to figure it all out. But we get in the way. I'm puzzled by how human beings get in their own way of having good will and peace among themselves.

**EDITORS:** How is the Denniston Hill project raising such questions for you?

**ROBBIE:** The theme of the Denniston summer is "exodus," so I'm bringing some writing that I'm doing now about where I am in terms of where I've been and where I'm going. I find myself examining spiritual questions and I find that exciting. I find myself examining my basic religious Christian upbringing because I have never really examined it in this way before. Of course, I grew up in a traditional Christian home and then I broke away from it. I'm not looking at this lightly, but I like the almost joke of it—orthodox agnostic—because that's more the spiritual realm that I live in. Agnosticism is kind of dismissed often. I'm examining myself in relationship to that because I've never quite given up the mythology of Christianity. And it is a mythology. However, in mythology there's truth.

**EDITORS:** Could you give an example of a spiritual question that's come up for you that you're thinking about or writing about?

**ROBBIE:** I think of prayer and I find myself praying. A friend of mine once told me that all thought is prayer, and that made a lot of sense to me. So I find ways of reaching out beyond myself to something I don't know. I don't have a face for it. I don't have a human image of a god, but when I do that, I trust that there's something beyond me that is a guide. And I make that a reality for me and it's very palpable.

And also, it's because I'm in that generation where I'm losing friends and, in a way, I can't let them go. I hear people's voices. Of course, I'm imagining it, but I find that very palpable. Their voices come out of nowhere. Laurie [Carlos] is always checking in. And older ancestors. That's also part of the African American way of keeping connection with forebears. When we talk about ancestors we are talking about a real phenomenon in our lives.

**EDITORS:** And this comes up through prayer?

**ROBBIE:** Yeah. Through just taking time alone.

One of the questions that I'm interested in for everyone is: What is there beyond reality for you?

**EDITORS:** "Beyond reality"?

**ROBBIE:** Reality imbued with imagination, creativity, and spiritual contemplation. I luckily have made time in this life to grapple with that. And I have begun to be more tuned in to lessons from ancestors, which for me as an African American woman feels natural. When I say "orthodox agnostic" that leaves me a way to codify something that is not demanded from someone else. I mean, I respect and am interested in wonderful practices like Buddhist meditation, but my nature is that I resist codes. Even the conduct. But I like to borrow from it.

**EDITORS:** Will the texts your intern/collaborators bring to Denniston Hill address the same questions?

**ROBBIE:** In the class that I did with them [Playing the Other at HB Studio], I asked them to bring material that was personal and bigger—their personal stories that addressed some of their larger, topical concerns. They'll bring the material and we'll find a way to talk to each other. The part that's experimental for me that I haven't quite done before, is to find a way to hear each other and create dialogue out of the individual stories.

**EDITORS:** Your collaborators are twenty-nine and fifty-four years old. There's half a century between you and one of them and a couple of decades between you and the other. Are there assumptions that you have that they don't have? Do they think about race differently?

**ROBBIE:** I think they're much more advanced in their thinking. There's so much more information, there's so much more access to differences. The old idea that one has to be taught to be racist is not as easy to teach anymore, because people have access to differences. Doesn't mean it's gone away, but I think generationally they're smarter and certainly these two people are easy to talk to about race. One is Taiwanese and one is Jewish American.

**EDITORS:** How is the theme of "exodus" guiding the work? Does it imply you are thinking about a promised land? Where do you imagine going?

**ROBBIE:** Well, you go to the desert and you find your way. My thought on the theme is: What are you leaving behind?

**EDITORS:** That's a hard question to ask a young person.

**ROBBIE:** Both of them had experiences of exiting from one place to another, from one sensibility to another.

**EDITORS:** What does it mean to leave a sensibility behind?

**ROBBIE:** One can shift their way of seeing, shift their vision. The young man I'm working with is gay and I think he's gone through his life having to come out and all of that, which is a way of changing how you live and experience the world. Tina made a journey from one culture to another, one language to another. In fact she speaks a couple of languages. She sees things differently that way.

**EDITORS:** What are *you* leaving behind?

**ROBBIE:** The idea of pedagogy as performance.

**EDITORS:** Which means?

**ROBBIE:** I've always thought of theater as a place for teaching and learning. I know many people would find that a problem. But I'm interested in asking an audience: What did you learn? What do you know now that you didn't know before? What I've been working with is to find the aesthetic in the pedagogy.

**EDITORS:** In *Sally's Rape*, there's the moment where you stand naked on the auction block and Jeannie Hutchins asks the audience to join in chanting "bid 'em in." Is this an example of the aesthetic in pedagogy? The audience experiences—and is invited to participate in—a horrifying spectacle enabled by a theatrical or aesthetic choice. You're not *telling* them something in a didactic way, you're creating an experience they can reflect on.

**ROBBIE:** And if they participate or not, they get something. The audience is like a pebble in the stream. They get a bit of it and will talk about it or do something out of it or criticize it or whatever, but one transmits something to the witnesses. When we did *Sally's Rape* at a women's prison in Virginia the women got into it because they knew what we were talking about. They were calling out numbers for bidding. "Fifteen dollars!" That was something.

**EDITORS:** How did you understand that response?

**ROBBIE:** They knew what it felt like to be the body being bid upon. I'm not sure what their stories were, but I can imagine that many of them have had their bodies sold in some way. They knew what it was to be objectified. Their responses were so immediately familiar with the idea of being bid upon.

When we performed *Sally's Rape* in Kentucky a panel had been set up to talk about the fact that I took off my dress and the white woman didn't and how shameful that was. But when they held the panel after they saw the play, they admitted that they had nothing to talk about. Another thing happened at that talk-back: A young Black man was weeping. He said, "I felt like I was on an auction block 'cause I couldn't save you." And a young woman just burst into tears. She said, "We can't do this. We can't, we can't let people see us like this."

**EDITORS:** Did she mean that we can't let *white* people see us like this?

**ROBBIE:** That's exactly right. I said, It's okay. We have to tell the real stories, otherwise who'll believe us? And I said, In vulnerability, there is strength. That's what we find in telling the story and it's okay for you to cry. When we don't allow ourselves to be vulnerable, it's hard to move. We put walls around our feelings and it's hard to move to the next place.

**EDITORS:** And harder to reach the audience?

**ROBBIE:** Yeah. For actors, vulnerability must be there in order to speak out of one's self. The more vulnerable you are, the more able you are to be fully present.

**EDITORS:** And the spectators experience something real.

**ROBBIE:** That's right. More powerful.

**EDITORS:** What life for these scripts do you imagine for the future? Can others play you?

**ROBBIE:** Yes. When I'm performing personal stories, I'm a character telling those stories.

**EDITORS:** Do you envision other actors performing *Sally's Rape*, for example?

**ROBBIE:** It has been done. I saw a tape of two students doing *Sally's Rape* and I was delighted. They did a very good job. I saw two others do it as a workshop in Boston. So that told me that the characters I'd written—even though they were myself and my acting partner Jeannie Hutchins—live on in the theater.

**EDITORS:** Do you see that for the other plays, like *Indian Blood* that are very much about your own family?

**ROBBIE:** I envision that. I had talked some time ago to the choreographer Jawole Zollar of Urban Bush Women about the possibil-

Robbie reminisces with Paula Elliott (left) and Donna Bivens (right) about their work in the early 1990s on *Turf*. "Robbie McCauley 'n Company: A Convening in Performance," co-produced by Sleeping Weazel and Emerson College, Boston, MA, 2017. Photo: © David S. Marshall.

ity of making a dance-theater piece based on it. The piece didn't come to fruition, but just having that conversation gave me a sense of how the piece could be done without myself. Because the stories live. And the character that I play is the teller. Someone else could embody that. I also saw the possibility of having various characters telling the story, and I'm interested in the theatrical elements. Simply put, I like the idea of pageants. And the idea of having different people embodying different characters in the story.

**EDITORS:** Does the person who plays your role have to be female or Black?

**ROBBIE:** That's a great question. I think stories can be told by anybody, but one has to invest in the aesthetics of the story. Someone else telling the story would have to find their own way. And if it works, it works. If it doesn't work, we'll find out.

**EDITORS:** What does it mean to "work"?

**ROBBIE:** I'm trying to think of an example. When we did the community project in Boston we had the actors do scenes playing the other—Black actors playing whites and vice versa. It was an exercise in the rehearsals, but we ended up having one excerpt we kept like that. We called it "White-Talk, Black-Talk." The audience understood we were making that exchange. That's something I'm really interested in. I know that there's much angst around representation, appropriation, and authenticity. I keep all of that in mind in making these experiments. "Experimental" is an important word for me. How do you experiment with having the other person hear one story?

**EDITORS:** How *do* you?

**ROBBIE:** One of the problems with racism is that people don't hear the other's story. People cut off because they have assumptions about the other. In the work, listening is the task. And it's amazing how hard it is to get people to hear the other's story. I know it's hard for Black people to hear white people's story because their assumptions are already there and I'm sure it's the same with white people. And so, in the work, we target listening as a process, and then, after that, there's cross-talk. There's talk about, "What did you hear?" And it's often surprising what is heard.

**EDITORS:** You mean, it's not accurate?

**ROBBIE:** Well sometimes it's more surprising than one thought, more familiar than one thought.

**EDITORS:** *Sally's Rape* would be pretty weird with actors playing across such lines. The dynamic of that play depends so much on Jeannie Hutchins being white and you being Black.

**ROBBIE:** Yeah. *Sally's Rape* says in the script "a Black woman and a white woman." Anyone who wants to experiment with casting it differently—it's up to them. But that process would need strenuous work, the strenuous work of finding what's in the material that could allow that to happen. One of the things that came up when I was working with Roxbury Repertory Theater was that the

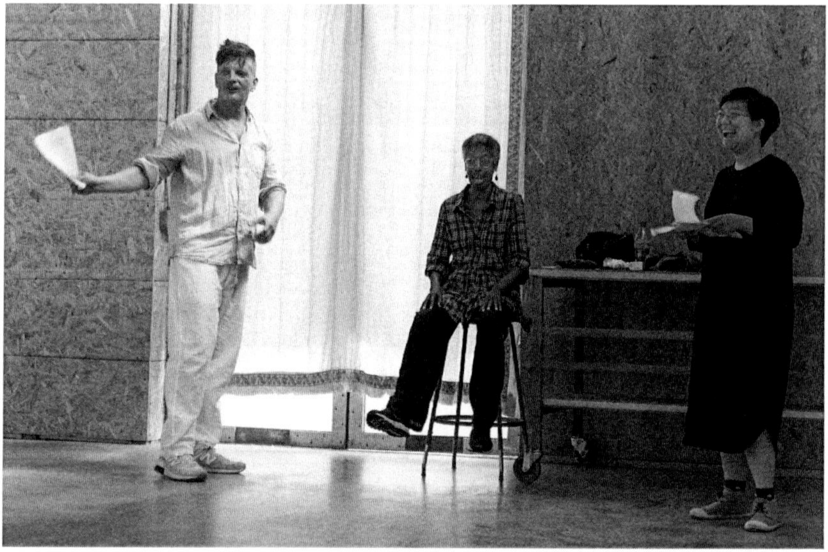

Robbie working with Eric Rasmussen (left) and Tina Ruan (right). Denniston Hill, NY, 2019. Photo: © Claudia Mandlik.

other artistic director, Marshall Hughes, and I always had conflicts around casting. He was into what's called "colorblind casting." And I was into what we call "race-conscious casting." It turned out we were both right. Some roles demand authentic representation and some can cross.

**EDITORS:** Do you think race is ever invisible on stage?

**ROBBIE:** It's not that the audience forgets. I'm not wanting them to forget. That's not the aim. It's just that that's not the most important thing they're looking at. Most important is the story. We did Williams's *A Streetcar Named Desire* with a white Blanche and a Black Stanley. After a moment he was just Stanley and she was Blanche. The landlady and her husband were a Black couple and Stella was white. We found that Williams had written that The Quarter was a multicultural neighborhood and we went with that. There's a Spanish-speaking character in the play as well. Several, in fact, because his card partners are mixed.

**EDITORS:** But you weren't pretending that Stanley wasn't Black?

**ROBBIE:** No, we weren't. We weren't trying to make the audience "colorblind." We wanted the audience to engage with the story in a different way. He played Stanley as a Black person, without changing a word of the script. It is rumored that Williams actually wanted Stanley to be Black, but it was 1938 so he had to go with Polish. In the stage directions Williams describes him as a beast. At that time, Polish was down on the list in terms of ethnicity for white people. But those images about Stanley were Black stereotypes. Of Black men. So we weren't hiding that and so the visibility was apparent.

**EDITORS:** And there is Stanley's sexual violence. How did you contend with the risk of playing into a terrible stereotype about Black men?

**ROBBIE:** I was making no apologies for that because I know that character from my own background. That's charged material—the idea of him being violent and a rapist. But who doesn't want to play Stanley? It's one of those characters. I said, "Let's play the play."

**EDITORS:** And you don't fight racism by making all the people of color into good people.

**ROBBIE:** Yeah. And all the people who are white, bad people. I think there's been progress on that.

**EDITORS:** Do you think white people see racial injustice with more attention or understanding than a generation or two ago?

**ROBBIE:** I think the best part of the media has exposed blatant examples of racism that can't be unseen. And these are the things that change people's minds. People's senses are assaulted through some media, especially by images of police violence. These images interrupt the habit of minimizing or of not bringing up what is painful. For Black people, as I'm sure is the case for other people who are targeted, pain is part of life. You just have it. And there's this sensibility among so many white people that they just can't be uncomfortable. Racism is huge. There is some progress in recognition. It's good to see some white people using the term "white supremacy": They *know*! But many white people don't admit it.

**EDITORS:** Do you still have faith in the theater as a valuable arena for confronting that failure? Your community projects have involved all kinds of people in excavating the truth.

**ROBBIE:** Absolutely. There are all kinds of ways of doing community theater. One is that you go and ask the community what they want to talk about. What I wanted to do was to bring the subject to the community and ask them to talk about it.

**EDITORS:** But of course that subject—a local racial conflict—was always there.

**ROBBIE:** Yes. One of the best things that came out of that for the work was a student who worked with me at Emerson, Tara Brooke Watkins, who has done a project in Tulsa, Oklahoma, about Black Wall Street and the anti-Black riots there in 1923. She's collected stories there and they have been playing it all over Tulsa. They've traveled with it and she has done the real work of community theater. She's left and the community is continuing to collect the stories and to play them.

**EDITORS:** Are the young people you're working with optimistic?

**ROBBIE:** That's a good question. *(Pause.)*

**EDITORS:** Are you?

**ROBBIE:** Well, for the first time in my life, I'm not. I worked very hard at trying to be optimistic and always hoping that things would get better, but that is now very cloudy.

**EDITORS:** Well, we're thinking of calling this collection, *The Struggle Continues*. Beginning with the association with the *struggle* of the civil rights movement, how does the phrase still resonate for you?

**ROBBIE:** Back then there was progress every day and now things tend to go backward. I think progress goes forward and backward. And right now, we're in a backward phase. I think politics are retracting and that that dynamic, that contradiction, is always there—as things move forward, they go backward. Through the arts, one can examine and enjoy the dynamics and the contradictions.

**EDITORS:** So does the phrase "the struggle continues" have a different meaning now than it used to?

**ROBBIE:** I think it's the same—it's just added to. Everything is connected in ways that we always knew. But now it's more obvious how things are connected. I think we're struggling for our lives right now. Yes, our whole lives.

I'd like to say something more positive about the work. I think what's in this book is what I've come up with so far and it's something that I continue to work from. I'm continuing to experiment, and hopefully may come up with more, in terms of finding ways to shift assumptions about how we see each other. My story comes out of a time in this country when the process of being able to take in others was fraught with danger. What I've learned for myself from the work is that I'm more and more able to take in differences between myself and others. And I think theater does that.

**EDITORS:** What are your thoughts and hopes for the Black Lives Matter protests that have apparently involved more Americans than any other protest movement in U.S. history?

**ROBBIE:** The recent use of personal media for exposing police homicides has cleared up the fog of denial in the minds and hearts of numerous white people. White supremacy is a deeply entrenched worldwide, longtime wrong that white people must delve way down into, confront, and dismantle.

**EDITORS:** Do the protests inspire you in your work in any way? Could you see making theater based on these events?

**ROBBIE:** I've recently been in touch with a theater company that creates work from real events. Their language is pretty much the same language I've been using for years, connecting personal stories to bigger topics, and they're not the only ones. That's heartening to me because the work is continuing whether they heard it from me or from John O'Neal* or from anyone else. Now is the time for that work to be more visible. And that work can make change because it is personal and it is breaking silences.

George Floyd. How he died. It makes me feel much more militant, because the work to be done—all this business about "the Black problem" is over with. I mean, white people need to accept what they're born into and clean it up.

The legacy of courage I come from inspires me to continue to work with or against white people to end the supremacist terrors. I wish I were younger and had more energy, and yet, "I can't," as the old James Cleveland hymn says, "get no ways tired."

*John O'Neal was the co-founder of the Free Southern Theater. His story circle technique inspired Robbie.

# ROBBIE'S IPHONE POEMS

Robbie often used her iPhone to record ideas about her work and responses to her physical condition, among other things, and shaped them into reflective gems that shimmer with insight and intimacy. She left a trove of them when she died in May 2021. Some of the pieces about acting might have been thoughts for a book she wanted to write on the subject. Thanks to Ed Montgomery, we had access to scores of them, written between 2016 and 2021, though many are undated and some untitled. We present a selection here. Robbie called them her "iPhone Poems." We organized them under two general rubrics: "Theater/Acting/Craft" and "Health /The Body/The Body Politic." Ed Montgomery has set some of them to music; these songs can be found on YouTube at:

https://www.youtube.com/watch?v=Af-AMn9A970

—eds

## THEATER, ACTING, AND CRAFT

Acting allows you to express yourself from the inside out.

Yes, acting can be pretending to be other people but when acting you are always revealing some self-knowledge, some inner truth. Preparing to express yourself in this way involves heightening your voice and physical presence.

[NO DATE]

### "STORIES" PEDAGOGY BOOK

"Stories" is the first title I gave a project I did at NYU, inspired by exemplary acting teacher and theater director Lloyd Richards, who told me to encourage students in my Voice for Actors to add content to the sound-making work in which they were being well educated. His comment made after observing my class literally sparked a vision. The Kristin Linklater Teacher Training I'd been fortunate to have taken was based in the actor's recognition of personal impulse. I had also learned somehow that the process of learning to speak is somewhat mysterious, that it most likely comes from parents—the mother's tongue—supported by culture and education.

2/8/2018

### PRINCIPLES AND PROCESSES

Radical Inclusion
Leadership by Inclusion
Respect differences
Receive stories
Allow feelings to emerge,
to be spoken, to flow
Allow silence
Allow discomfort
Welcome creative actions

4/1/2018 7:00 A.M.

I like to talk about my work in a cultural context. The United States at the time I write this in 2018, just after the Brett Kavanaugh confirmation, which exposes what many of us have known and struggled with for centuries—often unspoken tensions around differences based in race, class, historical events, gender, sexuality, and religion in this country. We all have individual stories reflecting these tensions.

As a theater worker, I started early on to learn and teach how the story is endemic to the art of theater. To do the art one must be able to call up and express images.

FALL 2018

As tiresome as it can be to get white people to break open denial of their complicity, I knew change needed their unspoken stories, and chose to chip away at their resistance.

1/27/2019

### TALKABOUT EXERCISE

What's the easy things for you to talk about that have to do with your race or culture?
—What's the hardest?

What's the easy things for you to talk about that have to do with another culture or race?
—What's the hardest?

What's the easy things for you to talk about that have to do with your economic class?
—What's the hardest?

What's the easy things for you to talk about that have to do with another economic class?
—What's the hardest?

What were you most struck about what you heard others say?
—Talk about it.

1/30/2019

### ART LEARNING

I learned by doing: what impulses (based upon observation) shaped into modes of expression, generate perceivable output, or art.

1/31/2019

### ABOUT THE WORK

So much about the body,
even as a body-based actor

who writes, I seldom paid attention to mine. For me the body was always more thought energy than physical stamina. Not either/or but a constant delicate balancing of the two which is why I like plastique and tai chi.

I went to the physical pain and emotional pain in *Sally's Rape*. Yes, *Sugar*, too. Tuned into the sounds to shape what I felt into words, imagined what life was like for Grandma Sally.

Put myself inside my body to confront the wreckage of my internal parts for *Sugar*—both inside and out. Harder to do than I had imagined.

But easy enough to step into after breaking to and through the pain, swimming around in it, shaping the words that emerge. The body absorbs and the mind articulates. With unexpected questions, enthusiasm comes.

Not to answer, not show, but to shape and color the energy of the passion dived into, and allow that.

5/8/2019

## THREADS

The body is the the thread
The words are the weave
The space is the canvas

Summer 2019

We are disciples of each other.

Leading and following and holding forth principles of process and production we each have taken chances to dare do.

Each has her own journey, journeys that we keep to ourselves or finally shape through the art. I need help. And happiness. I do not want to be Frida Kahlo. Though I'm sure her passion gave her relief.

8/6/2019

It's raining now. Early morning in October. I cover up. Sleep.

Performing herself over and over like a griot in a garden. Running from hard stories with the harsh men and feet on her back on benches in Florida or porches in Seattle. Looking while losing herself until she found and played the saga of her life before her life began.

10/3/2020

## MIXED MESSAGES

*(Teacher and Student face each other on a diagonal.)*

STUDENT: Should I keep acting?
TEACHER: Look at your question.
STUDENT: Please don't condescend to me, this is my life.
TEACHER: I think you are good at acting, if that's what you need to hear. But I think only you can decide to continue.
STUDENT: I don't know what to do. I don't know if I can make it.
TEACHER: Make what?
STUDENT: It . . . work a lot.
TEACHER: If you decide to, you're good enough to take that chance.
STUDENT: I want to be rich and famous.
TEACHER: Good luck.
STUDENT: I want to learn how to do that.
TEACHER: Not what I teach.
STUDENT: What the hell do you teach?
TEACHER: Ask and answer yourself if you're sure you work better now than when you first came to study.
STUDENT *(Relenting)*: Okay, but I don't know what and how I learned. I just know I work better.
TEACHER: You have learned to show up, to keep your body and senses alive, tune in to the material you are working with . . . and to be open to what you discover.
STUDENT: I want to win.
TEACHER *(Smiling)*: First you have to get nominated.
STUDENT: Are you making fun of me?
TEACHER: Yes I am. You're way ahead of yourself.
STUDENT: So what.

TEACHER: Bill Cosby once suggested that phrase as the best way to end an argument. Well he, as we all do, found out what "what" is.

STUDENT: My life in general.

TEACHER: Try one step at a time. Develop the script of your life as you go. Be guided by your desires and opportunities. And act moment to moment toward your objectives. When things aren't working as you like, find your way to the end of the scene. And move from what you discover.

[NO DATE]

Basic to acting is tuning into your pulse. Jazz again. If you find doing that bewildering (puzzling, a turnoff, or a block of any kind), breathe, sing, sigh, dance, or move your thoughts without lingering into the space occupied by your blockage. Taking as much time as you need (or have), begin to speak your material as rhythmically as you can find into that space. Spend as much time as you have or can on this exercise (minutes, days, weeks, years—I'm working now on Hamlet—always have something impossible, something you're not likely to be cast for, to work on when you don't have "a job"). Be open to discover what is repeatable for you. Repeatability—an intimate relationship with parts of the material that you long to play. If and when you/your pulse is connected to the material with little blockage or resistance, begin right away to discover the material's rhythms, allowing your pulse to vary.

[NO DATE]

Black people have personally experienced so many large political dramas. Growing up we identified with Emmett Till, Rosa Parks, sit-ins to dismantle segregation, the four little girls murdered in an Alabama church, and the Supreme Court's demand to desegregate public schools, to name a few. Fortunate enough to follow my dream to step into a wider world while viscerally retaining connection to my origins, I looked for, and took advantage of opportunities to make theater, to continue to learn, teach, and use the form to explore possibilities for telling untold stories and fostering dialogue between contentious racial and cultural groups of people. Neither scholarly nor physically energetic enough to study in a traditional academic way, I learned through my comfort with acting, teaching, and making theater in whatever venues were nearby me, or places I could manage travel to.

[NO DATE]

Regarding future discussions concerning Black theater, artistic, and thus political reparations: Can we start with works as profound and technically innovative as this one by Jackie Sibblies Drury? Don't settle for the dreck. Don't settle for a so-called art that presumably represents you. Usually that work has more to do with the so-called artist's will to success and very little to do with you, and a great deal to do with fame as power, fame as allure. Seek out and support those artists who see your complexity and want to take you deeper, past ideology, because we are not ideology, we are vast human beings. Usually, those artists have a hard time stretching a buck. Because it's not innovation that's rewarded, generally, it's liberal status quo garbage in tap shoes. Give Michael R. Jackson his own theater and make Adrienne Kennedy the dramaturg. If you settle for less than excellence in your own work, let alone the work those creatures of fashion are feeding you, that means you're rough-housing, still, in their playing field. Make your own field. And then grow other fantastic flowers in it.

[NO DATE]

My sense of theater has helped me get through life, has given me understanding that my life has purpose. My awareness started with stories, family stories that let me know I descended from people who lifted me up in their imaginations before I was born. My sense of theater, before I even knew what theater was, urged me to listen to the stories. I did know theater and, as with most cultures, drama for Black people emerged from religion—church, as we fondly call it. The call-and-response mode is endemic to the culture whether or not it started in the church. Both Paul Carter Harrison and Zora Neale Hurston write substantially describing the phenomenon in Kuntu Drama and the Sanctified Church, respectively.

Yes, I read Camus and listened to contemporary jazz, was charmed by the Beat Generation, and wrote and listened to poetry before spoken word or word were words. But how theater saved my life was my discovery that I had been the center of a bigger story all my life.

I began to know this understanding the process of personalizing the characters I played. Gloria Foster, the great American actress (which was the term we used back then), called it translating. She, who I had the pleasure of working with, told me translation does not mean substitution. It means to personally engage with the character. By the mid-1980s I had begun to create a character of myself in order to tell a bigger story. The first lines I wrote were these: "Seems like my father . . ."

[NO DATE]

Boston with its social contradictions around race felt less the presumption one might have of a northeastern politically liberal city. I found it fertile ground for my longtime interest in theater practice as a process for shining light on the unspoken tensions around racial and cultural differences. Two examples stand out. Teaching there at Emerson College where I also directed and was able to do other theater work, theater in the town, mainly at other colleges.

The first piece at Emerson I adapted from James Baldwin's film script on the life of Malcolm X, *One Day When I Was Lost*. I'd bought and read the paperback and immediately envisioned the dialogue spoken live interspersed with Baldwin's poetically described action shots. The senior class I was assigned to teach, except for one student from Panama, were all white. I presented the script to the students who gave me all kinds of expected resistance. They had learned to think they had no right to speak the words of Black people. I discussed the boldness required in experimental theater to break boundaries with respect to questions of appropriation aesthetics and authenticity. An arts program in the academy I suggested was a unique place to explore these questions on their feet. Reluctantly the students agreed. I got permission from the publisher to do an adaptation to be done only at the college. Titled *Malcolm X in White and Black*, the result was stunning for me. The process was interactive in that the students early on recognized that playing the situations of others expanded their inner voices and imaginations. The poetic action became a choral narrative sequencing dialogic vignettes from the script. With eyeglasses as a hand prop, different actors played Malcolm. The presentation was well received, especially by parents, many of whom had lived through the history. The student from Panama, who later became an award-winning producer on Broadway, tried very hard to get the rights to produce our adaptation in another theater venue. I did fantasize seeing it played elsewhere, but no go. The result of the hard work that goes into making such work may be only witnessed by a few, yet what happens can resonate deeply for the actors and widely for the witnesses/audience.

[NO DATE]

All my work life as an interdisciplinary theater artist I've made it possible for people to talk to one another rather than stay mad because of differences. Across these differences we have opened our hearts and minds among ourselves. We laugh, cry, and interrogate each other, and, to our delight, our daring to shape and perform from our interactions has resulted in enthusiastic feedback from others. People have said things such as being inspired to open up and shift their views toward positive change.

[NO DATE]

## HEALTH / THE BODY / THE BODY POLITIC

Time holds through night
Morning in the morning returns.
Worn out rhythms I welcome
as methods and moods
weave slowly.
Familiar moral action beautiful.
I trust old sentimental truths, as
Songs remember themselves.

10/26/2016

### BROKEN HEART REPAIR

Scratching itch
Feet and hair walls and floors
Cover colors and shiny doors
Nobody knows other people's language or hearts or guilty pleasures.
Cold bones inside and out, make it hard to yearn for treasures.

Floor has an unsteady feeling
Like Fred Astaire dancing on the ceiling
I too want to dance
Like Gene Kelly splashing past a fire hydrant
Head inside on fire.
Life slower. Time dire.
What's the future?
Will there be nature?
Is what's now past?
All moving slow fast.
Stop my head, it's turning blue.
I want to go to bed
And rest with you.

10/26/2016

## BODY THOUGHTS

Men think they are God
because they plant the seed.
Their bodies tell them that.
Women think we are earth.
Amen

4/6/2018

I notice how more annoyed
I am with white liberals
Than with regular racists.
I think I want liberals to be like they say, not realizing back then how encrusted whiteness how embedded supremacy was in all white people who'd not sat down and moved such thoughts around, like John Brown.

Regular racists were more predictable, more able to change, more familiar with us, like Lyndon Johnson and Jimmy Carter.
Ted Kennedy, though late,
came charged with change.
He would have been able to move
white people forward.

5/4/2018

Dancing and singing
Not easy for me
though rhythm sustains my core
Uncles bound and lost cousins
Rumble melodies
and my pin-pricked feet
move from inside out
Beating time
from way before
Time
Had a name.
Beating time
Before time
Had a name.

7/23/2018

Love and death are both
the scariest things.
At least love is
less mysterious, and death
more.

The end of everything,
the final fog,
alone not moving, unable to,
and no door.
Doors and light mean
coming back Kubler-Ross,
fear of sleep.

Welcoming rest rare nowadays.
The body knows
kicks your butt
to sleep.

Unspoken confessions again.
The sea of love conquers nothing,
it just is.
Helps to swim in it
fear of sharks and all.

4/3/2019

### THE FEET

lose feeling or hurt. Find yourself walking like old people you usta dismiss, and now yourself feeling invisible. So much of how you feel is how you see others see you. Some call that projection. In the air one becomes the other.

Because I was always skinny people thought I was a dancer. But never developed such strength. I only acted with my body. Once I did an exercise like this . . . moving every muscle I could imagine in my feet . . . which I'll do for a while . . . and see what comes out.

4/16/2019

Another time rhyme
Cataracts bad back
Kidney stones broken bones
Can't walk can hardly talk
What you say, can't hear today
Tomorrow is a day apart from
Failure of my pumping heart
Getting old I'm told

No hollandaise sauce,
said the undertaker,
Who's the boss,
said the salad maker,
Word faker,
said the lawyer
no case, no groundbreaker
on the face of the matter in the courts,
just a complaint of sorts,
the kind of thing a person fat from food
blames what he chewed
on the recipe of the cook
who went strictly by the book

And now ailing
from heart failing
Kinfolks say nothing's wrong
Don't want to hear
the mourning song.

All can be said when my boat
sails from the dock
is respect for Mister Time
and his conscientious clock.

5/7/2019

Yes, free speech is free.
though many may disagree.
You may be blamed
or shamed,
even condemned.
Thinking first I'd recommend.

6/19/2019

Making me was not so hard, but difficult moments felt like forever until I started seeing myself in a historical perspective. My family's spoken memories go back to slavery time. The 13th, 14th, and 15th amendments—and of course the 19th, were personal for me.

8/6/2019

Itching is annoying, especially the scalp. My skin used to be so pretty even before other people said Black was beautiful. Now my skin is old and though Black, it did crack. Another stereotype smashed. My skin is getting crackly, thin, and wrinkly. No other women in my family went like that. Aunt Jessie was smooth at ninety-three. I did live harder, thought I'd die young, and now am too curious to care much about how I look. I'm not afraid of the floods and the fires, but am pulling for the scientists and artists. Laurie my dear friend, now in heaven, put homemade pottery on the stage.

8/23/2019

How I found nice is not a problem though many disparage it. After years of jaw-clenching rage, I began . . . after my toddler daughter, now thirty-something, years ago told me when I was enraged about something or another, "Mommy, your face is not a mommy . . ." I began bit by bit to breathe deeper and flow thoughts out my mouth. Made me feel nice, and nicer. The rage I began to see as a loud cover for sadness pride shame fear, so many unspoken stories.

10/28/2019

Heart trouble
Inherited from Daddy
Whose anger snarled out
Mine eased out unseen
Twisted back in, couldn't
Breathe, look people in the eye
Acting the only relief
Being present onstage
More myself playing others or
Playing myself
Playing nice in real life
But too late for cure
Heart trouble'd be my nature
Little attacks until the big 'un
Got countrified calling Mama
Jesus Daddy God
All way up way beyond
Zoom circle prayers
So many health carers
Covid-19 didn't come
Surgery well done
Eight weeks till home
Now easy breath offstage and on
Love every where
From every one.

In the midst of the world
Birds fly . . . or flew
Cows chew

People cry and die
Take and give
Laugh and live.

Born Black
I fight back.

5/11/2020

F**k conversations
Pay reparations

If you want to talk
Take a walk
Up the hill
And pass a bill
For us who're Black
Pay us back

6/30/2020

### "HAPPY BIRTHDAY TO ME"

Happy Birthday to me
Starting again
My 78th year
Feeling like 19
Owning my wanderlust
My dynamic rage
Even with my body rust
Stricken with age
Able still to picture stamina
To move from within
From shapes of inner drama
Making structures to give
In order for to live.

The first was a tree
Who came up to me
Swinging branches
Making chances
in many ways
For my soul to breathe
to feel the air in my hair
to taste the light of sun rays.

Next was number two
Another one to view
To adore to want more
And life became a zoo
With zebras and monkeys
Uncaged running free
Climbing all over me

I hopped upon a merry-go-
roundup of baby bears
At a thousand county fairs.

People were the creatures
When I wake from the dream
On a bus to integrate a school
Headed by a fool
Who puts me in a room alone
Where on the wall is a phone
My mom says be brave for
all the nation you must save.
I decide instead
to stand on my head.

Little by little things began to change in schools on buses
On beaches and places to eat.
Pain now in my hands and feet
Arthritis rheumatism diabetes
No virus from the test
And worldwide protests
For Black Lives

And the heart
Surgery a success
Here's the best part
Living through it all
And I'm still on call.

7/8/2020

## OLD DEAD DICKS

From a long time ago
Should just lay on down

Or walk out the door

They don't do a thing
But get in the way
Have no idea about today.

Missed the boat to the future
Were left upon the shore
No one cares to see 'em anymore

Nobody cares about their false
Apologies explanations or
Their reputations and greedy expectations.

They can go to the graveyard
And dig up cover up with
Their crinkly old hands
And lie down under dirt
No longer have the nerve
No longer to hurt people
They were elected to serve.

7/24/2020

I have the discipline of wind
Motivated impulsively by forces without and yes from within
Making light and gentle breezes
Or a devastating storm bringing
High water that no one pleases
Sometimes I am only air
No damage anywhere
But now the earth is warmer
No fault of mine
We are running out of time
The ones with discipline
Should take charge
I'm just the air the window
Moving small or large
Necessary for all our breath

Without me only death.

7/26/2020

Racism is a health problem
Police brutality, a health problem
Not knowing who you are
Is crazy making causes
An inner loneliness

You are not
Who you think you are
You are ordinary
Not superior.
Sit in it.

2/1/2021

Broke heart
Sore feet
Sweat heat
Cold bones
Bye-byes all gone
Aching back
No body part has a lack
Of pain and dread
Except inside the head
Where thoughts are loud
Which is one way
To have something to say
To feel proud.

2/19/2021

Doctor spoke
Wadno joke
Toe has to go
Won't be there
No mo'
Double negative
Give me
Time to rhyme
Give me time
To mourn and beg
And be glad at least
It's not a leg.

2/20/2021

Big toe is for balance
There is a chance
I still can dance.

2/20/2021

# FURTHER READING: A PARTIAL BIBLIOGRAPHY

Becky Becker, "Robbie McCauley: A Journey Toward Movement." *Theatre Journal* 52, no. 4, December 2000: 519–42.

Sheila Bock, "'Grappling to Think Clearly': Vernacular Theorizing in Robbie McCauley's *Sugar*," *Journal of Medical Humanities* 36, no. 2, January 2015: 127–39.

C. Carr, "Talk Show," and "Deconstructing Dixies," *On Edge: Performance at the End of the Twentieth Century*. Wesleyan University Press, 1993 and 2008 (revised edition).

Cynthia Carr, *Our Town: A Heartland Lynching, a Haunted Town, and the Hidden History of White America*. Crown Publishers, 2006.

Elin Diamond, *Unmaking Mimesis: Essays on Feminism and Theatre*. Routledge, 1997.

Charles R. Garoian, *Performing Pedagogy: Toward an Art of Politics*. State University of New York Press, 1999.

Jennifer L. Griffiths, *Traumatic Possessions: The Body and Memory in African American Women's Writing and Performance*. University of Virginia Press, 2009.

E. Patrick Johnson, "An Interview with Robbie McCauley," in *solo/black/woman: scripts, interviews, and essays*, eds. E. Patrick Johnson and Ramón H. Rivera-Servera. Northwestern University Press, 2013.

Omi Osun Joni L. Jones, *Theatrical Jazz: Performance, Àse, and the Power of the Present Moment*. Ohio State University Press, 2015.

Omi Osun Joni L. Jones, Lisa L. Moore, and Sharon Bridgforth, *Experiments in a Jazz Aesthetic: Art, Activism, Academia, and the Austin Project*. University of Texas Press, 2010.

Lucy R. Lippard, *Mixed Blessings: New Art in a Multicultural America*. The New Press, 2000.

Robbie McCauley, "Lullaby for Jessie." *Broadside: The National Topical Song Magazine #151*, eds. Jaribu Hill and Jeff Ritter, May 1984.

McCauley, "*Sally's Rape* in Sally's Rape," *Black Theatre, USA: Plays by African Americans: The Recent Period, 1935–Today*, eds. James V. Hatch and Ted Shine. The New Press, 1996 (revised expanded edition). Also in *Moon Marked & Touched by Sun: Plays by African American Women*, ed. Sydné Mahone. Theatre Communications Group, 1993.

McCauley, *Shays' Rebellion*. Alexander Street Press, 2005.

McCauley, "The Struggle Continues," part of "A Forum on Black Theatre," *Theatre Journal* 57, no. 4, 2005: 583–85.

McCauley, "The Subject of Beauty," in *Heide Hatry: Not a Rose*. Charta, 2013: 158.

McCauley, *Sugar: A Work in Progress*, in *solo/black/woman: scripts, interviews, and essays*, eds. E. Patrick Johnson and Ramón H. Rivera-Servera. Northwestern University Press, 2013.

McCauley, "Surviving Virginia," in *Extreme Exposure: An Anthology of Solo Performance Texts from the Twentieth Century*, ed. Jo Bonney. Theatre Communications Group, 1999: 248–56.

McCauley, "Two Street Things," *Aloud: Voices from the Nuyorican Poets Cafe*, eds. Miguel Algarín and Bob Holman. Henry Holt and Company, 1994: 443–44.

Robbie McCauley with Laurie Carlos and Jessica Hagedorn. *Teenytown*, in *Out from Under: Texts by Women Performance Artists*, ed. Lenora Champagne. Theatre Communications Group, 1990: 89–117.

Robbie McCauley and Bill Rauch, "What Happened?: A conversation between Robbie McCauley and Bill Rauch." *Theater* 31, no. 3, Fall 2001: 109–17.

Katherine McKittrick, *Demonic Grounds: Black Women and the Cartographies of Struggle*. University of Minnesota Press, 2006.

Timothy Murray, "In Exile at Home: Tornado Breath and Unrighteous Fantasy in Robbie McCauley's *Indian Blood*," *Discourse: Journal for Theoretical Studies in Media and Culture* 16, no. 3, Spring 1994: 29–45.

Ann E. Nymann, "*Sally's Rape*: Robbie McCauley's Survival Art," *African American Review* 33, no. 4, Winter 1999: 577–87.

Vicki Patraka, "Obsessing in Public: An Interview with Robbie McCauley," *TDR* 37, no. 2, Summer 1993: 25–55. Anthologized in *A Sourcebook on Feminist Theatre and Performance: On and Beyond the Stage*, ed. Carol Martin. Routledge, 1996. Also in *A Sourcebook of African-American Performance: Plays, People, Movements*, ed. Annemarie Bean. Routledge, 1999.

Sandra L. Richards, "'I've got the sweetest hangover': Robbie McCauley's *Sugar*," in *solo/black/woman: scripts, interviews, and essays*, eds. E. Patrick Johnson and Ramón H. Rivera-Servera. Northwestern University Press, 2013.

Marc Robinson, "Dual Nationals: Squat, Squat/Love, and Robbie McCauley," *Theater* 19, no. 2, Spring 1988: 46–53.

Demetria Royals, dir. *Conjure Women*. Produced by Louise Diamond, 1995.

Rebecca Schneider, *The Explicit Body in Performance*. Routledge, 1997.

Alisa Solomon, "A New York (Theater) Diary, 1992," *Theater* 24, no. 1, Winter 1993: 7–18.

Deborah Thompson, "Blackface, Rape, and Beyond: Rehearsing Interracial Dialogue in *Sally's Rape*," *Theatre Journal* 48, no. 2, 1996: 123–39.

Lynne Tillman, "Interview with Robbie McCauley," *BOMB* no. 41, Fall 1992: 8–10.

Raewyn Whyte, "Robbie McCauley: Speaking History Other-Wise," in *Acting Out: Feminist Performances*, eds. Lynda Hart and Peggy Phelan. University of Michigan Press, 1993: 277–93.

Dana A. Williams, *Contemporary African American Female Playwrights: An Annotated Bibliography*. Greenwood Press, 1998.

David Willinger, "Developing a Concert for the Spoken Voice: *Solo Voyages* and an Interview with Robbie McCauley," *Intersecting Boundaries: The Theatre of Adrienne Kennedy*, ed. Paul K. Bryant-Jackson and Lois More Overbeck. University of Minnesota Press, 1992.

Kinga Witek, "Robbie McCauley's *Sally's Rape*—'Speaking the Unspeakable,'" in *Worlds in Words: Storytelling in Contemporary*

*Theatre and Playwriting*, eds. Mateusz Borowski and Małgorzata Sugiera. Cambridge Scholars Publishing, 2010: 127–46.

Harvey Young, *Embodying Black Experience: Stillness, Critical Memory, and the Black Body*. University of Michigan Press, 2010.

Young, "Touching History: Suzan-Lori Parks, Robbie McCauley and the Black Body," *Text and Performance Quarterly* 23, no. 2, April 2003: 134–53.

# CONTRIBUTORS

**CYNTHIA CARR** is the author of *Candy Darling: Dreamer, Icon, Superstar* (2024), winner of the National Book Critics Circle Award for biography; *Fire in the Belly: The Life and Times of David Wojnarowicz* (2012), winner of a Lambda Literary Award; *Our Town: A Heartland Lynching, a Haunted Town, and the Hidden History of White America* (2006); and *On Edge: Performance at the End of the Twentieth Century* (1993). Carr chronicled the work of artists as a *Village Voice* staff writer (with the byline C. Carr) in the 1980s and 1990s. Her work has appeared in *Artforum*, the *New York Times*, and other publications. She won a Guggenheim Fellowship in 2007. From 2016–17, she was a Fellow at the Leon Levy Center for Biography at CUNY Graduate Center.

**MARIE CIERI** is a social/environmental geographer, cartographer, arts producer, writer and artist based in Cambridge, MA. She founded and directs The Arts Company, and as such produced all three pieces in Robbie McCauley's Primary Sources series. She has taught at RISD, The Ohio State University, Cooper Union and Rutgers University; at Ohio State, she organized a two-week residency for McCauley that included research and a work-in-progress showing of *Sugar*. In her own work, Cieri often combines geographic techniques and perspectives with ones from the arts to create representations of space and place with and for people who have little access to tools and forums of the public sphere. Her work has been shown at art spaces in Brooklyn, Boston, Providence, and Los Angeles.

**ELIN DIAMOND** is professor emerita of English and Comparative Literature at Rutgers University. She is the author of *Unmaking Mimesis: Essays on Feminism and Theater* (1997) and *Pinter's Comic Play* (1985). She is editor of *Performance and Cultural Politics* (1996); co-editor, with Denise Varney and Candice Amich, of *Performance, Feminism, and Affect in Neoliberal Times* (2017); and co-editor, with Elaine Aston, of *The Cambridge Companion to Caryl Churchill* (2009). Her many essays on drama, performance, and feminist theory have appeared in *Theatre Journal, PMLA, ELH, Discourse, TDR, Modern Drama, Cahiers Renaud-Barrault, Art and Cinema, Maska*, and in critical anthologies published in the U.S., Europe, and India.

**DANIEL ALEXANDER JONES**'s critically acclaimed performance pieces include *Black Light* (Public Theater, Greenwich House Theatre); *Duat* (Soho Rep.); *An Integrator's Manual* (La MaMa, Fusebox Festival); and *Radiate* (Soho Rep and National Tour). His book of plays and performance texts, *Love Like Light* (53rd State Press) was published alongside *Particle & Wave*, a conversation with Alexis Pauline Gumbs. Jones has recorded six albums of original songs as his alter-ego, Jomama Jones, and created the digital project www.aten.life. Daniel received a Guggenheim Fellowship, a Doris Duke Artist Award, the Idea Award for Theatre, a USA Artist Fellowship, two Art Matters grants, the PEN/Laura Pels International Foundation for Theater Award, and the Alpert Award in the Arts from CalArts where he is a producing artist with the Center for New Performance.

**OMI OSUN JONI L. JONES**'s work rests on theatrical jazz aesthetics and Black Feminist politics. Her original performances include *sista docta*—a critique of the academy, and *Searching for Ọṣun*—a performance ethnography around identity. Her most recent book is *Theatrical Jazz: Performance, Àṣẹ, and the Power for the Pres-*

*ent Moment*. Omi is founder of the Austin Project—a collective of Global Majority women and allies who use art for re-imagining societies. Omi holds a Ph.D. from New York University and an Embodied Social Justice Certificate from Transformative Change. She is professor emerita from the African and African Diaspora Studies Department at the University of Texas at Austin, a mother, a Queer wife, and a curious sojourner.

**CHARLOTTE MEEHAN** is a playwright, professor (Wheaton College, MA), and artistic director of Boston-based multimedia theater company Sleeping Weazel. She has created and produced her own and others' socially progressive, multimedia theater and performance since 2012. She commissioned Robbie McCauley's *Jazz 'n Class*, a paean to jazz and the African American experience from slavery onwards. In March 2022, Sleeping Weazel partnered with ArtsEmerson (Boston) to premiere her multimedia play with dance, *Everyday Life and Other Odds and Ends*. The play, dealing with the vicissitudes of family life in the throes of Parkinson's disease, was sponsored in part by the NEA Challenge America grant and seen by many in the Parkinson's and LGBTQIA+ communities.

**EDWARD MONTGOMERY**, while training to be a filmmaker in his early twenties, took up the saxophone and pursued both music and filmmaking for the next fifty years. He now programs the music at a small venue in Berlin, Kühlspot Social Club, and composes and leads the Right Now band. In a posthumous continuation of many years of collaboration with Robbie McCauley, Ed and the band have been setting Robbie's lyrics to music.

**ERIKA MUNK** edited *Theater* magazine (Yale) from 1992–2004. Before that, she was a senior editor at the *Village Voice* for twelve years, editing the theater section and writing on theater, books, and politics. Even earlier, she was the founding editor of *Performance and Scripts*, publications of the New York Shakespeare Festival, and an editor of *TDR*. She published widely in newspapers and academic journals on twentieth century theater, particularly Brecht and the avant-garde, and from the countries of former Yugoslavia during and after the war of 1992–95.

**CARL HANCOCK RUX** is an American poet, playwright, librettist, novelist, essayist, recording artist, journalist, curator, and conceptual installation artist working in text, dance, ritualized performance, audio, video, and photography. He is the author of the poetry collection *Pagan Operetta*, the novel *Asphalt*, and the OBIE Award–winning play *Talk*. He has collaborated with artists like Gerald Clayton, Anne Bogart, Julia Wolfe, and Carrie Mae Weems. He's done sound installations at the Whitney Museum Biennale, Park Avenue Armory, and the Kaatsbaan. Rux is co-artistic director of the Mabou Mines theater company and associate artistic director of Harlem Stage. Rux has received a Doris Duke Artist Award, a New York Foundation for the Arts Prize, a Bessie Award, the Alpert Award; he is a Global Change Maker fellow.

**MAUREEN SHEA**'s (1950–2022) directing credits include Circle Rep and Music-Theatre Group in New York, the Philadelphia Drama Guild, Los Angeles Women's Shakespeare Company, and the Huntington Theatre, Coyote, the Nora, Theater Offensive, and Theatre on Fire in Boston. She was artist-in-residence at the Iowa Playwrights Lab and the Toneelacademie in Maastricht, the Netherlands, and directed *Henry V* and *King Lear* for the Company of Women, an all-female Shakespeare troupe led by Kristin Linklater and Carol Gilligan. Produced by ArtsEmerson, *Sugar*, directed by Shea, premiered in Boston in 2012 (Paramount Center), and was later presented by Brown University (Granoff Center), Boston College (Bonn Studio Theater), the HartBeat Ensemble (Hartford, CT), and in 2018 by Lumberyard Contemporary Performing Arts at New York Live Arts. Shea was a professor at Emerson College.

**PAMELA SNEED** is a poet, performer, and visual artist. She is the author of *Imagine Being More Afraid of Freedom Than Slavery*, *KONG and Other Works*, *Sweet Dreams*, and *Funeral Diva* which was featured in the *New York Times* and won the 2021 Lambda Literary Award for Lesbian Poetry. She has also won the Black Queer|Art|Mentorship Award, a BOFFO Residency, and was a finalist for New York Theatre Workshop's Golden Harris Commission. Sneed has published with the *Paris Review*, *Frieze*, *Artforum*, the Academy of American Poets, and many more. Her paintings have been featured in group shows at the Leslie-Lohman Museum of Art and at the Ford Foundation. She is a professor and guest artist at SAIC, and also teaches across disciplines in Columbia University's MFA program.

**ALISA SOLOMON** is a professor at Columbia University's Graduate School of Journalism, where she directs the MA concentration in Arts & Culture. A longtime theater critic, reporter, and dramaturg (most recently on several projects with Anna Deavere Smith), she is the author of the award-winning books, *Re-Dressing the Canon: Essays on Theater and Gender* and *Wonder of Wonders: A Cultural History of Fiddler on the Roof*. She is editor of *The Reverend Billy Project: From Rehearsal Hall to Super Mall with the Church of Life After Shopping* by Savitri D and Bill Talen, co-editor of *The Queerest Art: Essays on Lesbian and Gay Theater* (with Framji Minwalla), and of *Wrestling with Zion: Progressive Jewish-American Responses to the Israeli-Palestinian Conflict* (with Tony Kushner).

ACKNOWLEDGMENTS

### FROM ROBBIE MCCAULEY:

I am grateful to courageous community members and artists who dared to examine and perform and talk with me about race and class long before the necessity for such talk became dire in this country. Especially, I thank Edward Montgomery, the late beloved Laurie Carlos, and Jessica Hagedorn, whose love and encouragement sustained my efforts. I thank, also, the artist collaborators who contributed to this volume: my assistant Tina Ruan and, most especially, the editors—Alisa, Elin, and Cynthia, who beautifully joined with me to interlock the diverse material as I endeavor to do in making theater.

—2019

## FROM THE EDITORS:

We are grateful to the original publishers for permission to reprint:

"Thoughts on My Career, *The Other Weapon*, and Other Projects," originally published in *Performance and Cultural Politics*, ed. Elin Diamond (London and New York: Routledge, 1996), 265–82.

"Participatory Theatre: 'Creating a source for staging an example' in the USA," by Marie Cieri and Robbie McCauley, originally published in *Participatory Action Research Approaches and Methods: Connecting People, Participation and Place*, eds. Sara Kindon, Rachel Pain and Mike Kesby (London and New York: Routledge, 2007).

"Mississippi Freedom: South and North" originally published in *Theater* 24, no. 2 (Summer 1993): 88–98. Copyright © 1993 by Robbie McCauley. *Theater* is published by Duke University Press.

Also, warmest thanks to photographers whose powerful images help bring Robbie's work to life on the page: Marie Cieri, Paula Court, Martin Cox, Paul DeFrain, Joyce George, Claudia Mandlik, Paul Marotta, David S. Marshall, Dona Ann McAdams, Kirk J. Miller, Marlis Momber, Vivian Selbo, Martha Swope, Mirta Tocci, and Nancy Wasserman.

Thanks, too, to those who helped track down these images: Ed Cardoni, Marie Cieri, Ron Ehmke, Geoffrey Hull, Anita McCauley Henderson, Charlotte Meehan, Jessie Montgomery, Tina Ruan, Kevin Semagin, and Maureen Shea.

We are grateful for the enthusiasm and meticulousness of Terry Nemeth, Kelundra Smith, Kathy Sova, Emma Walsh, and their colleagues at TCG Books.

**ROBBIE MCCAULEY** (1942–2021) was a playwright, director, performer, teacher, and leader of collective creations who made a significant mark on America's theatrical and political landscapes. In addition to early work in the experimental and Black theater movements in New York, she performed in Ntozake Shange's *for colored girls who have considered suicide / when the rainbow is enuf* on Broadway. McCauley went on to write and perform regularly in cities across the country and abroad. Her play *Sally's Rape* won the 1991 Obie Award for Best New American Play and a Bessie Award for Outstanding Achievement in Performance. Other notable works include *Sugar*, *Indian Blood*, *Mississippi Freedom*, *Turf: A Conversational Concert in Black and White*, *The Buffalo Project*, and *The Other Weapon*.

Conducting interviews and group improvisations, McCauley pioneered a form of community projects in which local people addressed long-buried racial tensions in their communities. Among them, she created the *Primary Sources* series in Mississippi, Boston, and Los Angeles, produced by The Arts Company. In 1998, her *Buffalo Project*, produced by Hallwalls Contemporary Arts Center, was highlighted in the *Village Voice* as one of "The 51 (or So) Greatest Avant-Garde Moments," a roster that also included works by Igor Stravinsky, Pablo Picasso, and John Cage.

McCauley was a recipient of the IRNE (Independent Reviewers of New England) Award for Solo Performance and was selected as a 2012 United States Artists Ford Foundation Fellow. Her work has been widely anthologized, including the volumes *Extreme Exposure*, *Moon Marked & Touched by Sun*, and *Performance and Cultural Politics*.

McCauley taught at City College of New York, Hunter College, Mount Holyoke College, Boston College, Emerson College, and New York University Tisch School of the Arts.